T5-AGO-968

THE SECULARIZATION OF LEISURE: Culture and Communication in Israel

THE SECULARIZATION OF LEISURE: Culture and Communication in Israel

Elihu Katz & Michael Gurevitch

with the assistance of
Hanna Adoni
Gila Brand
Oved Cohen
Hadassah Haas
Leah Isaac

FABER & FABER 3 Queen Square
London

First published in 1976
by Faber and Faber Limited
3 Queen Square London WC1
Printed in Great Britain by
Western Printing Services Ltd
Bristol

ISBN 0 571 09848 7

In memory of Zalman Aranne

CONTENTS

PART FOUR: Mass Media and Home Culture

PREFACE

This book is based on an audit of participation in leisure and cultural activities in Israel. Although it is a case study of one small country – a new nation with a long past – we believe it raises issues which are relevant to students and practitioners of cultural policy everywhere.

At various stages in their evolution, societies have to solve and re-solve the problem of their identity, that is, of uniting the people in a culture of their 'own'. Some old, established nations are at present having to confront anew the integrative problem because of schisms of class and ethnicity. Analysis of the ideological meanings latent in the mass media, popular culture and social ritual is a scholarly reflection of this preoccupation.

Some new nations virtually have to invent the symbols of their integration: language, holidays, folklore, the myths of legitimacy. Other new nations, heirs to Great Traditions, are struggling with problems of orthodoxy vs. modernity. Yet even those most committed to social, economic and technical modernization are continually discovering that modernization itself requires the cultivation of a national identity but at the same time tends to undermine it. Modernization disconnects people from their traditions – it secularizes – and it invites an influx of mass-produced culture from outside – it homogenizes.

As in other new nations, it sometimes seems that Israel is too busy – modernizing, absorbing immigrants, defending itself – to be occupied with the planning of culture and leisure. But it is a fact that people 'consume' culture and spend leisure – that is part of daily life. And it is a fact that government, willy nilly, has a hand in broadcasting and the arts, and even in shaping the character of certain holidays. Moreover, the hand of history weighs on the shoulders of the Israelis; it is impossible to explain the emergence of the State or its present-day character and problems without reference to the continuity of Jewish tradition. All these are prerequisites to an understanding of Israeli society and planning for its future. It is the behavioural and functional aspects of these facts which we try to analyze in this book.

The field work on which the study is based was conducted in the early summer of 1970, midway between the wars of June 1967 and October 1973. The optimism which followed the Six Day War was everywhere in evidence during that period, despite the outbursts of terrorism and the long war of attrition with which Israel had to contend at that time.

A sense of confidence was pervasive; the standard of living was rising and participation in leisure activities was expanding.

With the hindsight of Yom Kippur 5734 some people have described this mood as 'complacency' and have sought to explain in this way how the War took Israel by surprise. Perhaps so. But if that is the case, the data reported here may be said to reflect the 'positive side of complacency'. Israel had a taste of peace, however fleeting and illusory, and we caught a glimpse of its prospects – and its problems.

The completed manuscript of this book was in the hands of the publishers in the spring of 1973, a few months before the War. Things have not been the same in Israel since, but we do not presume to analyze them here. Rather, we hope and believe that the portrait of society enjoying a sense of peace will soon come back into focus.

Elihu Katz
Michael Gurevitch

July 1975

ACKNOWLEDGEMENTS

Empirical research in the social sciences requires team-work, but that does not mean that members of the team need remain anonymous or that their specific contributions need be blurred by the corporate seal.

Indeed, while the two senior authors had overall responsibility for the project, there was a clear division of labour among all seven team members. Considerable autonomy was granted to, and exercised by, each within the collective framework while the team served as a source both of support and criticism. The joint effort produced the research report which was submitted to the Ministry of Education and Culture which sponsored the study. The report is the starting point for this volume.

Hanna Adoni had charge of the analysis of the data on the consumption of culture and on attitudes toward work and leisure. She drafted the chapter on reading of which her Master's Thesis in the Department of Sociology at the Hebrew University is an expanded version. Elihu Katz supervised this work and then collaborated with Mrs. Adoni in the writing of articles based on these materials for the UNESCO publication, *Diogenes*, and for the volume, *Lifelong Education in Israel.*

Gila Brand assisted Michael Gurevitch in the analysis and writing of the chapter on the introduction of television in Israel, and was responsible for the analysis in the chapter on time budgets. The latter is the basis for her Master's Thesis in the Communications Institute of the Hebrew University, for which Michael Gurevitch served as supervisor.

Oved Cohen analyzed the materials on values, and sought to find interrelationships among the values themselves and between different types of values and the patterns of consumption of culture. Mr. Cohen edited the manuscript of the original research report, the two mimeographed volumes of which were submitted to the Ministry in March 1972.

Hadassah Haas had charge of the analysis of the functions of the mass media in Chapter Thirteen. This work required considerable methodological inventiveness and great patience with detail. Katz, Gurevitch and Haas have published an article in the *American Sociological Review* based on part of this chapter. Mrs. Haas also prepared the materials on the functions of holidays.

Leah Isaac conducted the research on the supply of culture. She supervised the collection and coding of the posters and other information which constitute the basis for the chapter on this subject. The chapter in the present volume, however, represents only a fraction of the detailed report which she prepared.

The questionnaires for the survey were devised jointly by the entire team, inspired, in part, by the earlier (1966) study of leisure, culture and communication in Haifa and Ashdod in which the senior authors were joined by Rivka Rahat and Dov Shinar. As a first step we also reviewed all previous Israeli research on these subjects. This review, published separately by the Association for Adult Education in Israel, was edited by Oved Cohen. We thank Shlomit Kotik of the Association for her assistance.

Like much of our other work, the present volume is a joint product of the Communications Institute of the Hebrew University and the Israel Institute of Applied Social Research. Continuing research in the fields of public opinion and communication is possible only where there exists a sophisticated survey research organization. There are very few places in the world as fortunate as Jerusalem in this respect. Beyond the technical services rendered, our work throughout reflects the advice and encouragement of our colleagues at the I.I.A.S.R., especially Louis Guttman, Tsiyona Peled and Shmuel Shye.

Being the largest survey ever carried out at the Israel Institute of Applied Social Research – involving, as it did, some 4,000 respondents – we are especially indebted to the fieldwork supervisors of the Institute and, most particularly, to the staff of the computing department, Uzi Hayim, Avraham Uliel, Roni Fatal, Shmaya Seger and Naomi Mansur. A staff of over 200 interviewers and coders were enlisted in the study, and we are grateful to all of them. The fieldwork was directed by Oved Cohen. The sampling design was worked out by Leah Isaac with the assistance of members of the staff of the Central Bureau of Statistics.

It is fitting also to thank the interviewees, who gave freely and cheerfully of their time, sometimes as much as two hours of it. We hope that they will be able to identify themselves in this volume, even though all of the data, of course, are presented in the form of statistical summaries. Interviewees were chosen at random so as to represent a cross-section of the nation as a whole.

As noted at many points throughout this volume, the work as a whole was commissioned by the Ministry of Education and Culture. The late Minister, Zalman Aranne, initiated the discussions which led to the formulation of the study, and at its early stages we have had the benefit of advice and interest of Dr. Yoseph Melkman, Haim Tsipori, Dr. Dan Ronen and, later, of Leah Porat, Director of the Department of Culture in the Ministry, and of the Director-General, Elad Peled. In addition, a grant from the Israel Foundation Trustees, a subsidiary of the Ford Foundation, made it possible to expand the sections of the study dealing with the mass media, with particular reference to the introduction of television.

Michael Gurevitch was responsible for the preparation of the Hebrew volume published by Am Oved in 1973; Elihu Katz was responsible for preparing this version for publication in English. The time and facilities for doing so were provided by the University of Manchester through the Simon Research Fellowship which was awarded to Elihu Katz in 1972–3. The privilege of the Fellowship and the hospitality of the Department of Adult Education at Manchester and, particularly, of comrade and chairman, George Wedell, who acted as host, are very gratefully acknowledged. So, too, are the comforts of Broomcroft Hall, the companionship of fellow Fellows, and the opportunity of discussing her thesis on The Sabbath, with Dr. Ruth Salzberger.

We are also grateful to the *American Sociological Review*, *Diogenes* and the *Jewish Journal of Sociology* for permission to incorporate material which originally appeared in their pages. We wish also to thank Professor Alexander Szalai who allowed us to examine his monumental comparative study of time budgets prior to its publication (*The Use of Time: Daily Activities of Urban and Suburban Populations in Twelve Countries*, The Hague: Mouton, 1972).

PART ONE INTRODUCTION

CHAPTER ONE The Hard Work of Studying Leisure: An Introduction to the Study

This study originated in 1970, in the mind of the late Zalman Aranne, then Minister of Education and Culture in the Government of Israel. During his term in office, he had devoted himself primarily to education, and, in particular, to the role of primary education in the integration of the reunited tribes of Israel. But culture was always in the wings. The traditional *yeshiva* education of his boyhood continued to haunt him; his sense of participating in history directed his reading; his secret life as a poet sensitized him to the problems of creativity; and the constant delegations of artists and their managers – impresarios of the concert and the theatre, committees of writers, stars visiting from abroad – continually reminded him of his role as Minister of Culture and thus his power as Patron of the Arts in a welfare state.

1. *The Aims of the Study*

When he called us together he put a series of questions, which immediately reflected the sweep of his ideas about the state of Israeli culture. His questions came complete with answers – we would call them hypotheses – and it is sad that we can no longer report to him directly concerning where he was right and where he was wrong.

The Minister asked us (1) to describe the patterns of exposure to and taste in a large variety of cultural activities – from reading newspapers to buying paintings, from theatre-going to playing football; (2) to analyze the functions and meanings of these activities for those who partake in them; (3) to assess the extent to which these activities are uniformly available to all, or differentially available only to certain places and certain groups; (4) to examine the institutions responsible for creating and supplying the content of leisure and culture, and to report on their problems; (5) to study the relationship between patterns of cultural consumption and patterns of attitudes and values; (6) to study the influence of types of occupational pursuit, of ethnic and religious traditions, and of the events of contemporary Jewish history – the destruction of European Jewry and the establishment of the Jewish State – on the uses of leisure and culture and the values with which they are associated; and, finally, (7) to explore the social relations between the generations, among people at work and among the different ethnic groups, for a better understanding of the context in which culture is created and consumed in Israel.

When we told the Minister that he was asking us to research and write a Sociology of Israeli Culture, he was pleased. He liked the idea. But we told him we could not answer all his questions in a single study. The methodologically-oriented reader will already have noted that the method of the sample survey of a public will answer some of the questions, but not others. In response to the Minister, we proposed a national survey of the attitudes, values and behaviour of a large sample of the population, and some preliminary work on the supply of culture (his question (3) above).

Still lacking are two major components of the sociology of culture which must remain on the agenda for future research. Each is related, in its own way, to problems of the *content* of culture. First of all, we refer to content in its simplest sense. Thus, while we report here on how frequently the average Israeli attends the cinema, the theatre or the concert hall we do not know enough about the content of what he sees and hears or the meanings he finds there.

A second missing link in the analysis of the content of culture has to do with the dynamics of creating and distributing cultural products. The economic, social, political and cultural constraints affecting publishing, broadcasting, theatre or film-making are urgently in need of study if indigenous cultural creativity is to be given a chance against the barrage of imported culture. We proposed to the Minister that both these aspects of content be examined at a later date, and the concluding chapter, below, will recall this matter.

2. *The Design of the Study*

The study is based on nearly 4,000 personal interviews with a representative sample of Jewish adults, eighteen years old and above. Problems of continuity and change in the culture of the Arabs of Israel are of a very different order, obviously, and deserve a study of their own. The respondents were selected at random from fifty-six different settlements, which were themselves chosen from a stratified listing of all settlements ranging from the largest cities to the smallest villages and including new towns, kibbutzim and moshavim. The fieldwork was carried out over a period of approximately ten weeks between May and July 1970.

In order to collect all of the information we needed, without taxing the endurance of the respondents, the questions were divided between two questionnaires. One half of the interviewees were asked half of the questions and the other half were asked the other half. Certain key questions were included in both questionnaires. Despite this division, the average interview was over one and a half hours in length. Our impression is that respondents would have been willing to continue even longer had we asked them to.

The sampling design – the method by which towns and settlements were chosen from among all settlements, and the method by which respondents were chosen for interview within settlements – is detailed in the Appendix. It should be noted here that all cities above a population of 20,000 are represented in the study. Among the smaller settlements, we preferred to cluster more respondents in fewer settlements rather than fewer respondents in more settlements so that the cultural life of these settlements could be more accurately circumscribed.

Three kinds of data are derived from the questionnaires. One set of data refers to the *behaviour* of the Israel population, for example, the name of the last book read; the frequency of theatre-going; the exact division of time over all activities during the past twenty-four hours. A second set of data deals with the *attitudes* of the population toward such things as the adequacy of leisure time and facilities available for leisure, or the relative preference for home-produced rather than imported television programmes. The third set of data bears on the perceived *functions* of various cultural activities and institutions ranging from the media of mass communication to books on the Six Day War and on the Holocaust to traditional Jewish and secular holidays.

A pioneering aspect of this study – compared with other studies of leisure and culture carried out both in Israel and abroad – is the attempt to integrate data on patterns of *consumption* of culture with data on the *supply* of culture. Parallel with the collection of data from respondents, an independent effort was made to obtain data about the public events being offered in each of the fifty-six settlements sampled. The data on supply are based primarily on the announcements of events advertised on the billboards in the streets during the month of June 1970 when the survey was being conducted.

Just as there remain substantive goals unfulfilled by this study, so there are methodological shortcomings as well, and these deserve to be mentioned. Survey research in Israel suffers, for one thing, from the out-of-date records which constitute the basis for sampling. The 'mortality rate' for designated interviewees is therefore unusually high, as the Appendix explains. In general, we console ourselves in the knowledge that most of our analysis is based on comparisons among subgroups and that we do not attempt statistical descriptions of the population as a whole without first examining differences among groups. For the usual reasons, the sample is somewhat better educated than the population as a whole.

And because we are talking about a representative sample, another problem arises: some of the phenomena which seem to observers to be characteristic of the population are not easy to discern. This is partly because surveys report on large and representative groups and subgroups and not on small minorities, even if one must always be aware of the possibility that today's minority may be tomorrow's majority, or today's headline may be reflected in tomorrow's public opinion. It should also be noted that our data are discrepant from the alleged public mood because they were collected in the spring of 1970, almost four years ago. The question of social dynamics – of following the indicators of social change in a systematic way – is being much discussed nowadays and this is not the place to do more than underline its importance. For the present purpose, however, we wish to state that we think our portrait was probably as true at the time of writing as it was when the data were collected, even though still portraits and majority portraits understate dynamic processes and vocal minorities – by definition.

In analyzing the data, we chose to give primary emphasis to the variables that seemed to us most important: education (which stands essentially for socio-economic status), age, ethnicity, city size, religiosity and sex. These – but education above all – make for important differences in attitudes and behaviour. Still, we now feel that we may even so have under-emphasized certain factors – differences between men and women, for one – and perhaps overlooked certain others.

But, as Kenneth Roberts emphasizes, social studies of leisure may be over-concerned with differences and not enough concerned with *similarities* in patterns of modern leisure, not only among subgroups within a nation but among nations themselves.[1] It is quite striking, for example, that the proportion of people outside their homes on an average weekday evening is very much the same in Britain and in Israel, or that the number of hours of television viewing hardly differs from country to country. The effect of television on radio-listening and cinema-going is everywhere very great, and its effect on reading is everywhere very negligible. Young people are the group who 'go out', and only formal education overcomes the urge to 'stay in' that accompanies growing older. Rest and sleep define leisure for the lower classes. Everywhere, it is women who are the more interested in the arts or in reading fiction, for example.

We are warned, therefore, to beware treating any one country as unique or making too much of small differences among subgroups. There is a pervasive homogenizing process at work in the rhythms of modern work and leisure. Even if this is so, however, we shall argue that there are certain characteristic differences among countries that are noteworthy, and that cultural policy-makers would do well to consider fostering their continuity. Moreover, we shall argue that the meaning of ostensibly similar activities may vary from one group to another, even within the same society. And if universal forms are emerging – as indeed they are – it is interesting to see how they evolve from different origins. These are some of the major purposes of this study.

3. *The Contents of the Book*

This volume is the result. It presents in an encyclopedic fashion information about leisure, culture and communication in Israel. It treats both Culture – in the sense of participation in cultural activities; and culture – in the sense of attitudes, values and behaviour. Each, of course, is a setting for the other.

The aim of the volume, however, is not simply to present detail. The reader interested in detail – in use of public libraries, for example, or participation in sports, cinema attendance, time spent on housekeeping, attitudes toward the five-day week or the traditional Israeli Sabbath – will find a lot of it. He will find even more in the Hebrew version which is designed also to contribute practical information to the planning of policy in the fields of leisure and culture. The larger aim of both volumes, however, is to attempt to integrate these data into a meaningful whole.

At the very outset, therefore, we take our stand: the following chapter proposes a framework within which to read the book. Referring to five themes in the traditional Jewish culture of the diaspora, it argues that contemporary Israeli culture reflects both the continuity of these themes and their gradual transformation. The transformation, in large measure, can be accounted for by the secularization of such traditional values as Jewish peoplehood, study, Sabbath and holidays.

There is a chapter on attitudes to work and leisure, followed by a chapter on the Sabbath and holidays. The round of life for the population as a whole, and for subgroups within it, is then summed up statistically in the chapter on time budgets. In this chapter, the use of time – that scarcest of human resources – by Israelis is compared with its use in other countries.

The stage is then set for an analysis of the consumption of culture. First, as already mentioned, there is a brief report on the supply of cultural activities which was available to the population of the fifty-six sampled settlements during the period of the study. This is followed by an attempted overview of the patterns of consumption of these activities. Comparisons are made by generation, by educational level, by ethnic origin, by degree of religiosity and by city size. The detailed analysis that follows is divided into the consumption of culture outside the home, and inside it.

Two cultural activities are singled out for special attention. They are the oldest of the mass media, the book, and the newest, television. During the period of this study, the diffusion of television sets in Israel soared to almost six in ten households, and over 80 per cent of the population had easy access to a set. We describe the effects of the new medium as it is perceived by the public, and our own estimates of those effects. The fate of the book, the classical medium of Jewish civilization, is then examined. We find that while the extent of reading is high in Israel, compared with other nations, the functions of the book appear to have changed.

In a separate chapter, we explore in detail this question of the functions of the several media of mass communication. First, we attempt to specify the 'needs' or 'goals' which the Israeli public singles out as important. Then, we attempt to identify the role of the mass media in the satisfaction of these needs comparing the media among themselves, on the one hand, and the media with other sources of gratification, on the other.

Needs, of course, represent valued things. The final data-based chapter of the book turns explicitly to values, particularly to those values associated with the continuity of Jewish tradition and with the character of Israeli society. The respondents are asked to discuss the values which form the basis of their identities as Jews and Israelis. Then, an analytic effort is made to relate differences in these values to observed differences in the patterns of use of leisure and culture. It is difficult, as has already been said, to discern such relationships.

The concluding chapter comments on the findings overall, but concentrates on their possible implications for policy-making in the field of culture.

4. *Policy Research and Research Policy*

The object of this study is not only to describe and to analyze but to *contribute* to policy-making in the fields of culture and communication. We do not believe, however, that this can be done by means of appended lists of 'recommendations' drawn up in academic detachment. Our experience in the field of applied social research has repeatedly taught us that only the *shared effort* of researcher and policy-maker to interpret the results of a study, to consider alternative courses of action and to explore the likely consequences of these alternative courses, has any chance of success. Only in this way can the translation of research findings into policy implications be effectively accomplished, and only in this way can the constraints operating on the policy-maker be adequately taken into account in the formulation of new policy.

The effort required for such joint endeavour is great, and few research projects find their way into policy for this reason. Policy-makers are busy people, and their decisions can rarely be timed to the prolonged process of serious research. Researchers, too, busy themselves with the next project almost before the previous one is complete. Yet, we repeat, the implicit ideas for action in this report can be uncovered only through serious exchange between researcher and policy-maker. Data do not speak for themselves and policy implications do so even less.

Yet, it is clear that the issues of cultural policy in Israel and elsewhere will inevitably attract more and more attention. The Government plays a major role in the provision of the facilities and franchises for leisure activities, and any challenge to these priorities forces leaders and officials, however reluctantly, to make explicit what is often implicit and unformulated. While arguing that minorities who are willing to pay for their leisure tastes can easily escape the alleged levelling of culture, Roberts nevertheless agrees, for Britain, that certain of the arts – opera, broadcasting, certain sports – would be 'forced out of existence if their current sources of subsidy were withdrawn. . . . In the future it is to be expected that coherent policies guiding the dispensation of patronage for leisure interests will be adopted, and these policies, in view of the growing importance of leisure in society, could possibly become political issues commanding considerable public debate and attention.'[2]

NOTES – CHAPTER ONE

1. Kenneth Roberts, *Leisure*, London: Longman, 1970.
2. Roberts, ibid., pp. 81 and 85, is here arguing both for and against the more paternalistic policies of writers such as Joffre Dumazedier, *Toward a Society of Leisure*, New York: Free Press, 1967.

CHAPTER TWO The Transformation of Tradition

While this book – and the social survey on which it is based – is concerned with the patterns of spending leisure and consuming communications, we have tried throughout to place these patterns in a broader context. Thus, we do not discuss leisure without discussing work. Leisure and work, in turn, are placed within the context of the twenty-four-hour round of daily activity. We attempt to place the round of daily activity alongside the more festive occasions of Sabbath and holidays. And all of these are considered in relation to the social structure and the values that characterize the society.

Despite these efforts, the reader will often find himself occupied, justifiably, with the detailed report of one or another aspect of leisure. He may find himself intrigued with the patterns of leisure attitudes and behaviour which distinguish the generations, or the social classes, or the several ethnic groups.

The object of this introductory chapter, therefore, is to make certain that the trees are not permitted to obscure the view. We think the forest is there to be seen. After analyzing what nearly 4,000 Israelis had to say about their leisure and culture, we began to discern a framework – a latent structure – which brings order to what they told us. Since facts never speak for themselves, however, we cannot be certain that this ordering is correct. Perhaps there are other, equally valid, ways of imposing order on these data. The reader, of course, must judge. But it is important, we think, to present a framework at this point – rather than in a concluding chapter – so that the reader may employ it, if he chooses, as he makes his way.[1]

But before we proceed, a brief prologue about our approach to the data seems in order. While seeking to find a way of presenting this huge array of detailed data as a meaningful whole, three quite different approaches suggested themselves. We rejected two, and adopted a third. It will serve some purpose, we think, to share these deliberations with the reader.

Three Approaches to Ordering the Data

One approach would have been to report on Israel as a small state with modest but essentially modern patterns of leisure and culture. We can demonstrate that Israelis are not very different from the English, for example, in the proportion of the population who are outside their homes on a weekday evening, or in the number of books which they read; and not so different from the French in the time they spend caring for children. A good case can be made for the contention that modern societies are growing homogeneous in their patterns of spending leisure, and that Israel – for all its ostensible difference – is moving in the same general direction.[2]

Another way in which these findings might have been summed up is in terms of changes which are believed by some to be taking place in Israeli society today. Thus, it has become routine for journalists, some of whom are sensitive observers, to find materialism and pleasure-seeking on the rise in Israel: they suggest that officials and businessmen are more corruptible than before; they find more aimlessness and crime; they say tension among ethnic groups is increasing; they argue that there is a desensitizing to human suffering; they find that the interdependence of the Jewish people is a matter of decreasing concern to young Israelis.[3]

We have rejected both of these approaches. The first seems to us overly behaviouristic and too matter of fact; it ignores nothing less than the long saga from which Israel arose, the short and dramatic history of its nation-building, and the imprint of both of these – Judaism and Zionism – on its culture. To say, in behaviouristic zeal, that it resembles other small European states is to ignore its idiosyncratic meaning: where it has come from, what it is about, and the choices that lie before it.[4]

We have rejected the second approach because, while it has time perspective and is concerned with values, it is too near-sighted. It is based on a too facile romanticization of the recent past, very selectively recalled. It is based on the behaviour of very small groups and on sensational cases. Perhaps some of these indictments are correct. Indeed, our own data do give some support – though far less dramatically – to some of the allegations. For example, we find that Israeli youth are somewhat less convinced than their parents of the mutuality of dependence of the Jews in Israel and abroad. But this is a far cry from the radical changes that are alleged, and a finding that is counterbalanced by the essential *similarity* which characterizes the Israel-born generation and its parents even in this matter. Altogether, as we shall argue, we find very little evidence of a generation gap. Perhaps today's exceptional and sensational will some day prove to be the rule; perhaps the sensibilities of today's minorities are portents of tomorrow's majorities.[5] But for the moment, and in the absence of serious and much needed longitudinal studies of Israeli values, we demur. We shall be unable to say that we were not warned.

Our choice is a third way. The story in our data, we think, is neither one of small-nation normalcy nor of drastic demoralization, but of the transformation and secularization of tradition. Our thesis, in a word, is that the predominant patterns of leisure and culture in modern Israel are anchored in a set of traditional Jewish values which are undergoing a process of transformation. It might be better to say that these data describe both the ways in which Israeli society has incorporated traditional values in its rapid evolution, as well as the ways in which these values are transformed in the course of their secularization.[6] Perhaps the end-result will be normalcy and/or demoralization, but in the meanwhile, it is the process that it is important to see – and perhaps to do something about.

Secularization is presumably one of the attributes of modernization. Nowadays, however, some observers are not so sure; others would grant only that life has become more compartmentalized, and that certain institutions are governed by sacred norms and others by secular ones.[7] All agree, however, that the concept has been used in a variety of ways and deserves clarification. One writer has even pleaded for a moratorium on its use.[8]

Applying the concept of secularization to Judaism is even more problematic because Judaism, from the beginning, was infused with secular elements. It is, first of all, a national religion, albeit with a universalistic God and a universalistic ethic. It is, moreover, preoccupied with history, making it all the more difficult to decide, for example, which elements of which holidays are sacred or secular. Indeed, its overall strategy was to sanctify the secular, not in the sense of mystification but in the sense of giving religious significance to the round of everyday life. It is a religious culture which emphasizes observance and form, perhaps more than belief. Nevertheless, if the society and values of modern Israel are viewed against the backdrop of the traditional Jewish society of not-so-long ago, some meaningful comparisons can be made.

It is in this sense that we find the concept of secularization applicable to the situation we want to portray. Sometimes, we refer to the secularization of form but continuity of traditional consciousness – as in the transformation of the age-old longing for a return to Jerusalem into the business of irrigating deserts and electing parliaments.[9] Sometimes we refer to the secularization of consciousness but continuity of form – as in the re-infusion of nationalistic and naturalistic meaning into religious holidays. In either case, there appears, at first glance, considerable continuity with traditional Jewish values. In fact, however, the process of secular transformation, while preserving external forms or internal meanings, is sometimes subversive of that which it purports to continue.[10]

The themes which seem central to this framework are the following: (1) the traditional collectivity orientation of the Jewish people, opposed to the primacy of individual self-interest; (2) the traditional centrality of the nuclear family; (3) the traditional idea that the content of leisure – and indeed, the entire round of life – is normatively prescribed rather than freedom to do your own thing; (4) the traditional conception of 'the chosen people' and its reappearance in Zionist thought as a 'spiritual centre' for Jewish and humanistic creativity; (5) the traditional qualities of asceticism (sobriety) and reality orientation as opposed to hedonism and free-floating fantasy.

1. *Collectivity Orientation*

It is a nice paradox that the establishment of modern nationhood was probably easier – psychologically speaking – for the Jews than for embryonic nations that were living on their own soil. Jewish nationalism did not have the difficult job of overcoming loyalties to village and region that stood in the way of the unification of other nations. Jewish loyalties always reached beyond the local community to regional, national and international alliances with other Jewish communities everywhere, all of which shared the memory of the collective national experience in the past and of its promised renewal in the future. It was easy to adapt this image to the conceptions of European nationalism.

It hardly takes an elaborate empirical study to establish that the materialization of this dream is at hand. 'To feel pride that we have a State' tops a list of thirty-five personal, social and other 'needs' presented to the sample of respondents. Similarly, of all the holidays about which we inquired, Yom Haatzmaut (Independence Day) is the one which holds meaning for everybody – young and old, religious and irreligious, educated and uneducated, Europeans and immigrants from the East – while Yom Kippur, the holiest of the religious holidays, by comparison, is alleged to have 'no meaning for me' by 16 per cent of the population. Again, the 'readiness to sacrifice oneself for the national ideals' – which was associated, in our question, with the traditional concept of *kiddush hashem* (sanctification of the Name) – is adjudged one of the most characteristic of contemporary national traits by religious and irreligious alike.

The nation is united not only by the fact of the State and not alone by memory of the collective experience of long ago, but by more recent experience as well. The fact of the Holocaust of European Jewry preoccupies a majority of the population. The extent of reading on this subject is pervasive, and there is disquiet lest something like it happen again. It is true that this concern is more characteristic of older persons and of Ashkenazim but it is a matter of no small concern to younger people and Eastern immigrants as well.

The feeling of connection with Jews abroad is also strong. The feeling that Jews abroad are spiritually dependent on Israel is shared by all segments of the population. The feeling that Israelis, in turn, are dependent on diaspora Jewry is also high, but younger people are less likely to agree to this than their parents.

Israelis see little difference between their identities as Jews and as Israelis. Whereas Professor Herman, in his book, *Israelis and Jews*, finds that religion is a component of Israeli identity only for religious Israelis but not for irreligious ones, the present study finds the same thing holding true for *Jewish* identity![11] That is, non-religious Israelis find it possible to maintain their identity as Jews (not just as Israelis) without making room for religion. For a significant proportion of the population, in other words, the religious element has been subtracted from both Jewish and Israeli identities whereas it is present in both sets of identities for religious persons. Indeed, it appears that the two sets of identities are virtually synonymous. For all its contribution to integration of the society, here are first warnings concerning the consequences of a facile transformation of the traditional collectivity orientation of the Jewish people into the typical forms and symbols of nationhood. We shall see the manifestation of this problem again in the discussion of the transformation of traditional holidays.

We find very little evidence of a generation gap. The youth hold values and attitudes very similar to those of their parents – that is, the statistical distribution of the opinions and attitudes and behaviour of youth with respect to almost any issue is almost exactly like that of the parent generation. Where youth and parents differ, both parties know exactly where the other stands; there is no confusion about the fact that the parents are somewhat more ascetic and that the youth are more present-oriented and claim a stronger sense of social justice!

The lines along which the population does divide are educational and religious. Education is generally much stronger than ethnicity, with people of different ethnic backgrounds acting and thinking similarly given similar educational attainments. Of course, 'holding education constant', as we say, is easy to do statistically; that ought not to blind us to the fact that the educational gap is still very wide. Religion stands out as potentially the sharpest dividing line in the society. Religious people – while concentrated in the lower educational groups – not only differ in their outlook and behaviour on many things, they are also more solidary among themselves than the non-religious population. The educated religious person is at the vanguard in upholding values and practices which have a bearing on the religious outlook. Yet, religious identification does not interfere with national identification at all. The religious groups in our sample (certain extremist groups are under-represented) are, if anything, *more* Zionist than the non-religious.

How are these integrative tendencies represented in the institutions of culture and leisure? For one thing, people rely very heavily on the newspaper, the radio and on television for the feeling of being close to what is going on. These are the media of involvement with State and society, and they are very heavily used for this purpose. The newspaper is the medium *par excellence* in this respect.

Secondly, we are impressed that internal tourism (the *tiyul*) is a major integrating mechanism. There is a very large amount of travelling within the country. Upwards of two-thirds of the country have been to visit Caesarea, Hebron, Safad, the Negev. Three-quarters have visited a kibbutz. Half of the country has been to the Israel Museum. Even if *tiyul* may not be a Zionist invention – Jacob Katz, in *Tradition and Crisis*, suggests that it was popular even in Eastern Europe before emancipation[12] – there seems little doubt that the country meets each other on the road and at historical and national sites.

The holidays are major integrating events as well. As we will note below, most of them are still very viable not only for religious persons but for the irreligious as well.

Again the shared experience of the Holocaust and the Six Day War – both the actual events and the reporting of them – symbolizes the common fate. The reading of books on these two subjects has cut across all of the dividing lines of the society.

Finally, there is a strong trend towards homogenization in the consumption of culture in the country. More explicitly, if one compares a person with eight years of education in Dimona with a person of like education in Tel Aviv, the chances are very good that they will have both been to the theatre, to the movies, on a *tiyul*, etc., with about the same frequency. The chances are very good – though we did not check this explicitly – that they saw the same films and plays and visited the same sites. This is quite remarkable in view of the great disparity of cultural offerings between large towns and small ones. This does not mean that Dimona or similar towns are satisfied; they are not. Their residents complain that their leisure is impeded by inadequate facilities and unsuitable companionship. Moreover, the proportion of well-educated people is much smaller in the development towns than in Tel Aviv, and one should beware – we caution again – of generalizations based on 'holding education constant'. Nevertheless, we repeat, the homogeneity of cultural consumption – holding education constant – is remarkable. And, of course, this homogeneity is only abetted by national radio and television broadcasting and a national press. The two afternoon papers are read by 69 per cent of the population.

2. *Familism*

An equally familiar trait of Jewish civilization is the dedication to the family, and to the extended family as well. The data from this study find the family at the centre of the society's conception of itself. Along with the pride in having a State, the need 'to spend time with my family' is of foremost importance.

These are not just expressions of values or of attitudes. Familism is expressed in action. Three-quarters of the adult population of Israel (whose parents are alive) visit their parents at least once a week, and parents report visiting their married children with equal frequency! Education and social class make almost no difference here; unlike other societies, higher education if anything increases the frequency of visits.

One has the impression that Israelis – despite or because of the uprooted character of the society – are very sensitive to familial continuity: a large majority of the population feels that it has a good idea of how life was lived in grandfather's house.[13]

The time devoted to household care is not outstanding in Israel society; familism is not expressed, apparently, in housecleaning. On the other hand, the time devoted to care for children is high compared with most other nations.

When people are asked to imagine what they would do with an extra day of leisure if the five-day working week comes to pass, the most frequent answer, by far, is: 'I would spend the time with my family'. That a man 'should' spend most of his leisure time with his family is affirmed by 71 per cent.

How does the family spend its time? What cultural activities bind it together? At the moment, television is the mass medium that contributes most to family solidarity; families spend an average of one to two hours around the television set every night. Television is rather less effective in keeping adolescents and young adults, or persons with higher education, at home.

Other activities that go on inside the home are more particularized: reading, hobbies, listening to records, study. Radio-listening, too, has become a much more private affair since the advent of the transistor and the introduction of television. All these activities increase with increased education. Indeed, the culture of the home is primarily a function of education (whereas the selection of activities outside the home is governed at least as much by age). Persons of lower education spend more of their leisure sleeping or caring for their households.

Far more important than television as a medium for family solidarity are Saturdays and holidays. The Sabbath is the day which families spend together. It is the day for visiting and for more leisurely meals. For the religious, it is the day of prayer and rest. For the non-religious, it is a day for family trips and cleaning house.

A clear majority of the population wants to preserve the quiet, homey character of the Sabbath eve as it exists today in Israel. This holds equally true for young and old alike. On the other hand, when asked more explicitly whether public transportation should operate on the Sabbath and whether theatres, concert halls and movie houses should be open, they are rather less traditional in their response. Still, even here, there is a clear differentiation between more 'cultural' activities – such as community houses and theatres – and the cinema, for example. Far fewer (about 40 per cent) are in favour of opening the cinemas on Friday night. While the scriptural definition of the Sabbath is by no means the guiding ideal, it is obvious that there is a 'cultural' ideal that is shared by a good part of the population. (Only the stoutly irreligious among the well educated want a drastic change in the character of the Sabbath eve.) Once more it should be said that while there are clear signs of cultural continuity here, one should not make the mistake of assuming that no changes are at work: a drive in the family car, or playing chamber music or watching television – however cultured the content of these activities – is not what our forebears had in mind for the Sabbath.

Still another sign of the commitment to family and tradition in connection with the Sabbath is in the preference expressed for Friday, rather than Sunday or another weekday, for the second free day of the desired five-day work week. The preference for Friday – from the point of view of the quality of the culture – will have very different consequences, if adopted, than will a Saturday–Sunday weekend. The Friday–Saturday weekend implies a day of 'preparation' – as Friday is today – followed by the holy day. The Saturday–Sunday weekend provides for tension-release at the conclusion of the holy day. While Saturday night is the popular night for going out even now, if it is followed by a day which is normatively unstructured, the risk of anomie and its accompanying malaise increases. Partly this depends on what kind of cultural activities will be available for the coming extra day of leisure. The questions of (1) whether an extra day? (2) which day? and (3) what provisions will be made for cultural activities on the extra day? – are major questions for cultural policy-makers.

3. *Normative Prescriptions for Spending Leisure*

Traditional Jewish culture, like nature, did not tolerate vacuums. It made certain it sanctified activities governing the entire round of life – not just prayer time or *rites de passage* but eating time, and sleeping time and leisure time. It is another one of those nice-sounding paradoxes to say that the Jews invented leisure (in the institution of the Sabbath) and then took it back again by minutely prescribing how to spend it. Indeed, spending leisure was not left at all to the individual's discretion on weekdays either; normatively, his every moment – and all the more so if he could free himself from work – were to be devoted to sacred study. Like other norms, this one was not easy to live up to, but people were well aware of it – and tried. Nor is there reason to think that it was experienced as oppressive; quite the contrary appears likely. Moreover, as with other aspects of Jewish religious strategy, certain things that people wanted to do – like making parties, for example – were subsumed and legitimated in terms of the *halakhah* in the same way as the things they had to do – such as eating. Thus (cf. J. Katz) parties could be legitimately given on certain occasions – such as when group study of a book of the Talmud was completed or on certain holidays; then the party became a *mitzvah* and was not considered mere frivolity organized at the expense of study. And days off from work (and study) were called holidays, and each of these was a legitimation of leisure too.

The modern, secular city is at the opposite pole. Its ideal-type, at any rate, makes available the widest variety of individual choice to suit all tastes and proclivities. And modern leisure, say today's prophets, is a time for individual self-expression.

Israel (and most other places) is in-between, though it is likely that Israel is on the more traditional side here, too. First of all, there is a six-day working week. This obviously spares the society the problem of deciding what to do with a non-normatively prescribed leisure day.

Moreover, in so far as people can foresee how they would spend another free day when one becomes available, it is safe to say that they do not have very radical ideas. Most would spend more time with their families; some would rest; some would take care of their household duties; others would go on trips. The main thrust of most of these replies is that people would do more of or better in the roles to which they are already committed. Most of this extra leisure would be spent close to or inside the home. It is interesting that reading is ahead of any of the arts or the media in the list of things people say they would do with more time.

The need for rest appears to be particularly acute for certain elements of the population: the working woman, first of all; then people employed in commerce; and workers in building, industry, services. All these are tired; and want a five-day week. Agricultural workers are tired, too, but they are not enthusiastic about a shortened work week since they would not benefit much from it and might only feel deprived that others are off. Persons with low incomes are also tired, and are also unenthusiastic (relatively) about a shortened work week – perhaps because they fear reduced income, perhaps because they have little idea of the potentialities of leisure. While these groups are the more likely to relate leisure and rest, the equation of leisure and respite and of leisure and privacy (or familism) is a predominant emphasis of almost all groups. It is important to emphasize that while physical rest certainly figures in the traditional conception of leisure, so does its sacred and public aspects: the Sabbath, in the tradition, is a day of 'rest and sanctity'; and it is a day of assembly – for festive prayer and study. Moreover, it is noteworthy that the idea of spending leisure in public, and of devoting it to collective rather than private pursuits, also underlies the idea of political participation. It is not only Jewish ideals that require the normative use of leisure for their fulfilment.

Revealing evidence of the preference for normatively prescribed leisure rather than for do-your-own-thing leisure is evidenced in the attitudes of Israelis toward the holidays. The traditional holidays, in general, continue to have meaning for persons who are not religious. Unlike Sylvester or the First of May, for example, the holidays of Purim, Passover, Rosh Hashana, Hanukka – and even Shavuot (Pentecost) or Lag Ba'Omer – have retained their meaningfulness for most people. Once again, as in the case of the Sabbath, these are not the original meanings, but rather transformed meanings which represent the elevation of familial, historical, natural and other aspects of the holidays to primary positions. Thus Passover, for example, becomes a holiday whose primary meaning for many is to provide a feeling of connection to past generations and to history; Shavuot connects them to the changing seasons, etc. They might have answered – as some people did – that the holiday has no meaning for them, or that it is a day for rest or doing what I please. But they did not so answer. Interestingly, as was noted earlier, Yom Kippur is said to have 'no meaning for me' by fully 16 per cent of the population – because it is incapable of undergoing secular transformation. It is not a day on which one can go out for a picnic, or even celebrate national or social emancipation. It is a holiday for which Jewish tradition provides no alternative other than personal confrontation with God.

To a certain degree, unprescribed leisure time is made available to young people. They go out often, and engage in a variety of activities involving a mixture of friends, movies and light entertainment. Their going out is probably more aimless than the outings of their elders. Even in the case of young people, however, the need to feel that leisure is being spent constructively is an important need.

But what of the classic prescription to employ leisure time for study? Here, again, we have an example of a secular transformation of a traditional concept. Relative to other countries, Israelis spend more of their leisure time reading books. Compared with the countries of Western Europe, a larger proportion of Israelis read at least one book last year, and more are 'active readers' (eight books or more per year). The proportion of 'active readers' among all readers is about as high as in

England and the Scandinavian countries, and is somewhat higher when looked at as a proportion of the population as a whole.

So, maybe the Israelis still deserve the title of the People of the Book (an appellation given to Jews by the Moslems, incidentally). Still, even if that is so, it is important to distinguish between the classical conception of the People of the Book and the secular transformation of that concept.

The traditional idea of the People of the Book is that an entire people is simultaneously – indeed, almost continually – occupied with the same set of symbols and metaphors in terms of which their society and their perception of the world is organized. The Book is the source of rules, and the constitution by which all members – leaders included – are bound. It is an ongoing collective creation, contributed to by each generation. The secular transformation of the concept, People of the Book, is people of books, or people of reading; something quite different, obviously. There is nothing shared about the experience any more, reading is now a private experience and everybody is reading a different book. There is no little irony in the fact that something of the collective experience which once derived from the Book is now to be had from viewing television, for a majority of the population spends its evenings tuned to Israel's one channel. In this sense, television is more like the original conception of the Book than are books! But *Mission Impossible* is no match for Genesis.

4. *Chosenness*

Book-reading relates, in turn, to the conception of a 'spiritual centre' which, in turn, is a modern transformation of the concept of 'chosenness'. When asked: 'Do you think Israel should be more actively engaged in culture and learning than other nations?', 70 per cent said yes.

There is some reason to believe that they mean it. Not only are there more readers than in other countries, but there are also more people who study. (As many as a third study regularly – on their own, or with teachers.) They express a strong interest in the possibility of formal study – not necessarily for credit or degrees. They say that radio and television might be used for this purpose, even at the expense of prime-time programming. Indeed, judging from the response to this idea, if television were to devote one night a week to courses in adult education, there is a good likelihood that it would be well received. But the emphasis must *not* be on the instrumental career-oriented learning, but on learning for learning's sake. People say they want that: why not believe them?

The argument that adult education via television requires another channel because the present one is 'full' is based on the assumption that *Family Affair* and *Bewitched* and *The Saint* are the kinds of programmes people will not do without. Indeed, people say they are satisfied with these programmes – but neither do they want more of them. What they do want more of, however, is Israeli programmes – home-made programmes – in preference to the technically superior imported ones.

And for the same reason they are enthusiastic about Israeli-made movies. The loyalty to Hebrew-speaking movies is remarkably high.

That is not the case, however, for original Hebrew books. While 70 per cent of the population reads books in Hebrew almost exclusively, the large proportion of these are translations into Hebrew of foreign books. Only about 20 per cent of the population says it reads original Hebrew books 'frequently'.

It is clear that we are very far from a spiritual centre as far as indigenous creativity is concerned. It is ironic that the spectacular achievement of teaching the Hebrew language to an entire nation should result in the use of that language for translation. Israeli Culture – television, films, books – is a culture in translation, or even better, a culture in subtitles. This is true of television (50 per cent or more of programmes are imported), of film, of theatre, of books. Another of the great problems in fulfilling the dream of a 'spiritual centre' is how to foster indigenous creativity in the theatre, in film, in television. The audience is there waiting.

The idea of 'chosenness' is alive in Israel far beyond the field of adult education and learning. There are a number of other areas in which Israelis feel that their country should set a moral example. The notion of 'national purpose' is still alive in Israel, struggling with the competing idea of 'normalcy'. This is the schizophrenic aspect of the Zionist dream: to be a nation like all the others, and, at the same time, to rally to the idea of mission. The dilemma is probably more difficult now than it was in ancient Israel.

5. *Reality Orientation*

The final concept which is appropriate to our analysis is the Jewish commitment to looking soberly at the world. It is based on an ever-alert concern with what is dangerous in the environment and the need to mobilize to combat it.

Israeli culture still partakes of this kind of asceticism and reality orientation. Israelis perceive the mass media as existing more for news than for entertainment. Although there is demand for more light entertainment, too, the role of the media – even television – is thought to be primarily informational. Probably for the same reason non-fiction is far more popular than in other countries.

Still another sign of this same phenomenon is in the low importance ascribed to escapist needs – 'the need to escape from the harsh realities of everyday life', for example. And at the same time, high importance is ascribed – as has been noted – to the need 'to spend leisure constructively'. Physical indulgence – sport, for example – is also little engaged in, perhaps as another sign of asceticism.

While our study did not examine the prevalence of other media of 'escape' – liquor or drugs, for example – Israel is well known for the near-nonexistence of the problems of alcoholism, and drugs seem to be making very little headway in the society. The importance of orientation toward the future – at the expense of hedonistic gratification in the present – is a predominant emphasis of Israeli public opinion. When asked whether time spent at work or at leisure is more important, the former outdistanced the latter by far – though the proportion answering that 'both' work and leisure are important is higher still. Altogether the characterization of Israeli society as 'puritan' seems not too far off the mark. On the other hand, the high percentage who feel that luck is a major component of success, and the high proportion of participation in the several national lotteries argue in another direction. Nor is higher productivity or pride in work – attributes which were not explicitly examined here – especially conspicuous to the observer of this society. Still, orientation to reality and a general sense of sobriety and of purpose appear to be important basic values.

6. *Summary*

The threads of continuity are still clearly visible in Israeli culture. The Jewish values of collectivity orientation, familism, learning, sense of purpose and orientation to reality are all much in evidence. Some of these values remain intact it appears. Others are undergoing transformation. Thus, the People of the Book has become the people of reading; the religious festival is transformed in meaning; ethnicity and national identification appear to be subsuming religious integration.

In all of this, the generation gap does not seem much in evidence. There are some differences. The young (18–25 in our study) feel less dependent on diaspora Jewry; their thoughts turn less often to the European Holocaust; they seek more immediate gratification, as compared with the future-orientation of their parents; they may be somewhat less religious. But on the whole, they are not very much different. And will be even less so, one suspects, when they get older.

The big question is whether the transformation will preserve any semblance of the uniqueness of traditional Jewish culture. What will become of Yom Kippur, if secular Jews find trouble investing it with transformed meaning? What will become of religious holidays that have –

once again – returned to the nature, family and nation whence they arose? What will happen to the tradition of learning if it is oriented to individualistic rather than collective experience, and to career rather than learning for its own sake? Will the sense of peoplehood become standardized patriotism? Will chosenness become mere chauvinism? These are some of the major questions raised by this study.

Another set of problems has to do with artistic and cultural creativity in a small nation bent on reviving an ancient culture in a modern world. Will the satellite leave room for indigenous expression on the airwaves? Will the book written locally and in Hebrew be able to hold its own against the avalanche of imported translations? Will the nascent Israel film have a chance against the subtitled films of Hollywood? Indeed, will traditional holidays survive the electronic transmission of other people's celebrations? Will Judaism survive Zionism?

All these matters require policy decisions. There is no use evading the fact that the Government *is* actively involved in cultural policy: it subsidizes certain theatres; it gives tax rebates to certain films; it designs the Independence Day celebrations; it does not concern itself with the high cost of books; it makes the public performance of Richard Strauss very difficult; and so on.

Yet, cultural policy is rarely made explicit. The Ministry of Education and Culture is just now beginning to face up to the latter part of its name. Public discussion of the issues has hardly been encouraged, partly because of the competing interest and sensitive issues involved.[14] But perhaps the time for it has come, and perhaps the data of this study will help.

At the same time, the education of the consumer of culture needs to be cultivated. Learning how to view a television programme, or how to read a newspaper is one aspect of this. Pondering the contemporary meaning of traditional holidays is another. Contemplating how – or whether – to give expression to the national quest for moral purpose is still another. Adult education – in its broadest sense – is the challenge of Israeli culture. It is, potentially, also the most important link to the kind of continuing education which was the most distinctive aspect of traditional Jewish culture. Thought and resources must be made available for its cultivation.

If this introductory chapter provides some stimulus and some structure for the thought that these problems deserve it will have served its purpose. Its purpose – as will be recalled – was to reveal the major themes which seem to us to underlie the mass of empirical materials which went into the making of this book.

NOTES – CHAPTER TWO

1. We refer throughout this chapter to data which are reported and discussed in the chapters that follow. We do not cite chapter and verse here. Nor do we emphasize what should already be clear from the previous chapter: that the data are based on responses to a questionnaire about attitudes, meanings and behaviour with respect to the consumption of culture, communication and leisure.
2. For a persuasive argument that students of leisure focus too much on national and subgroup differences and too little on the similar rhythms of modern societies, see Kenneth Roberts, op. cit.
3. In fact, the collection of our data pre-dates much of this writing. This is of some import inasmuch as it is the *relative* decline in concern over security problems which is blamed for some of these alleged changes. This is another possible reason why our data do not reflect them (or why we did not focus on them as directly as we might have, if our study were being designed today). It is certainly true that a decline in the pre-occupation with security brings the domestic problems of social and economic relations to the fore; Israel will have to grapple with these. It is also true that in circumstances of ostensible calm the newspapers have more room, and more time, to put these problems on society's agenda.
4. This is the objection to all purely behavioural analysis, of course, whether of the Kinsey-type studies of human sexual behaviour or of behavioural studies of the uses of time, where one kind of act is equated with another so long as they consume the same amount of time. There is much to be learned from such data, however; indeed, as noted above, a considerable part of our own analysis is based on such materials. But, clearly, they are not 'sufficient'.
5. Survey research based on random sampling gives every respondent an equal vote. But radical social change is, of course, not usually accomplished by majority vote. Methodologically, it suggests that several parallel lines of social inquiry must be carried out at the same time, and with different populations. And that each of these lines of investigation must be continued over time.
6. We are sidestepping the question of how Israeli culture and leisure are different from that of Jewish communities in the diaspora. Clearly, the process of secularization in Judaism did not begin with Israel, or even with Zionism. And the tension between ethnicity and religion has marked the history of modern Jewish thought not only for the irreligious but for the religious as well; indeed, this is part of what Reform Judaism was (is?) all about. We ask forgiveness of those who would have liked us to face this larger question head-on. We hope, nonetheless, that this portrait of Israel will contribute to the larger discussion, in which the role of Israel – as the Jewish State – features so prominently.
7. See, for example, Andrew Greeley, *The Denominational Society*, New York: Scott, Foresman, 1972.
8. David Martin, *The Religious and the Secular*, London: Routledge & Kegan Paul, 1969. See especially Chapter 1, 'Toward Eliminating the Concept of Secularization', and Chapter 4, 'Secularization: The Range

of Meaning'; Michael Hill, *The Sociology of Religion*, London: Heinemann Ed. Books, 1973, Chapter 11, 'Secularization: the varieties of meanings'.

9. The distinction between secularization of social structure and of consciousness is Peter Berger's in *The Social Reality of Religion*, London: Faber and Faber, 1968. In discussing Israelite religion, Berger tends to see the Jews as de-mystifiers of primitive religions and hence a secularizing influence from the beginning. Our outlook is rather different, as noted above.
10. Here we disagree with writers like Andrew Greeley who argue that secularization is not rampant in modern society and that the sacred and the traditional are holding their own, at least as well as in earlier societies. For the case reported here, the evidence of the continuity of tradition is there to be seen; indeed, that is the point of this chapter. But the process of secularization and its ultimate subversion of the sacred seems equally apparent. One can remember what Passover used to be like in one's parents' home and, re-enacting its forms, infuse it with secular meanings. But even if the result can be institutionalized one cannot transmit this *process* to another generation; that is the problem.
11. Simon Herman, *Israelis and Jews*, New York: Random House, 1970.
12. Jacob Katz, *Tradition and Crisis: Jewish Society at the End of the Middle Ages*, New York: Free Press, 1961.
13. This is one of the points at which a comparison between second- and third-generation Israelis and their cousins in Britain or the United States might be very revealing. One has the impression that immigrants to America did not give their children much of a picture of what life was like in their parents' home in Eastern Europe, whereas Israelis of comparable origin have a clearer picture. But this is just a guess – and eminently worth studying, though the picture grows cloudier with each new fiddler on each old roof.
14. For a discussion of certain of the areas of conflict over cultural policy, see S. N. Eisenstadt, *Israeli Society*, London: Weidenfeld and Nicolson, 1967, pp. 372–90.

PART TWO WEEKDAYS AND FEASTDAYS: THE ROUND OF LIFE

CHAPTER THREE The Allocation of Time

Time, like money and power, is a scarce resource. Time is even scarcer, perhaps, since human beings can never be certain how much of it they have. While scarce resources such as time, money and power are things most people want, some people would gladly forgo them if they could. For example, those who have *only* time – some old people, prisoners, the unemployed – do not know what to 'do' with their time. Others think that possession of these resources is corrupting, whence come ideologies such as the religions of labour (and the fear of free time), of abstinence and frugality (and the fear of money), and of turning the other cheek to power.

The ways in which societies use their scarce resources – time, money, power – reflect their values. The same thing is true of individual members of society – at least to the extent that they have access to these resources, and a certain amount of freedom to deploy them. The areas of discretion in spending time or money or power, even when these are available, are hedged in by all kinds of restrictions stemming from obligations imposed on individuals by the roles which they have assumed or been assigned. Hence 'free time' is often equated with non-working hours, whereas, in fact, these hours may be no less strongly spoken for – by family, or by commutation trains, or by religious precepts – than the working hours.[1]

Some theorists would say that the only truly 'free' time is when individuals can freely elect to 'do their own thing'. All this, ultimately, confronts us with the classical problems of defining freedom – something which we are not free to do just here. Here we shall note only that the traditional Jewish conception of leisure is at once highly progressive and highly conservative. Judaism invented leisure, so to speak, in the institution of the Sabbath. But the Sabbath, as has already been noted, is not just a day of rest, but a day of sanctity and obligation in which prayer and study and care for family are prescribed activities. The Sabbath is a good illustration of the Jewish attitude toward 'free time': it is very largely spoken for. Indeed, the entire round of life is normatively prescribed in Judaism, as we have already said and shall continue to say.

Does Israel continue in these footsteps? The answer is yes and no, as the facts will show.

1. *The Method of Time-Budget Research*

One of the oldest of social science methodologies is the time budget.[2] This method studies the way in which societies or subgroups allocate their time among a variety of activities during the course of a day. Since all modern societies count time in terms of minutes, hours, days and weeks, this method is attractive for comparative study. In the last few years, a study of the use of time in twelve different countries has been carried out under the direction of Alexander Szalai and similar work has been done in Japan, Britain and elsewhere.[3] It was Szalai's work that gave us the idea of including time budgets in the present study. While our method is not an exact replication of Szalai's, we believe it permits comparison nonetheless.[4] Thus, we shall not only be able to describe the ways in which Israelis use their time, but also the extent to which Israel is similar, in this respect, to other nations. Luckily, we also have some of our own comparative data from a study in two Israeli cities carried out in 1966 – prior to the introduction of television![5]

During the course of the interview respondents were asked to reconstruct the way in which they had allocated their time during the day before.[6] People who were interviewed on a Friday, for example, were asked to think back and tell us exactly what they had done for the 24 hours beginning at 4 o'clock on Thursday morning and ending at 4 a.m. on Friday. They did so according to a list of 48 different activities with which we provided them. They told us how long they had engaged in a particular activity, where the activity took place, who else was with them, and whether any other activity was carried on at the same time.

This method, then, permits us to say how much time is given by society, or some group within society, to a particular activity, be it housecleaning or prayer. When, where and with whom the activity took place can also be summed up. The time-budget method can also portray what is going on in a society on Thursday evenings or Saturday mornings. It must be borne in mind that the figure given for each activity represents the average amount of time over a 24-hour period invested in an activity by a group or society: if 4·3 hours is the amount of time given to paid employment in Israel on an average weekday, it may mean *either* that every adult works 4·3 hours, *or* that some people work 7, 8 or 9 hours while other people are not gainfully employed. Only a comparison of subgroups – by sex, for example – can provide the answer. There are many other methodological problems in time-budget research, some of which will become apparent.[7] But it has its distinct advantages as well.

2. *National Differences: Israel and Other Countries*

The first thing we shall do is to compare the time budgets of Israelis with ten of the nations studied by Szalai in 1965–6. To make the comparison more valid, only urban Israelis are included in Table 3.1, since all of Szalai's data refer to city-dwellers. In addition, the 48 categories in our study are collapsed to make them comparable to Szalai's. Note that the table averages activities for an average day, thus combining weekdays and weekends. For ease of reading, the figures are presented in hours and tenths of hours (one tenth of an hour equals 6 minutes) and each column adds up to 24 hours.

The first activity given in Table 3.1 is gainful employment. The figure for Israel is low in comparison with that of other countries. Israelis appear to work fewer hours, on an average day, than do people in other countries. This rather low figure, as was hinted earlier, is due to the smaller proportion of women in the full-time labour force. Only 27 per cent of female respondents were employed, compared with 40–50 per cent in the Western countries and 60–90 per cent in Eastern Europe.[8] Thus, while the norm for a working day in Israel is 7–8 hours, the smaller proportion of women in the labour force reduces the average daily total invested in work *by the society* to a figure roughly comparable to that of the United States and Germany.

The high proportion of non-working wives is not reflected in housekeeping (line 2 of Table 3.1) but *is* reflected in child care (line 4). In attention to children Israel and France lead the list of eleven countries cited here. Here is a first fact about the family-centredness of Israel.[9]

The amount of time devoted to sleep and rest is higher than in any but the three countries of Western Europe, and Israel spends a lot of time at the dining-table, too. In both these activities, Israel is more like Western Europe than Eastern Europe, and these figures, presumably, are related to the amount of time spent on the job.

Among the leisure activities (lines 8–16) Israelis stand first in time devoted to 'social life' – that is, to entertaining, or being entertained by others. This confirms the image of some that the national pastime of Israelis is visiting friends and relatives. Israelis spend a lot of time reading books and newspapers, comparatively speaking; the Russians spend even more, however.

Among the remaining activities, Israel is distinctively low in the amount of time devoted to commercial non-home recreation – movies, theatre, discotheques, night clubs, coffee houses, etc. It is not that they spend all their time at home – as the amount spent on 'excursions and travel' or visiting will show; nor is it that they go infrequently to movies, theatres and museums – evidence to the contrary will be presented later. These data apparently mean that other forms of commercial

TABLE 3.1 *Time in Hours* Devoted to Various Primary Activities in Selected Urban Areas in Eleven Countries†*

Activities	Bulgaria (Kazanlik)	Hungary (Gyor)	U.S.S.R. (Pskov)	Yugoslavia (Maribor)	Poland (Tourun)	Czechoslovakia (Oloumouc)	W. Germany (100 urban areas)	France (6 cities)	Belgium (national sample)	U.S. (Jackson, Michigan)	Israel
1. Gainful employment	5·6	5·4	5·4	4·5	4·9	4·7	3·7	4·3	4·4	4·1	3·9
2. Household care	2·4	3·4	2·3	4·1	2·7	3·1	3·4	2·9	2·6	2·2	2·1
3. Shopping	0·4	0·3	0·4	0·3	0·5	0·6	0·4	0·4	0·3	0·6	0·4
4. Child care	0·3	0·4	0·4	0·4	0·4	0·4	0·4	0·6	0·3	0·4	0·6
5. Sleep and rest	8·5	8·1	7·9	8·2	8·1	8·2	8·8	8·8	8·8	8·2	8·7
6. Eating	1·2	1·0	0·8	1·1	1·1	1·0	1·5	1·7	1·6	1·1	1·4
7. Personal care	0·8	0·9	0·8	0·8	0·9	1·2	0·9	0·9	0·7	1·0	0·8
8. Reading	0·5	0·4	0·8	0·5	0·6	0·6	0·4	0·4	0·6	0·6	0·7
9. Radio	0·3	0·2	0·1	0·1	0·2	0·2	0·1	0·1	0·1	0·0	0·2
10. Television	0·3	0·7	0·7	0·7	1·1	1·1	1·0	0·9	1·4	1·7	0·9
11. Social life‡	0·2	0·4	0·3	0·6	0·6	0·4	0·8	0·6	0·7	1·2	1·3
12. Conversation	0·2	0·2	0·2	0·2	0·2	0·2	0·3	0·3	0·3	0·3	0·3
13. Walking	0·4	0·2	0·3	0·3	0·2	0·3	0·6	0·2	0·2	0·0	0·2
14. Sports	0·1	0·1	0·1	0·1	0·0	0·0	0·2	0·0	0·1	0·1	0·0
15. Other non-home recreation§	0·6	0·2	0·5	0·3	0·3	0·4	0·3	0·5	0·7	0·4	0·2
16. Excursions, travel	1·3	1·2	1·3	1·1	1·2	0·9	0·6	0·9	0·9	1·2	1·2
17. Other	0·9	0·9	1·8	0·7	1·0	0·7	0·6	0·5	0·3	0·9	1·1
TOTAL	24·0	24·0	24·0	24·0	24·0	24·0	24·0	24·0	24·0	24·0	24·0

* Based upon an average of 7 days of the week. Figures are hours and tenths of an hour.
† Data from other countries collected in 1965–6, as reported in Szalai, ed., *The Use of Time*, The Hague: Mouton, 1972.
‡ Includes visiting, hosting, parties, dances, games.

recreation – 'going out' to a pub, restaurant, coffee house, night club, etc. – occupy rather less time in Israel than elsewhere.

Considering that television was only two years old at the time of the study, that there were few hours of broadcasting and that only about 60 per cent owned sets, the time spent watching TV in Israel seems quite high. It equals that of France which has about a like proportion of sets but has many more broadcast hours. The viewing time was only half that of the United States which had, however, twice the proportion of sets[10] and, of course, television broadcasting almost around the clock.

By comparison with ten European countries, then, Israelis invest their time rather more like the people of Western Europe than Eastern Europe. This is reflected particularly in time spent working, resting and eating. Israelis spend a lot of time, comparatively, in attention to children and in reading.

The contrast with Japan is much more striking.[11] Japanese spend more time working and less time resting than even the Eastern Europeans. On the other hand, their rate of radio and television consumption is surely the highest in the world. An average day finds the average Japanese sitting before his television set for three hours and listening to the radio for half an hour. Time spent in reading is almost as high as in Israel, but social intercourse and other out-of-home leisure activities are afforded far less time in Japan than in Israel.

3. *Subgroup Differences in Time Allocation*

Cross-national comparisons provide only a framework for a deeper understanding of the differential allocation of time to various activities. There is no 'average Israeli', of course, and the sample must be broken down into more realistic units. We do so here according to sex and employment, education, and type of community. The tables refer to *weekdays only*.

Table 3.2 compares the time budgets of employed men, employed women and housewives. Here the problem of working hours becomes clear at a glance. Men who work do so, on the average, 7·4 hours per day; employed women work rather fewer hours. Adding the obligations of work and household (lines 1–4) finds working women devoting 8·6 hours per weekday to these pursuits, working men 8·4 hours, and housewives only 6·9 hours – or 1·5 hours less than their working sisters.[12] Housewives also spend more time eating, sleeping, resting, watching television and socializing. The fact that working women spend more time reading, studying and 'going out' suggests – what we know to be true – that they are also better educated, but chances are that they are more alert to the Big World as well.

TABLE 3.2 *Time in Hours Devoted to Primary Activities on an Average Weekday, by Sex and Employment Status*
Weighted

	Men employed	Women employed	House-wives
1. Gainful employment	7·4	5·7	0·2
2. Household care	0·6	2·0	4·9
3. Shopping	0·1	0·3	0·8
4. Child care	0·3	0·6	1·0
5. Sleep	7·2	7·4	8·0
6. Rest	0·9	0·9	1·5
7. Eating	1·4	1·1	1·5
8. Personal care	0·9	0·9	0·8
9. Prayer	0·2	–	–
10. Studies	0·2	0·2	0·0
11. Clubs, organizations	0·1	0·0	0·0
12. Newspapers and periodicals	0·4	0·3	0·3
13. Books	0·2	0·4	0·2
14. Radio	0·2	0·1	0·1
15. Television	1·0	0·8	1·1
16. Social life*	0·8	1·0	1·2
17. Conversations	0·2	0·1	0·2
18. Walks	0·1	0·1	0·2
19. Sports	–	0·1	–
20. Hobby, creative activity	–	0·1	0·2
21. Excursions, pleasure trips	0·1	0·1	0·2
22. Other non-home recreation†	0·2	0·3	0·1
23. Work trips	0·9	0·9	0·1
24. Non-work trips	0·3	0·4	0·6
25. Other	0·3	0·2	0·8
TOTAL	24·0	24·0	24·0
Total leisure time (11–22)	3·3	3·4	3·8
Unweighted N =	(647)	(215)	(359)

* Includes visiting, hosting, parties, dances, games.

† Includes cinema, theatre, museums, exhibitions, concerts, light entertainment, coffee houses, night clubs, discotheques.

Indeed, education makes a very big difference in time budgeting as it does in almost every other activity or attitude to be reported in this volume. Consider Table 3.3. The most educated group (University degrees) contributes most working hours: this is because professionals and executives actually spend more time at their work and because there are more working women in this group. They also travel longer and probably further in connection with work (line 23). The more education, the less time spent on household care, on shopping, and on sleep and eating. And the less time spent in prayer. Notice that time spent on child care is not affected by education. Indeed, time spent on child care – as a primary activity – seems to be almost invariant regardless of the factor considered – including number of children![13]

Thus, although the better educated may spend more time, or no less time, at work, they do spend less time at some of the 'obligatory' activities – such as sleep, prayer and household care – and thus have *more* time for leisure. The amount of leisure time summarized at the foot of the table increases with education.

How do the well educated spend their leisure? The main differences apparent in the table are in the amount of time spent reading newspapers and books (lines 12, 13) and in study (line 10).[14] Excursions are also positively related to education (21). *Only* the well educated belong to voluntary organizations (11): but radio, television and sociability are not related to education – and these daily activities account for almost half of the society's leisure time. Putting it more precisely, the table suggests that radio, television and sociability (14–16) peak among those with middle levels of education, tapering off, but only slightly, at the two extremes of the highs and the very lows.[15]

In sum, the better educated spend more time at their jobs, and more time at their toilette. They travel more – for business and pleasure – read more and study more. They spend less time than the less educated in housekeeping, sleeping, resting, eating and praying. The society is almost as one man as far as time spent with the electronic media and in sociability.

Most of these differences in education are reflected in a comparison of the time budgets for different kinds of settlements – large urban centres, developing towns and kibbutzim. In comparing these, as Table 3.4 does, note that more time is spent on household care, prayer, sleep, rest and food in the development towns than in the cities. But the educational advantage of the city is not the only explanation for these differences: note the low level of sociability in the new towns (line 16). The time spent on social life in the city is twice the amount in development towns, and we know that sociability is *not* closely related to education. In discussing the leisure problems of the new towns, we shall discover that the perceived lack of appropriate companionship is

TABLE 3.3 *Time in Hours Devoted to Primary Activities on an Average Weekday, by Years of Schooling*
Weighted

	Years of Education						
	0	1–4	5–8	9–10	11–12	12 + (no degree)	12 + (with degree)
1. Gainful employment	2·2	4·4	4·4	4·1	4·5	4·1	5·6
2. Household care	4·8	2·8	2·3	2·4	1·9	1·6	1·1
3. Shopping	0·4	0·5	0·4	0·5	0·4	0·3	0·2
4. Child care	0·7	0·5	0·5	0·6	0·6	0·3	0·6
5. Sleep	8·2	8·0	7·7	7·7	7·4	7·4	7·0
6. Rest	2·2	0·9	1·3	1·1	0·9	1·0	1·0
7. Eating	1·4	1·4	1·4	1·3	1·4	1·3	1·2
8. Personal care	0·7	0·8	0·8	0·9	0·9	0·9	1·0
9. Prayer	0·2	0·2	0·1	0·1	0·1	0·1	–
10. Studies	–	0·1	0·1	0·1	0·4	1·6	0·4
11. Clubs, organizations	–	–	–	–	–	0·1	0·1
12. Newspapers and periodicals	0·0	0·1	0·3	0·4	0·5	0·5	0·6
13. Books	0·1	0·1	0·2	0·2	0·3	0·5	0·6
14. Radio	0·1	0·3	0·2	0·2	0·2	0·3	0·2
15. Television	0·7	0·9	1·2	0·9	0·9	0·7	0·8
16. Social life*	0·8	1·0	1·0	1·0	1·1	0·9	0·8
17. Conversation	0·2	0·2	0·2	0·2	0·2	0·2	0·1
18. Walk	0·1	0·1	0·2	0·3	0·2	0·1	0·2
19. Sports	–	–	–	–	0·1	–	–
20. Hobby, creative activity	0·0	0·1	0·1	0·1	0·1	0·1	0·1
21. Excursions, pleasure trips	–	–	0·1	0·1	0·1	0·2	0·3
22. Other non-home recreation†	0·1	0·1	0·1	0·1	0·1	0·1	0·1
23. Work trips	0·3	0·5	0·6	0·5	0·7	0·7	0·8
24. Non-work trips	0·4	0·5	0·5	0·5	0·4	0·5	0·6
25. Other	0·4	0·5	0·3	0·7	0·6	0·5	0·6
TOTAL	24·0	24·0	24·0	24·0	24·0	24·0	24·0
Total leisure time (11–22)	2·1	2·9	3·6	3·5	3·8	3·7	3·9
Unweighted N =	(134)	(95)	(442)	(288)	(416)	(152)	(78)

* Includes visiting, hosting, parties, dances, games.

† Includes cinema, theatre, museums, exhibitions, concerts, light entertainment, coffee houses, night clubs, discotheques.

TABLE 3.4 *Time in Hours Devoted to Primary Activities on an Average Weekday in Three Types of Settlement*
Unweighted

	Large urban centres	New development towns	Kibbutzim
1. Gainful employment	4·3	4·6	5·3
2. Household care	2·2	2·7	0·7
3. Shopping	0·4	0·3	0·1
4. Child care	0·5	0·4	1·3
5. Sleep	7·4	7·7	7·0
6. Rest	1·0	1·3	1·6
7. Eating	1·3	1·5	1·5
8. Personal care	0·9	0·8	1·0
9. Prayer	0·1	0·2	–
10. Studies	0·5	0·2	0·9
11. Clubs, organizations	0·1	–	–
12. Newspapers and periodicals	0·5	0·2	0·5
13. Books	0·3	0·3	0·5
14. Radio	0·3	0·1	0·4
15. Television	1·0	0·9	0·4
16. Social life*	1·1	0·6	0·9
17. Conversation	0·2	0·2	0·1
18. Walk	0·2	0·2	–
19. Sports	–	–	0·1
20. Hobby, creative activity	0·1	0·1	0·1
21. Excursions, pleasure trips	0·1	0·1	0·1
22. Other non-home recreation†	0·2	0·3	0·3
23. Work trips	0·6	0·6	0·4
24. Non-work trips	0·5	0·4	0·3
25. Other	0·2	0·3	0·5
TOTAL	24·0	24·0	24·0
Total leisure time (11–22)	4·1	3·0	3·4
N =	(578)	(196)	(51)

* Includes visiting, hosting, parties, dances, games.

† Includes cinema, theatre, museums, exhibitions, concerts, light entertainment, coffee houses, night clubs, discotheques.

one of the persistent complaints heard from new-town dwellers about the state of their leisure.[16]

The kibbutz makes an interesting contrast to both types of urban communities. The fact that women's place in the labour force is taken for granted in the kibbutz raises the average number of hours worked. Moreover, since the 'Sabbath' is, to some degree, a rotating day in the kibbutz these weekday figures probably underestimate the total average of working hours which would be higher still if averaged over seven days. The strikingly low figure for household care and shopping also reflects the communal life of the kibbutz which relieves most of its members of these tasks and puts them in the hands of members whose job it is to prepare food or to do the laundry for the entire community.

According to the data, kibbutz members spend almost an hour more in child care than do respondents from the city or development towns. To some extent, this sharp difference may be an artefact of the coding system which takes account only of primary activities; that is, of activities which were the chief content of a particular unit of time. Since kibbutz life is planned in precisely such terms – where time is set aside, in the nursery, or in the member's rooms – for giving undivided attention to a child, it is relatively easy for a kibbutz member to respond in these terms. In the city, however, while the child may be in contact with his parents more of the time, attention to him may be interspersed among other household activities. Attending to his physical needs may at times stand out as a central activity, but less well-defined interactions between parent and child may go unrecorded in time-budget interviewing and coding. This explanation is confirmed by other time-budget data which show that most daily activities go on in the presence of children, whether or not the children are explicitly the objects of the activity. In sum, urban and kibbutz parents spend an equal amount of time with their children present, but kibbutz children have more of their parents' time exclusively to themselves.

Kibbutz members spend much more time in studies and book-reading than do urban dwellers, and less time viewing television. The communal location of television sets may explain the latter finding, while the educational level of kibbutz members and the strong affirmative attitude toward study explain the former. Interestingly, the time spent on sociability – visiting, etc. – is lower in the kibbutz than in the city. But, then, kibbutz members are interacting with others all day long in the course of activities which, in the city, would normally be carried out in private or in the nuclear family.[17]

4. *Weekdays and the Sabbath*

In presenting time budgets for the various subgroups, we have been discussing weekdays only. Preliminary investigation revealed that the method is not sensitive enough to discern the very subtle differences which make the 'culture' of Thursday, say, different from the culture of Monday or Tuesday. Perhaps there are no such differences, thus belying the children's limerick of what each of the days is for.

For the present purpose, we have thrown Sunday through Thursday together and averaged them into a 'weekday', and now we want to compare this average weekday to Fridays and Saturdays. The Israeli weekend begins some time on Friday afternoon – most people get off a little earlier, and most shops are open until noon. It ends on Sunday morning, when work begins as usual.

In Table 3.5, we compare the 'culture' of these three days as it is expressed in the time-budget data, and in the column at the right, data are presented for the holiday of Shavuot (Pentecost) which occurred during the survey period.

Surprisingly, there is very little increase in leisure time as between Fridays and weekdays. People do work less, but they spend more time housekeeping and on personal care. And, of course, there is the festive Sabbath meal on Friday evening which takes more time than weekday meals, just as Sabbath prayer takes more time than weekday prayer. All these, considered normatively obligatory, reduce the discretionary leisure time (lines 11–22) on Fridays.

Compared with an average weekday, more time is spent on Fridays in socializing and reading newspapers; in fact, the weekend newspapers are published on Friday and there are no Saturday editions. But these activities, along with more festive dining, are really a part of the culture of the Sabbath which continues from Friday sundown to Saturday sunset. This would have been the better unit for time-budget analysis from the point of view of the Jewish calendar.

Such an analysis would show what we have already seen, and more. The Friday afternoon hours would emerge as a time of 'preparation' of the self, the household and the automobile. A lot of cleansing goes on on Friday afternoons. And there is newspaper-reading and resting.

On the Sabbath eve – Friday night – a strong spurt of sociability may be discerned: the festive family meal, a rise in visiting and being visited, and in group activity generally. Television viewing increases, too – since the same overall amount of time is devoted to TV, despite the abstention for religious reasons of over 20 per cent of viewers. And television is a sociable act: it is a family affair. (It is much too elitist and simplistic to say that television is only a stifler of conversation.)[18]

On the Sabbath day, there is rest, first and foremost. While the average person retires somewhat later on Friday nights, he rises much later on Saturday mornings. Compared with weekdays, people sleep or rest for two and a half additional hours on Saturdays. Of course

TABLE 3.5 *Time in Hours Devoted to Primary Activities on an Average Weekday, Friday, Saturday, and Shavuot*
Weighted

	Weekday	Friday	Saturday	Shavuot*
1. Gainful employment	4·3	3·6	0·5	0·2
2. Household care	2·3	2·7	1·1	1·5
3. Shopping	0·4	0·3	0·0	0·1
4. Child care	0·5	0·6	0·6	0·2
5. Sleep	7·6	7·3	9·3	9·4
6. Rest	1·2	1·4	1·9	1·8
7. Eating	1·3	1·6	1·7	1·6
8. Personal care	0·8	1·0	0·8	0·8
9. Prayer	0·1	0·3	0·7	0·4
10. Studies	0·3	0·2	0·2	–
11. Clubs, organizations	–	–	0·1	–
12. Newspapers and periodicals	0·4	0·6	0·5	0·7
13. Books	0·3	0·2	0·2	0·4
14. Radio	0·2	0·1	0·2	0·3
15. Television	0·9	0·9	0·8	1·3
16. Social life†	1·0	1·2	2·1	2·0
17. Conversation	0·2	0·2	0·4	0·3
18. Walks	0·2	0·2	0·5	0·6
19. Sports	0·0	0·1	0·1	0·2
20. Hobby, creative activity	0·1	0·0	0·1	0·1
21. Excursions, pleasure trips	0·1	0·1	0·8	0·5
22. Other non-home recreation‡	0·2	0·2	0·3	0·6
23. Work trips	0·6	0·5	0·1	0·2
24. Non-work trips	0·5	0·3	0·5	0·3
25. Other	0·5	0·4	0·5	0·5
TOTAL	24·0	24·0	24·0	24·0
Total leisure time (11–22)	3·6	3·8	6·1	7·0
Unweighted N =	(1614)	(320)	(267)	(27)

* Shavuot data are unweighted due to the small size of the sample.
† Includes visiting, hosting, parties, dances, games.
‡ Includes cinema, theatre, museums, exhibitions, concerts, light entertainment, coffee houses, night clubs, discotheques.

more time is devoted to prayer. As for leisure, two types of activity predominate: socializing and excursions. People seek out each other, and they go on family trips and walks.

On Saturday night, after sunset, the theatres and the coffee houses open, and while the level of social intercourse remains high, the mood has changed. Of course, time-budget data cannot show changes of mood, but participant observation can.

To this behaviouristic portrait of the Sabbath three more aspects contributed by this study can be added. First, what has been said already can be made more vivid by comparing the evening hours of weekdays, Fridays and Saturdays alone – in terms of the number of people who are engaged in various activities. This can be done by the time-budget method. Secondly, it is of obvious interest to separate out the time budgets of religious and secular persons. Finally, we want to examine not just behaviour on, but *attitudes* toward, the Sabbath. The first and second of these three tasks are undertaken in Tables 3.6 and 3.7. The third is the central theme of the first part of Chapter Five.

Table 3.6, then, reports on the percentage of participants in leisure activities from 7 p.m. to midnight. At first glance, it might seem that the home-consumed media fare badly at the weekend. But, as was already pointed out, this is misleading inasmuch as a fifth or more of the population do not tune in the radio or TV on Friday nights because they do not switch on electric light or power.[19] Expressed as a percentage of the *potential* audience, therefore, television has four-fifths of it on Friday nights.

Evening radio-listening, on the other hand, is simply not an event for the weekend; and the drop in religious listenership cannot explain that fact away. Newspaper-reading is up on Friday nights, but sharply down on Saturday nights, when, of course, there is nothing but yesterday's newspaper to read. Reading books is also sharply reduced on weekend evenings, but these are good nights for listening to gramophone records.

The increased visiting of Friday and Saturday nights is evident in the table. Friday night, more than Saturday, is for chess and card games, while Saturday night is for the cinema and the coffee house. There is much strolling in the streets on weekend nights – especially on Saturday – a function of people being out because they are 'going somewhere' or being out 'anyway'. The 'passegiata' is a familiar sight in Israeli small town and village streets.

The difference between weekdays and the Israeli weekend becomes clearer still from a comparison of the activities of religious and non-religious persons, as is done in Table 3.7. Because of a methodological difficulty, religious persons – for the purpose of this table – are defined behaviourally as those who say they do not tune in their radios on the Sabbath.[20]

TABLE 3.6 *Percentage of the Respondents Participating in Various Leisure Activities* between 7 p.m. and Midnight on an Average Weekday, Friday, and Saturday*

Weighted

	Weekday evening	Friday evening	Saturday evening
Mass media			
Television	53	50	48
Radio	43	27	31
Newspaper	21	24	8
Book	15	8	7
Periodical	2	2	1
Gramophone records	1	3	3
Social life			
Conversation	20	20	19
Visiting	16	18	21
Hosting	11	14	13
Parties, dances	3	5	3
Games	2	4	3
Non-home recreation			
Cinema	4	2	8
Theatre	1	1	1
Light entertainment	1	1	–
Night clubs, discotheques	1	2	–
Coffee houses	1	1	3
Museums, exhibitions	–	–	–
Concerts	–	–	–
Other leisure activity			
Walking (in town)	5	8	13
Hobbies	3	1	1
Excursion, pleasure trips	1	1	2
Letter-writing	1	–	1
Unweighted N =	(1614)	(320)	(267)

* As a primary or a secondary activity.

TABLE 3.7 *Time in Hours Devoted to Primary Activities, by Religiosity**
Weighted

	Weekday		Friday		Saturday	
	N.–R.	Rel.	N.–R.	Rel.	N.–R.	Rel.
1. Gainful employment	4·6	3·5	3·9	3·2	0·6	0·3
2. Household care	2·0	3·0	2·6	2·9	1·3	0·5
3. Shopping	0·4	0·4	0·3	0·4	–	–
4. Child care	0·4	0·5	0·5	0·7	0·6	0·6
5. Sleep	7·6	7·9	7·1	8·2	9·2	9·5
6. Rest	1·0	1·3	1·4	1·7	1·7	2·3
7. Eating	1·3	1·3	1·6	1·7	1·7	1·9
8. Personal care	0·9	0·8	1·0	1·0	0·8	0·8
9. Prayer	–	0·3	0·1	0·8	0·1	2·3
10. Studies	0·3	0·4	0·1	0·1	0·1	0·2
11. Clubs, organizations	–	–	–	–	–	–
12. Newspapers and periodicals	0·4	0·2	0·6	0·4	0·5	0·5
13. Books	0·3	0·2	0·2	0·2	0·2	0·2
14. Radio	0·2	0·2	0·2	0·1	0·2	0·2
15. Television	1·0	0·7	1·1	0·3	0·9	0·5
16. Social life†	1·0	1·0	1·4	1·7	2·2	2·1
17. Conversation	0·2	0·2	0·2	0·3	0·4	0·4
18. Walk	0·2	0·2	0·1	0·3	0·4	0·9
19. Sports	–	–	0·1	–	0·2	–
20. Hobby, creative activity	0·1	0·1	–	–	0·1	–
21. Excursions, pleasure trips	0·1	0·1	0·1	0·0	1·1	0·1
22. Other non-home recreation‡	0·2	0·2	0·3	0·1	0·4	0·2
23. Work trips	0·6	0·5	0·4	0·4	0·1	–
24. Non-work trips	0·5	0·5	0·4	0·2	0·6	0·2
25. Other	0·5	0·5	0·3	0·3	0·6	0·3
TOTAL	24·0	24·0	24·0	24·0	24·0	24·0
Total leisure time (11–22)	3·7	3·1	4·3	2·4	6·6	5·1
Unweighted N =	(1012)	(344)	(197)	(71)	(189)	(70)

* Religious defined as those who reportedly do not turn on the radio on the Sabbath, non-religious defined as those who do.

† Includes visiting, hosting, parties, dances, games.

‡ Includes cinema, theatre, museums, exhibitions, concerts, light entertainment, coffee houses, night clubs, discotheques.

On weekdays, there are some differences between the two groups. In large part these are due to the lower educational level of the religious group. But the differences between the two groups on Fridays and Saturdays are far greater than the weekday differences, and reflect the influence of religious practice.

Consider Friday. Religious persons do not watch television on Friday nights and they do less socializing. What do they do with this 'extra' time? They pray; they stroll; and they go to bed. On the average, they are in bed an hour earlier than the non-religious.

On Saturday, religious persons spend over two hours at the synagogue. What do the non-religious do with this time? They spend an hour or so in household care and another hour on pleasure trips. They also try their hand at sports and hobbies, though these activities are not very widespread. Religious people also rest more, eat more, study more and walk more on the Sabbath day.

The 'total leisure time' for the two groups is a very good summary of this discussion. On both Fridays and Saturdays, non-religious persons have much more leisure – the sum of lines 11–22 – two hours more on Fridays and over an hour on Saturdays. This is because the religious groups are engaged in more 'obligatory' activities by our definition– prayer is the obvious one, but even food and rest and bed (yes, sex) are prescribed by the tradition!

5. *A Note on Television*

Television already consumes some 20 per cent of all 'discretionary' leisure (lines 11–22). Another fifth of this time, approximately, is given to reading of newspapers and books, rather more to the former than the latter. The ratio in Britain is 3 to 1 in favour of television (23 per cent for TV, 7 per cent for reading).[21] But in Israel television has only just begun. There will be more broadcasting hours and more set owners. What then?

While it is difficult to answer the question for the future, something can be learned from the past. In 1966, in a survey of leisure and culture in two Israeli cities, we collected time-budget data. This was before the advent of Israeli television, though some Israelis had purchased sets in order to watch the programmes from across the border. It is possible, therefore, to compare pre-TV Haifa of 1966 with post-TV Haifa of 1970, as is done in Table 3.8.

As is noted in the table, one should beware of making too much of the differences because the methods used in the two studies differ somewhat. The table makes clear, at any rate, that among the leisure activities, television time has displaced time formerly spent in radio listening. Socializing and other forms of non-media recreation appear to remain completely unaffected. There is a hint – but the differences should not be taken seriously on the basis of these data alone – that newspaper-reading and cinema-going have also been affected; as will be demonstrated in a later chapter, the 6-minute per person per day drop in cinema-going shows up as a very large number in box-office statistics.[22]

TABLE 3.8 *Time in Hours Devoted to Activities* in Haifa: Summer 1966 and Summer 1970*

	Haifa 1966	Haifa 1970
1. Gainful employment	4·2	4·5
2. Household care	2·1	2·0
3. Shopping	0·5	0·4
4. Child care	0·5	0·4
5. Sleep and rest	7·8	8·4
6. Eating	1·8	1·3
7. Personal care	0·8	0·8
8. Prayer	–	0·1
9. Studies, lectures	0·2	0·3
10. Clubs, organizations	0·1	0·1
11. Newspapers and periodicals	0·7	0·6
12. Books	0·3	0·3
13. Radio	0·9	0·3
14. Television	0·2	1·0
15. Cinema	0·2	0·1
16. Social life†	0·9	1·1
17. Conversation	0·4	0·3
18. Walk	0·3	0·2
19. Sports	–	–
20. Hobby, creative activity	0·1	0·1
21. Other non-home recreation‡	0·1	0·2
22. Excursions and other travel	0·8	1·3
23. Other	1·1	0·2
TOTAL	24·0	24·0
Unweighted N =	(887)	(258)

* In the 1966 data, no distinction was made between primary and secondary activities; 1970 data include only primary activities.

† Includes visiting, hosting, parties, dances, games.

‡ Includes theatre, museums, exhibitions, concerts, light entertainment, coffee houses, night clubs, discotheques.

6. *Summary*

This is a behaviouristic portrait. It shows Israel more like the Western countries than the Eastern ones as far as the rhythms of work and leisure are concerned. Sociability, child care and reading are attributes in which Israel ranks high.

Education and religiosity, as we have seen, exert a lot of influence on time budgets. The well educated contribute more hours of work to the society (partly because more women work among the better educated), but they also devote more time to caring for their own persons. They read more, study more and travel more. These things are done at the expense – measured in time – of sleep, rest, housekeeping, food and prayer.

Much the same things differentiate religious from non-religious persons. In part, this is because religiosity and education overlap; in part, it is because tradition prescribes the differences. The latter are especially marked on Fridays and Saturdays. Time spent in prayer is the most obvious difference, and time spent in study is perhaps the least obvious, since religious persons of lower educational levels spend more time in study than their non-religious counterparts, since study is, of course, also a religious injunction.

The Friday afternoon hours are hours of 'preparation' in Israel – of household, self and car. Friday evening is for a festive meal and socializing. The religious go to sleep early; the non-religious watch television. Saturday, for the religious, is a day of rest, sociability and prayer. For the non-religious, it is a day of rest, sociability and travel – and some catching up on household care. Saturday night is for 'going out'.

NOTES – CHAPTER THREE

1. The problems of defining leisure have been grappled with repeatedly, and we have nothing useful to add. Cf. Roberts, op. cit., pp. 6–7; Max Kaplan, *Leisure in America*, New York: Wiley, 1960; J. Dumazedier, op. cit.; Sebastian de Grazia, *Of Time, Work and Leisure*, New York: Twentieth Century Fund, 1962; Stanley Parker, *The Future of Work and Leisure*, London: MacGibbon and Kee, 1970; G. Friedmann, *The Anatomy of Work: The Implications of Specialization*, London: Heinemann, 1961.
2. See Philip E. Converse, 'Time Budgets' in *International Encyclopedia of the Social Sciences*, New York: Crowell Collier and Macmillan, 1968.
3. Alexander Szalai, ed., *The Use of Time: Daily Activities of Urban and Suburban Populations in Twelve Countries*, The Hague: Mouton, 1973; Iwao Nakajima, 'Leisure Situation in Japan', *Studies of Broadcasting*, 8,

Tokyo: NHK 1972, pp. 111–42; BBC Audience Research, *The People's Activities*, London: BBC, 1965.

4. The important difference is that Szalai asked respondents to keep diaries of their use of time and an interviewer collected the diary and helped the respondent complete it if necessary.
5. Rivka Rahat, *Patterns of Use of Leisure Time: A Report on the Population of Haifa and Ashdod*, Jerusalem: The Communications Institute, The Hebrew University, 1969 (mimeo, in Hebrew).
6. In our study, all information was gathered by personal interview. Respondents were interviewed about their activities 'yesterday' – the day before the interview – from 4 a.m. to 4 a.m. Data on Friday and Saturday were collected in Sunday interviews. Note that, unless otherwise specified, tables refer to 'primary activities' – that is, the focal activity of a particular time period, whatever else was going on together with it. Data on secondary activities – e.g. listening to the radio while cooking – are also available. The number of activities studied is 48, but these categories have been grouped for presentation; the number of groupings varies to facilitate comparisons. Inasmuch as our sample somewhat under-represents the least well-educated sector of the population, these time-budget data are weighted by education so that the proportions correspond to the structure of the population, as reported in the *Statistical Yearbook of Israel 1970*.
7. Consider two: (1) 'Thus by using a strictly quantitative assembly-belt conception of time – time as a moving belt of equal units – one ignores the significance of most activities. A moment of awe in religion or ecstasy in love or orgasm in intercourse, a decisive blow to an enemy, relief in a sneeze, or death in fall is treated as equal to a moment of riding on the bus, shovelling coal, or eating beans.' S. de Grazia, op. cit. (2) 'In short Mrs. Quest was like ninety-nine per cent of humanity; if she spent an afternoon jam-making, while her mind was filled with thoughts envious, spiteful, lustful – violent; then she has spent the afternoon making jam.' Doris Lessing, *Landlocked*, London: Panther, 1967, p. 81.
8. Data are from 1965, based on the surveys in Alexander Szalai, ed., op. cit., p. 119. However, more recent data from *A Survey of Europe Today*, London: Reader's Digest Association, 1970, show much lower proportions of working women in Western Europe. Still another source, the Manpower Survey of the Ministry of Labour, 'Women in the Labour Force', Jerusalem: 1965, confirms that the proportion of Israeli women working is lower than that in the United States, Canada, France and Denmark. While the picture is by no means clear, it appears that the proportion of Israeli women working is rising and that it is approaching that of other Western countries.
9. Note that we are talking about the 'primary activity' of caring for children, not the presence of children during the conduct of other activities.
10. Differences in the rate of TV-set ownership and the number of hours of broadcasting are of obvious importance here. In the Szalai studies, op. cit., homes with TV numbered about 50 per cent in Hungary, Yugoslavia, and Russia; Poland, France, Germany and Belgium were in the

60–70 per cent range; East Germany exceeded 80 per cent, and the United States was effectively 100 per cent.

11. NHK, Public Opinion Research Institute, *How Do People Spend Their Time in Japan?* Tokyo: NHK, 1971.
12. This table omits the small numbers of men who are not working – mostly students and elderly people. The proportion of working men married is 83 per cent, and the proportion of working women married is 28 per cent.
13. Note, once more, that the subject is child care as a *primary* activity.
14. The next-to-last column, 12 years of school without a University degree, includes a high proportion of students currently working toward degrees. The high proportion of time spent at studies underlines this.
15. In many things, as we shall see throughout, the best educated and most poorly educated groups resemble each other. This is a phenomenon noted also in our previous leisure survey. See Rivka Rahat, op. cit.
16. See Chapter Seven, p. 121.
17. For a detailed analysis of the time budget of kibbutz members, see Michael Gurevitch and Gila Brand, 'Ideology, Social Structure, and the Allocation of Time: An Analysis of Urban and Kibbutz Time Budgets'. Jerusalem: The Communications Institute, The Hebrew University, 1973 (mimeo). For the authoritative statement on family relations in kibbutzim, see Yonina Talmon, *Family and Community in the Kibbutz*, Cambridge: Harvard University Press, 1972.
18. Much more research is needed on this question. Obviously some television stimulates conversation, though there is some evidence to suggest that this happens more in better educated homes. Nor do we know how much conversation there was before TV – except for the hint in Table 3.8 that perhaps conversation time has decreased slightly; but these are not really reliable data, as is pointed out. What is certain is that the family does sit around the TV set as a unit. It is also quite certain that they are not usually sitting in rapt attention – at least that is the experience of countries already accustomed to TV.
19. In terms of religious regulations, it would be technically acceptable if the set were tuned in before the Sabbath, and left on and untouched.
20. 26 per cent are 'religious' by this definition. It includes some 5–6 per cent who are not. It is presumably the latter who watch TV on Friday nights; in the summer months it is also possible to squeeze in some viewing before sunset.
21. Derived from *Midlands Activity Survey*, London: ATV Network, 1972.
22. See Chapter Eight, p. 126.

CHAPTER FOUR The Six-Day Week: Attitudes Toward Work and Leisure

Now that we have seen how people actually spend their time, we want to find out how they feel about it. In this and the following chapter we shall examine attitudes toward work and leisure and toward the Sabbath and holidays. We shall pay particular attention throughout to the fact that the Israeli work week is six days long.

The survey found 4 of every 5 men working full-time and almost 3 of every 10 women. As has been noted already, these figures are rather like those of the Western European countries.[1] The peak years of employment for men are in the age range 25–54, with rather lower figures for the under-25 – many of whom serve in the Army or are students – and the over-55 age groups. For women, on the other hand, the peak is reached before the age of 25 – when 44 per cent of female respondents are working – and there is a steady decline thereafter accompanying the change in marital and family status.[2]

1. *Satisfaction with Work*

How do people feel about their work – and about work in general? About two-thirds report themselves satisfied (26 per cent are 'very satisfied'), and a third are not so satisfied (10 per cent are 'entirely unsatisfied').[3] In general, the less educated, the less satisfied. Among the four areas of dissatisfaction about which we inquired, most dissatisfaction was concentrated on inadequate wages. A third of all employed persons said this was the reason. Uninteresting work, unsatisfactory working hours and poor relations at work each caused dissatisfaction to about 15 per cent of the employed population. On the other hand, half reported themselves 'satisfied', or better, with the interest and the human relations they encountered at work.

2. *Satisfaction with Leisure*

The desire for more leisure is characteristic of the well educated of all age groups, and particularly of the middle years when people are at the peak of their obligations both to work and to family.

Asked whether they have enough leisure time, too much, or too little, the population divides pretty evenly between enough and too little.

Within each education level, the demand for more time is most vocal in the 30–50 age range. It is important to note that in the group of people over 50, education makes a substantial difference: a large proportion of the less well educated (one-fifth of those with less than 4 years of schooling) say they have 'too much' time. While the size of this group will dwindle over time – inasmuch as the Israeli-born generation will have at least 10 years of schooling – the problem is a very real one now.

The high rate of dissatisfaction over the *amount* of available time is not carried over into dissatisfaction 'with the *way* in which you spend your free time'. In answer to this question, two-thirds reported themselves satisfied (14 per cent 'very' satisfied) and one-third not so satisfied (10 per cent 'entirely dissatisfied'). It will be noted that level of overall satisfaction with one's work is higher than the level of satisfaction with one's way of spending leisure: about twice as many are 'very' satisfied with their work.

Here, too, we find – exactly as we did in the case of satisfaction with work – that the better educated are more satisfied. This is true at all age levels, but perhaps particularly among the oldest group, the over-50s. Men are more satisfied than women of this age, and the same holds true for the youngest age group. Women's satisfaction with leisure matches that of men only in the middle group, age 30–50.

The close parallel between patterns of satisfaction with work and with leisure suggests that the two are correlated. And indeed they are: holding education constant, those more satisfied with work are also better satisfied with their way of spending leisure. The same is true for estimates of whether one has sufficient time for leisure: those more satisfied with their work – again, education held constant – are more likely to report that the amount of time they have for leisure is adequate. This latter relationship is somewhat surprising in view of the fact that we found the better educated happier at work, happier at leisure but somewhat *more* likely to complain of lack of time. But, when education is held constant, it appears that those who are happiest at work are not only happy with their way of spending leisure but also less likely than their peers to say they have too little leisure time available to them! Further, these people are less likely than their peers to complain of tiredness or lack of time as obstacles to spending leisure – problems to which we now turn.

A set of obstacles to spending leisure 'as you would like to' was presented to respondents for evaluation. Lack of money, energy and time are the chief obstacles: one-third of the population point to each of these. Lack of adequate facilities for leisure and the absence of suitable companions were next, named as primary problems by about 20 per cent. Transportation and baby-sitting come next (15 per cent), and rather fewer people – but still sizeable in terms of absolute numbers – mentioned dependence on spouse (or friend), and insufficient knowledge of the Hebrew language. Army reserve duty was sometimes mentioned, but our concern that outlying settlements would be troubled by 'security problems where you live' was not justified.

In addition to this set of items, a small number of respondents volunteered that care for their parents was a problem which we had not taken into account. Had we asked about this explicitly, it is possible that this problem would have loomed larger.

From Table 4.1, which examines the major obstacles implicated by the several age and education groups, it is clear that different kinds of problems are characteristic of each of the groups. The group aged 30–50, as we have already seen, feels the lack of time most keenly. This is the group that is also most troubled by lack of financial resources for leisure. Education – which is also a measure of income – is of great importance here: the better off complain less about money. This is not as self-evident as it sounds.

Age is responsible for feeling tired, but, interestingly, education affects tiredness almost as much. At each age level, persons of lower education are very much more likely to complain of tiredness than their better-educated age peers.

Tiredness is so basic an obstacle to the use of leisure that we continued in pursuit of its origins. Age is a physiological constraint, but we have seen how education, as if by magic, seems to relieve tiredness. Is this because well-educated persons tend to work at white-collar jobs and are therefore less tired? Is it because the better educated have less monotonous jobs? Or is it, perhaps, because they have a different perspective on the day and do not experience tiredness until they have completed both work *and* play?

To look for additional clues, we examined the influence of occupation on feeling tired. The most tired persons in the society, we find, are working women and the business sector.

In third place are manual labourers. Although it may not be apparent at first glance, all three of these groups actually do work 'harder'. The time budgets, as we have seen, show that working women put in more hours. That gives them a fair enough reason to be tired. Manual labour is manual labour. But what explains the weariness of persons engaged in business? At least one explanation is that the siesta system is really anachronistic, at least as far as the well-being of the sales force is concerned. Except for business, the Israeli worker or salaried employee typically begins work between 7 and 8 in the morning, has a very short sandwich break, and quits between 2 and 3 in the afternoon if he is an office worker, and between 3 and 4 if he is a manual or skilled labourer. Certain services – such as garages – work from 8 until 5, with longer

TABLE 4.1 *Major Obstacles to Spending Leisure, by Age and Education*

	Total* (N = 100%)	Per cent who say: Lack of money	Fatigue	Lack of time	Inadequate facilities	Unsuitable companions	Lack of transport	Baby-sitting problems	Dependence on spouse	Other problems
Age 18–29										
0–4 years education	(24)	46	50	25	38	29	25	50	29	27
5–10 years education	(228)	35	21	18	38	29	15	21	10	9
11+ years education	(319)	20	16	27	30	16	18	16	10	12
Age 30–50										
0–4 years education	(174)	66	52	44	27	23	21	33	17	27
5–10 years education	(426)	47	39	33	24	19	13	19	11	13
11+ years education	(326)	22	29	37	18	17	12	17	11	9
Age 50+										
0–4 years education	(115)	52	59	25	10	15	15	3	12	23
5–10 years education	(329)	40	45	21	14	15	9	2	12	20
11+ years education	(238)	21	38	28	12	8	15	2	8	8
TOTAL POPULATION	(2179)	36	35	29	22	18	14	15	11	14

* This table, and subsequent tables of this form, are to be read as follows: (1) there are 24 persons aged 18–29 who have 0–4 years of education; (2) of this group of 24 persons, 46 per cent claim lack of money as an obstacle to their leisure and 54 per cent do not; 50 per cent claim fatigue as an obstacle, and 50 per cent do not; 25 per cent claim lack of time, and 75 per cent do not, etc.

Percentages appearing in parentheses (in subsequent tables) are based on less than thirty cases. They should, therefore, lunch breaks. But the business sector works to a pattern of 9–1 in the morning, midday closing, and 4–7 in the afternoon.

Looking more specifically at the problem of women, however, 'lack of time' is shown to be a more important differentiating factor than fatigue (see Table 4.2, Part A). Compared with housewives, working women are much more likely to complain about lack of time as a serious obstacle to spending leisure. This condition is the result of two things: first, that working women feel more pressed for time than working men; and, second, that housewives do not complain much about lack of time. That is not their problem.

TABLE 4.2 *Fatigue and Time as Obstacles to Spending Leisure, by Sex and Occupation*

	Total (N = 100%)	Per cent who say Fatigue	Per cent who say Lack of time
A. *Sex, marital and occupational status*			
Men, working	(1664)	36	31
Women, working	(645)	40	47
Women, not working and housewives	(777)	35	22
B. *Men, by occupation*			
Professional, technical and scientific	(350)	27	37
Managers and officials	(257)	28	27
Business, sales	(103)	52	53
Agriculture, fishing	(104)	40	33
Transportation, communication	(97)	33	33
Building, mining, etc.	(102)	55	30
Craftsmen, factory workers	(338)	44	31
Services, entertainment, etc.	(164)	42	29
Not working	(149)	22	12
C. *Women, by occupation*			
Professional, technical and scientific	(175)	36	40
Managers, officials, secretarial	(152)	31	26
Business, sales	(62)	76	65
Agriculture	(33)	60	40
Transportation, communication	(4)	*	*
Crafts, factory worker	(100)	33	37
Services, entertainment	(119)	36	34
Housewives, not working	(777)	35	22

* Too few cases on which to base percentages.

3. *The Five-Day Week*

One way of expanding leisure time is to institute a five-day working week. Motions to do so have been put before the Knesset on a number of occasions, but, curiously, have failed to arouse much enthusiasm. Even the General Federation of Labour seems uninterested. Work is still a central value in this society, and there is the concern that the demand for consumer goods would increase as added leisure brings added shopping.

The most ardent supporters of a five-day week are probably the religious parties. Another day off would provide religious persons with more 'discretionary' leisure than the norms of the Sabbath permit. Moreover, if there were a second free day, the religious groups could ask their neighbours to transfer some of their more blatant secular activity – football, for example – from the Sabbath day. People who cannot get to the beach on Saturday – because they cannot afford private transportation – would have another day on which to get there by bus. But the religious groups have, so far, not prevailed. In a recent motion, they even proposed a compromise: to revive the ancient custom of taking a holiday on the first day of the new moon.

But sooner or later the five-day week will come. There is already research – from the Labour Federation's own research group – to prove that the same number of working hours spread over five, rather than six, days will probably not decrease productivity. And it would save the economy the time and the money spent on travel to work on short Fridays. From the point of view of the national planning of leisure, the five-day week is *the* great challenge to policy-makers. Will they be prepared to guide society in making choices for spending its new-found time? Will the options be made clear? Will facilities be made available?

While there is no pressing public demand for a five-day week just now, when we put the question to respondents the answer was clearly in the affirmative. As Table 4.3 shows, about two-thirds of the population are in favour. Another 10 per cent say 'Yes, but not while we are living in a state of emergency'. The distribution of replies to this question by age and education corresponds to what we have already seen: the more educated and the 30–50 age group are most heartily in favour.

When the same question is examined by religiosity, there is no apparent association. Surprisingly, religious persons are not more favourable to the five-day week than their non-religious neighbours of comparable education, despite the lobbying of the leadership of the religious parties.

TABLE 4.3 *Attitudes Toward Five-Day Work Week, by Age and Education*

	Total (N= 100%)	Per cent who say: In favour	Favour but not while emergency lasts	Against	No opinion	
Age 18–29						
0–4 years education	(44)	48	2	32	16	100%
5–10 years education	(381)	59	10	26	5	100%
11+ years education	(548)	68	8	20	3	100%
Age 30–50						
0–4 years education	(260)	50	10	23	17	100%
5–10 years education	(689)	69	8	18	4	100%
11+ years education	(525)	75	10	12	3	100%
Age 50+						
0–4 years education	(199)	45	9	21	25	100%
5–10 years education	(515)	56	7	23	12	100%
11+ years education	(421)	58	14	21	6	100%
TOTAL POPULATION	(3582)	63	9	20	8	100%

4. *Which Day?*

If there is to be another day of leisure, which day should it be? This is another easy-sounding question which, however, conceals more than it reveals. Friday? Sunday? A day in the middle of the week? A different day for different groups? All these are possibilities – but each has different implications.

'Friday' is the most conservative answer. A plurality of respondents (41 per cent) chose it. Friday is the Sabbath eve. As we have seen it is a day of washing-up – physically, and perhaps even spiritually. If Friday were the added day, the weekend would consist of a day of 'preparation' followed by the Sabbath. If all else remains unchanged, Friday night would continue its sedate, homey way, and moderate tension-release would continue to characterize Saturday night – moderate, because work begins early on Sunday morning. This presumably was the Western Christian pattern until the Sabbath eve became Saturday night!

Friday is a conservative choice for another reason: a non-work day, it would be the day on which the economy stands least to lose and self-interest has least to gain. On any day other than Friday, the individual would have more hours to gain. He is already working fewer hours on Friday and thus if he chose another day, he would gain a whole day without losing the extra hours that are his, anyway, on Friday. But if Friday is to be the extra day, shops would have to stay open, and shopkeepers would have to take off some other time. Friday without last-minute shopping is unthinkable.

TABLE 4.4 *Which Day? Proportions Preferring Friday, Sunday or a Day in Midweek as an Additional Free Day, by Age and Education*

	Total (N = 100%)	Per cent who say Friday	Sunday	Day in mid-week	No opinion	
Age 18–29						
0–4 years education	(42)	29	26	26	19	100%
5–10 years education	(372)	34	31	25	10	100%
11+ years education	(536)	45	30	19	6	100%
Age 30–50						
0–4 years education	(260)	41	13	25	20	100%
5–10 years education	(672)	40	29	23	8	100%
11+ years education	(523)	45	35	15	5	100%
Age 50+						
0–4 years education	(197)	33	10	23	33	100%
5–10 years education	(506)	37	18	22	22	100%
11+ years education	(404)	47	22	17	13	100%
TOTAL POPULATION	(3512)	41	26	21	12	100%

Twenty-six per cent of the respondents said 'Sunday'. This would be a very different weekend, of course. The prescriptive Sabbath would be followed by a day of complete 'discretion' with no distinctive normative character. The choice of Sunday as the second day of the weekend would almost certainly create a Western style 'Saturday night'. The Saturday–Sunday weekend would lean in a Western direction, including the Christian day of rest. The Friday–Saturday weekend, on the other hand, would incorporate a gesture to the holy day of Islam.

An almost equal number prefer 'another day of the week' in preference to both Friday and Sunday. This means, of course, that there would be no weekend at all, but simply a 'day off' in the middle of the week for rest, arrangements, or whatever.

Who prefers which days? While the first choice of every group is Friday there are certain differences among age-education groups which are worth noting. A higher proportion of the better educated prefer either Friday or Sunday, while preference for 'another day' is negatively related to education. This seems to mean that the idea of a two-day weekend matters to the educated; the less well educated are simply thinking of more rest.

As far as age is concerned, the data suggest that older people prefer Friday more than younger people, and younger people prefer Sunday more than older people. It fits our analysis rather well that young people prefer the open-ended Saturday night and the normatively unfettered Sunday, while older persons opt for the more family-oriented Friday–Saturday weekend. But the differences – it should be borne in mind – are small indeed. Note the large percentage of 'no opinion' among the over-50 age group.

Religion plays a more important role here than it did in expressed preference for the five-day week. Its role is complicated, however. While a preference for Friday increases with education among the two non-religious groups, the religious and traditional groups behave in the opposite way. Among the religious, the more educated groups are *least* enthusiastic about Friday. Among the well educated, it is the religious and traditional groups who are most likely to express a preference for 'another day' rather than Friday or Sunday. Indeed, the choice of Friday as a second day of leisure would probably bring least added benefit to educated-religious persons. Being not only religious but educated as well, their norms and life style are influenced not just by the religious fraternity but by others of like education (though not necessarily religious) with whom they associate. From this reference group, it is likely that they would have developed expectations about what they would want to do in their leisure. But if they have to be home at 2 or 3 p.m. on winter Fridays because the sun sets so early, the added leisure of a free Friday will hardly benefit them. They want a real extra day – for the same reasons that the educated non-religious want Friday or Sunday. Religious persons of lesser education are presumably quite content to have more time on Friday to make even better preparations for the coming of the Sabbath; to make even better chicken soup, so to speak.[4]

If they had an extra day, what would people do with it? Few people have original ideas. Most people would stay close to home. The largest group would spend their time with the family (27 per cent), others would rest (14 per cent), or work around the house (11 per cent). Over 50 per cent, in other words, would stay very close to home. Some want to take trips (15 per cent); as we shall see later, this is an important pastime in Israel. Some would see friends, read and study (13 per cent), do hobbies or sports (7 per cent). Almost nobody names media, except for reading (7 per cent books, 1 per cent newspapers). One per cent want to be more active in voluntary organizations, and 1 per cent want to spend more time at the theatre. On the whole, these seem to be honest answers, of people who want to do a little more of what they are already doing. It is up to the policy planner to suggest some additional options, or to make extant ones salient. Family activity, however, seems to be the major frame in which suggestions should be made.

5. *Summary*

Few people in Israel question the worth of work. Work is an accepted value. Although a sizeable group wants more leisure time and is in favour of the five-day week, there is no active demand for these social increments. Most people are satisfied with their work, and satisfied with the way they spend their leisure; indeed, there is a correlation between the two even when education is constant. The better educated, on the whole, are happier at work, happier at play, but feel the shortage of time more keenly.

The main obstacles to spending leisure as one would like are lack of money, tiredness and lack of time. The business sector and manual labourers are the most tired groups in the community. Working women are tired, too, but despite the many hours which they work on the job and at home, the problem of lack of time looms even larger. The business sector also suffers badly from lack of time for spending leisure.

Friday is the day preferred for a second non-work day, when the time comes. A plurality of all groups is in favour of Friday, but the least support for Friday comes from the educated-religious.

Better educated people want a consecutive two-day weekend; the concentration of support for another day in midweek is among the less well educated. Older persons, persons with families, want the Friday–Saturday weekend; there is some interest among young people in the Saturday–Sunday weekend. Most people would spend the added day with their families and close to home.

Policy-makers in the field of leisure and culture would be well advised to plan for the advent of the five-day week.

NOTES – CHAPTER FOUR

1. As noted in the previous chapter, the multinational study of time budgets (1965), reports that Belgium, Germany, Yugoslavia, France and the U.S.

each has 40–50 per cent of women in the active labour force. Most of the Eastern European countries range between 60–90 per cent. Cf. Szalai, ed., op. cit., p. 119.

2. About 20 per cent of the employed report that they work, at least occasionally, on Saturdays. A larger proportion – about one-quarter of employed respondents – sometimes works nights. There is considerable overlap between these groups, that is, half of the total who work on either nights or Saturdays work on both occasions.

   These overtime workers are made up of two rather different groups. Those who report working nights tend to come from the ranks of the lower educated; they are, apparently, manual labourers. On the other hand, 'nights *and* Sabbath' is more characteristic of the better educated, that is of the white-collar class, the professionals and the managers. This is because their work sometimes pursues them, or because they pursue it, or because they hold a second job. As many as one-quarter of University graduates hold a second job.

3. This is a composite index based on degree of reported satisfaction with (1) wages; (2) hours; (3) human relations at work; and (4) interest in work. The overall estimate of satisfaction is based on our inference from this four-item scale.

4. An alternative interpretation for the preference of educated-religious persons for another day is that they want it not so much for themselves as for others: they want a day which is at a distance from the Sabbath.

CHAPTER FIVE The Meaning of Sabbath and Holidays

The time budgets showed how Israelis spend their time, and the preceding chapter began to explore how they feel about it. The commandment to observe the seventh day is preceded by the commandment, 'Six days shall you work.' And Israelis, so far, affirm the latter no less than the former. There is an interest in additional leisure, however, and many religious people seem to feel that God might actually favour the five-day week. As we have seen, a majority of all groups in the society would welcome a second day of rest. In imagining what such a 'weekend' would then be like, most people foresee something like this: a full day off on Friday rather than just a few extra hours; more time to spend with the family, at home, on occasional trips, and 'preparing' for the Sabbath.

In this chapter, we want to explore more deeply how Israelis feel about their Sabbath. In analyzing the data of the previous chapter, we have already alluded to some of the attitudes toward the Israeli Sabbath which characterize different groups. These matters will be pursued in detail here. And then we shall turn from the Sabbath to the other holidays – religious and secular – to explore the contemporary meanings of these feastdays of the old-new Israeli calendar.

1. *Attitudes Toward the Sabbath*

Respondents were asked about the character of the Sabbath today, and whether they approved of it. Specifically, we put the following question: 'As you know, the Sabbath eve in Israel is quiet and homey by comparison to other nations. Do you believe that this is the way the Sabbath eve should be in our country or would you rather it were otherwise?'

Even if Moses had gone in for attitude surveys, it is unlikely that he would have put this question to the Children of Israel. When they received the Torah in the wilderness of Sinai, they had just come out of slavery, so the idea of the Sabbath was doubly new. It was new for all mankind, as a fundamental human right, and it was new, *a fortiori*, for ex-slaves. Indeed, one of the reasons Sabbath eve was 'given', scripture says, is to commemorate the exodus from Egypt. Manna was dropped twice on Fridays, to preclude the need to gather it on the Sabbath day. So everything was provided for by the authorities, and as far as we know, there were no complaints registered against the character of the Sabbath.

The quintessence of the modern, however, is the idea of choice, and most people know that there exist social models which are different from their own. Israelis certainly know that there are alternative models for the Sabbath. Most of them came to Israel from elsewhere, as migrants. All of them, practically, see alternative models at the movies. But their knowledge is even more immediate: the character of the Sabbath is something which is actively being fought over in Israel. Certain religious groups in Jerusalem throw stones at those who drive cars on the Sabbath. Trains and buses do not operate on the Sabbath, and one must rely on taxis for transportation; some people take violent objection to this, while others stand vigil lest the buses begin operating too early on Saturday night. To remain open on the Sabbath, industries must prove that their continuous operation is vital to the national security or economy or that shutting down would do serious damage to the plant.[1] Most theatres are closed, as are most coffee houses and restaurants. Like manna, the newspapers publish supplements on Fridays and the milkmen deliver a double quantity of milk. All shops are closed. What do people think about this? If Moses had asked, the people would have replied: 'We will do and we will obey' (though he encountered occasional dissidents). But what do the Children of Israel have to say about this in 1970?

In answer to our question about whether the present-day character of the Sabbath was to their liking, 60 per cent said, 'Certainly. That's the way it should be.' Only 6 per cent objected strongly to the existing situation, and another 19 per cent said that some changes might be desirable. About three-quarters of the adult population of Jews in Israel, then, positively affirm the 'quiet and homey' Sabbath – and most of these choose to say so categorically. Even more interesting is the fact that there is no difference by age in the proportion endorsing the quality of the Israeli Sabbath. Table 5.1 makes clear, in the first column, that after education is taken into account, age makes almost no difference. That is, while increased education is associated with a lesser degree of certainty that the present situation is a desirable one, age is not associated in this way.

If we hadn't known already that most people would use additional leisure to spend more time with their families, to go on (family) trips, to rest and to care for their households, we might have had different expectations. We might have expected larger proportions – and especially the young – to voice the wish for more excitement, more activity, more public entertainment. Indeed, one often hears that rising delinquency rates in Israel are associated with the fact that the youth have 'nothing to do' on Friday nights. Perhaps this feeling is more characteristic of teenagers, or of certain groups of younger people, but as far as young adults are concerned – our sample begins at age 18 – there is almost no evidence to support the argument that younger people are more restive or more actively dissatisfied with the restrictive character of the Israeli Sabbath. It seems fair to conclude, therefore, that education is strongly related to satisfaction and dissatisfaction with the existing culture of the Sabbath, but that age is not related.

When more specific questions are put to respondents about the character of the Sabbath, rather larger proportions are desirous of change. Adding together all those who favour change (i.e. those who appear in Table 5.1 as 'certainly favour' plus those who are more mildly in 'favour' but do not appear in the table), 61 per cent say they would like to see public transport on the Sabbath; 69 per cent want community centres (literally 'culture houses') to remain open (many of them already do, without necessarily violating the Sabbath injunctions); 53 per cent want the theatres and concert halls opened; and 43 per cent favour cinema openings. Thus, in spite of the overall endorsement of the 'quiet and homey' character of the Sabbath eve, about half of the population wants some liberalization in the availability of facilities for entertainment and culture.

There are, however, marked differences in the proportions favouring public transportation and community centres, theatres and concerts, and movie houses. The ranking obviously expresses a dominant sentiment: the more 'cultured' the activity, the more people are in favour. The notion that Friday night ought to have a cultured flavour is clearly reflected in this scale.[2]

It is important to note, once more, that age makes no difference in these matters. Young people of each educational level distribute themselves in exactly the same way as their elders. This is a remarkable fact: the young are no more in favour (or no less against) the opening of theatres and cinemas than their elders. This, in spite of the fact that age is an important determinant of participating in public entertainment (as will be demonstrated in Chapter Seven) and that we should not have been surprised had we found a concentration of young people in the vanguard of change. But we most emphatically do not.

It is no surprise, on the other hand, that religious observance is associated with attitudes toward the quality of life on the Sabbath. The demand for change is centred in the group which is educated and non-religious. Only a third (36 per cent) of this group strongly endorse the existing character of the Sabbath, and half of the group strongly favours the opening of cinemas. Larger proportions favour public transportation and the opening of theatres and concert halls. A small minority (5–14 per cent) of the most religious group concurs.[3]

The overall picture, then, adds up to this: when asked to contemplate the private, family-oriented character of the Israeli Sabbath in contrast with a more cosmopolitan weekend night, a large majority of Israelis

TABLE 5.1 *Attitudes Toward the Character of the Sabbath, by Age and Education*

		Per cent who say				
		The Sabbath eve should 'certainly' be quiet and homey	'Certainly favour' Sabbath opening of:			
	Total (N=100%)		public transport	cinema houses	theatres and concerts	community centres
Age 18–29						
0–4 years education	(29)	(66)	(17)	(10)	(10)	(17)
5–10 years education	(206)	54	41	29	33	39
11+ years education	(335)	52	49	31	43	53
Age 30–50						
0–4 years education	(120)	75	20	13	15	17
5–10 years education	(397)	65	46	26	33	44
11+ years education	(317)	54	59	39	49	60
Age 50+						
0–4 years education	(111)	80	15	11	12	16
5–10 years education	(282)	66	42	27	32	44
11+ years education	(260)	50	54	33	42	58
TOTAL POPULATION	(2057)	60	45	28	35	46

seem satisfied with the traditional mode which they now have. On the other hand, sizeable minorities strongly favour making available public transportation and public entertainment. A preference is expressed even here, however, for the special character of the Sabbath eve as a 'cultured' evening. Sabbath concerts are not exactly what the rabbinic tradition has in mind, of course. But the spirit of the replies of our respondents strongly suggests that they are at once respectful of the home-centred character of the Jewish Sabbath, and while open to the idea of change, it is the idea of a 'cultured' evening which they endorse.[4]

2. *The Meaning of the Holidays*

It is clear, therefore, that Israel is still 'keeping' the Sabbath. At least there is a strong consensus concerning how people 'ought' to behave on that day and a lot of evidence that they actually do so. Most of the population have a sense that the Sabbath is more than just a day of rest, 'a day off'. The non-religious – in large numbers – seem to agree that it is also a day of spiritual communion, where the spiritual, however, is translated into 'culture' rather than study or prayer. The sense of solidarity with family is even more salient, whether this be expressed in the festive dinner, in visiting with relations, in a pleasure trip – or even in watching television. These activities, as has been noted, are not those which the tradition prescribes, but they are *transformations* of traditional observance, and they have the quality of festivity, collective experience and shared meaning.

This is the essential difference between holidays and mere days of rest. Days of rest give individuals a chance to do the things they want to do. Unlike holidays, mere days of rest have little *collective* significance; they do not prescribe the feelings which people 'ought' to have or the activities in which they 'ought' to engage as members of a collectivity or a society.

Some holidays change their meanings over time. Some take on added meanings. Certain religious holidays have become quite secularized over the course of history, while certain secular holidays have taken on a religious aspect. Other holidays have lost all collective significance and have simply become days of rest.

Judaism is particularly complicated in this respect. In one sense Judaism may be said, from the first, to have imposed secular increments on religious holidays. The ideas of freedom and exodus associated with Passover, for example, represent historical and ethical additions to earlier cultic holidays of spring and fertility.[5] These elements, recombined, are seen by the tradition as a revelation of 'the finger of God'. If we now argue, as we shall, that family and freedom and exodus and spring are Passover for non-religious Israelis, we must also admit that the process of secularization began long ago.

Any investigation of contemporary leisure, therefore, must take account not only of days of rest, but of holidays and their meanings. Some holidays bring people closer to the central values of the society. Other holidays have transcendental meanings, emphasizing the relationship of the individual as a group member to God. Different holidays – no less collective in their observance – permit a letting off of steam or a last fling, as do carnivals and fiestas. But all of these, as we have said, are different from holidays which have become mere days 'off'.

As a preface to this subject, the interviewer said: 'The meaning of holidays is different for different people.' Then we listed eight different functions, as shown in Table 5.2, and asked: 'What is the principal thing that Passover (for example) means to you?'[6] We also gave the respondents the opportunity of answering 'The holiday gives me nothing; the holiday has no meaning for me.'[7]

The holidays about which we asked were Purim (The Feast of Esther), Passover, Yom Kippur, Lag Ba'Omer (the thirty-third of the fifty days of ritual counting between Passover and the Feast of Weeks), Shavuot (Feast of Weeks), the Jewish New Year (Rosh Hashana), Independence Day, New Year's Eve (Sylvester), May First, and Hanukkah. Some of these are imported holidays; we wanted to see how they have become acclimatized in Israel. Most are of traditional, even biblical, origin. Some, like Hanukkah or Lag Ba'Omer, are post-biblical but of very ancient origin. Some are brand-new. We wanted to see what contemporary meanings are assigned to these holidays, and what meanings, if any, the traditional holidays hold for non-religious persons.

No single question could hope to get at these subtle and complex matters.[8] Nevertheless, some things are clear (Table 5.2): several of the holidays have clear-cut meaning for a majority of the population. Thus Independence Day, Purim and Yom Kippur are, respectively, for feeling patriotic, merry and religious. Rosh Hashana and Passover also carry traditional associations for about half of the population.[9] Shavuot, Hanukkah and Lag Ba'Omer have much more diffuse meanings. Sylvester (New Year's Eve, i.e. Dec. 31st) and May First have almost none.

In a certain sense, the subsidiary meanings attributed to the holidays are more revealing than their primary meanings.[10] For sizeable minorities, Independence Day is considered an opportunity to rejoice; Passover gives a sense of historical connection, while Shavuot is associated with the seasons. It is a nice sidelight that even the religious groups prefer to say that Purim is for merrymaking because, of course, making merry *is* keeping the tradition. It proves, at least, that religious people are not simply conditioned to say 'yes' each time they hear the words 'religion' or 'tradition'.

TABLE 5.2 *The Principal Meaning of the Holidays*

'What is the principal thing the holiday gives you?'	Per cent who say: Independence Day (May)	Passover (April)	Purim (March)	Jewish New Year (September)	Hanukkah (December)	Yom Kippur (October)	Shavuot (June)	Lag Ba'-Omer (May)	New Year's Eve (Dec. 31)	May First
Opportunity to rejoice, make merry	30	9	67	8	22	1	13	21	17	3
To keep the tradition; to have a religious experience	1	47	11	57	27	72	31	19	0	0
To feel close to family	1	14	3	10	2	3	7	4	0	0
To feel part of nation	63	3	3	4	9	2	3	3	0	2
To feel connection with generations past and with history	2	17	7	6	24	3	8	15	0	1
To express a great social or ethical principle	1	2	1	2	2	4	2	1	0	8
To experience the changing of nature and the seasons	0	3	0	4	1	0	16	4	1	0
To be free to do things (excursions, reading, attend to personal matters)	1	3	3	6	3	4	11	5	2	17
Has no meaning for me	1	2	5	3	6	12	9	28	80	69
	100%	100%	100%	100%	100%	100%	100%	100%	100%	100%

But if we cannot hope to cope with the complexities of the changing meanings of these holidays, there is something very useful which we can do with these very data: we can analyze those who find *no meaning at all* in these holidays. For this purpose, we reasoned that the reply, 'to be free' (to do what I like) and the reply, 'the holiday has no meaning for me' are alike in that they de-emphasize the normative and collective in favour of the discretionary and private. It is only a collective sense of ritual and meaning – a shared norm – which makes a holiday more than just a day off, by our definition; hence our interest in those who opt out. Table 5.3 gives the basic data cross-tabulated with our measure of religiosity.

The holiday with meaning for everybody is Israel Independence Day. Only immediately following Independence Day in the list of 'meaningful' holidays comes a group of four holidays: Passover, Purim, Rosh Hashana (the Jewish New Year) and Hanukkah. Fewer than 10 per cent of the population say that these holidays are without meaning.

These four holidays ostensibly have little in common. Passover (April), the holiday of *matzot* (unleavened bread), celebrates the ideals and the miracles of the redemption from slavery and the coming of spring. Purim (March) celebrates the turning of the tables on the wicked Haman who was the victim of his own plot to destroy the Jews, thanks to the intervention of Queen Esther. Hanukkah (December) celebrates the triumph of the Maccabean revolt against the Greeks and the miracle of the flask of oil that burned for seven days. Rosh Hashana (September–October), the Jewish New Year, signals by the blowing of the ram's horn that summer is over and that a new year – with all its uncertainties – is about to begin.

On closer inspection, however, three of these holidays – Passover, Purim and Hanukkah – may be seen to have something central in common: they all celebrate victories. In each of them, with the help of God and a hero (Moses, Esther, the Maccabees), the weak Jews emerge triumphant. In each case it is faith in God which brings strength. The miracles of each holiday are recounted in ritualized form, celebrated in the synagogue, enriched with ritual symbols in the home, and keyed, in the tradition itself, to the active participation of children. The religious significance of these holidays is to be found in the thanksgiving to God for deliverance and in the triumph of spirit over might. The holidays of Purim and Hanukkah are comparatively minor from a religious point of view, but of great national importance. Passover, on the other hand, harbours great ethical and religious concepts. If the popularity of these holidays is, indeed, in their symbolic significance for Jewish national and spiritual survival, it would seem fair to add Yom Haatzmaut (Israel Independence Day) to this group, although the latter is still a long way from the treasuries of symbol and ritual which are the heritage of its more ancient models.

TABLE 5.3 *Holidays Without Meaning, by Religiosity*

Frequency of synagogue attendance	Percentage who say holiday 'Has no meaning for me' or is just 'Free Day'									
	Independence Day (May)	Passover (April)	Purim (March)	Jewish New Year (September)	Hanukkah (December)	Yom Kippur (October)	Shavuot (June)	Lag Ba'-Omer (May)	New Year's Eve (Dec. 31)	May First
Daily or all Sabbaths and holidays	2	2	3	3	2	1	4	13	93	88
Occasional Sabbaths and holidays	2	2	3	4	5	2	11	22	86	84
High holidays only	1	5	9	6	9	7	22	37	76	85
Does not attend at all	2	11	14	22	17	46	36	48	73	86
PERCENTAGE OF TOTAL POPULATION	2	5	8	9	9	16	20	33	82	86

Rosh Hashana differs altogether. The secret of its popularity, perhaps, lies in its seasonal aspect and its ushering in of the Days of Awe, with their richness of traditional association. Like Passover, Rosh Hashana marks a season. Like Passover, it is a time for family reunion. Like Passover, Hanukkah and even Purim (though it takes some sleight-of-hand to make Purim such) are holidays which are more than one day long. Religious meaning is important in these holidays, but they make room – in their very origins – for social and ethical transformations to satisfy the secular tastes of Jews where sentiments are national and cultural, if not religious.

Shavuot (Feast of Weeks) and Lag Ba'Omer fare much less well. Substantial proportions, even of the relatively traditional groups, say that these holidays are without meaning for them. The Feast of Weeks is also a seasonal holiday – of rich significance as an agricultural festival – but little more than a marker of the coming summer. Indeed, those non-religious Jews who find meaning in Shavuot see it primarily as a signal for the changing season. Again, this latter function, along with the religious one, has strong roots in the tradition, and thus is not alien to the 'collective' aspect of the holiday for the society. But it is clearly more difficult to accomplish this secular transformation for Shavuot than for Passover. And it is a lot of work for a one-day holiday, even though the two holidays have equal status in biblical tradition.

Lag Ba'Omer (May) marks an intermission in the fifty-day count-down between Passover and Shavuot. It is associated, in the tradition, with the story of a Jewish rebellion led by Rabbi Akiba and, as a result, the abstentions required during the seven-week period are lifted for the one day; weddings and other festivities are permitted on that day. Lag Ba'Omer has become a children's holiday; bonfires are lit everywhere and enemies of the Jews are burned in effigy. The future of this holiday, like that of Shavuot, seems precarious outside the religious community.

But the most interesting case is surely that of Yom Kippur. Sixteen per cent of the population – and almost half of the non-religious – say that Yom Kippur is meaningless for them! This, for the most sacred day of the Jewish calendar! And yet, the reason seems clear in the light of the discussion so far: this most religious of the traditional holidays is least easy to fill with familial, seasonal or social meanings. It is based on a dialogue between man and God, through the instrumentality of the community. But it is not a day for picnics, or for other family gatherings; it makes no mark on nature. It *has* a universal message and a moral, but the message and the moral are about soul-searching and soul-searing to heal the relationships between man and man, and man and God. People who are ideologically anti-religious have seized on Yom Kippur as the symbol of their rejection of the faith, and some have even tried, defiantly, to picnic on Yom Kippur. But it doesn't work. When they say that Yom Kippur 'has no meaning for me' perhaps it implies they are still struggling with its meaning, or struggling against it; perhaps not. Some thoughtful groups of religiously 'progressive' Jews, many of whom are members of kibbutzim, are explicitly engaged in a search for renewed meaning.[11]

The key to the fate of the traditional holidays, then, appears to be in their transformability. As far as the irreligious are concerned the traditional holidays largely continue to be 'meaningful' but the meanings ascribed to them tend to override their religious significance. Indeed, as we have seen (however cursorily), the very origin and history of these holidays represents a mix of the religious, the national, the ethical, the seasonal and the familial. So it is not difficult to give secular meanings to these holidays and still 'keep' them, and the unity of the collective experience which they imply.

Some of the holidays have more significance for the young than for the old. Purim and Sylvester are the best examples. About one-third of young adults find in New Year's Eve 'an opportunity to be happy'. It remains to be seen whether the holiday survives among these young people as they grow older. In any event, Purim is the holiday of happiness, far outdistancing Sylvester even for the young. But holidays for being happy clearly command the attention of the young.[12]

Most of the other holidays have more significance for older people than for younger ones perhaps because of their familial character, and perhaps because of their more sentimental associations with childhood. Young men (18–29) find less meaning in the traditional holidays than young women. This is almost certainly due to the fact that women in this age group are more likely to have assumed family responsibilities than the men and this is when the Jewish holidays become more meaningful. It is also likely that young women are more traditional in general than their age peers among the men. Among women, interestingly, there is a hint of *decline* in the meaningfulness of certain holidays with increasing age, the explanation for which, once more, would seem to be associated with the maturing of their children.

3. *Summary*

In sum, the secular holidays of Sylvester and May First have very little meaning in Israel with the exception of the young adults who find in Sylvester an 'opportunity to be happy'. But, for feeling 'happy', Purim is the undisputed source.

Like Purim, whose primary religious definition (the commandment to be happy) coincides with its secular significance, the other traditional holidays are taking on secondary secular meanings – national, familial, seasonal, spiritual – which, while different from their primary religious emphases, are still compatible with them. The triumphant holidays which celebrate the triumph of nation and spirit (man's and God's) are meaningful to all, religious and irreligious alike. These are Israel Independence Day, Passover, Hanukkah and Purim.

The only other holiday, of those we have chosen for study, which has a comparable level of meaningfulness is Rosh Hashana, the Jewish New Year. Shavuot (The Feast of Weeks) and Lag Ba'Omer, which are thought to mark the changing seasons, appear to be falling behind.

Alone among the holidays, Yom Kippur – the most sacred day of them all – appears to be incapable of secular transformation. Those who cannot find it in themselves to say that Yom Kippur provides them with a religious experience choose to say 'it gives me nothing'. The number who say so is not large, but it is symptomatic of the status of the traditional holidays in Israel.

NOTES – CHAPTER FIVE

1. A special research institute, headed by the physicist, Professor Zev Lev, is on constant look-out for technological solutions to the problems which keep certain industries in operation on the Sabbath. The object of the exercise is not only to minimize work on the Sabbath, but to reduce the likelihood of discrimination in the hiring of observant Jews as a result.
2. We are here accepting, of course, the popular stereotype that theatres and concerts represent 'higher' culture than the cinema. Cinemas are extremely popular in Israel, although – as we shall see – theatre-going is popular as well. Only a third (35 per cent) feel strongly that cinemas should be open. The 'brow' continuum does seem to underlie these judgements. That the young share this opinion of 'their' medium, the cinema, is noteworthy.
3. For the record, synagogue attendance by sex and age is as follows:

Synagogue Attendance, by Sex and Age

Frequency of attendance	Per cent Men 18–29	Men 30–50	Men 50+	Women 18–29	Women 30–50	Women 50+
Daily	5	9	20	1	1	2
Sabbaths and holidays	16	21	15	5	6	13
Occasional Sabbaths and holidays	24	21	18	14	19	18
High holidays only	28	29	25	52	43	38
Not at all	28	20	21	38	31	29
TOTAL POPULATION (N = 100%)	(238)	(413)	(380)	(332)	(436)	(277)

4. Indeed, the traditional notion of forbidden 'work' may be interpreted as including a strong taboo on what we might call 'creativity'. Creativity, of course, is what God rested from on the Seventh Day. The *Encyclopedia Judaica* attributes this interpretation to Samson Raphael Hirsch. Cf. 'The Sabbath', Vol. 14, pp. 557–72.
5. Peter Berger makes this point in Chapter Five of his *Social Reality of Religion*, op. cit. He argues that this historicism of early Judaism, together with its de-mystifying tendencies and its objectifying of a remote God, contributed to the secularization of primitive religion and, later on, to the secularization of Judaism itself (and of the other Western religions).
6. Retrospectively, the list of functions seems to us not entirely satisfactory: 'to keep the tradition . . .' is at too general a level, and sometimes, indeed, the 'tradition' enjoins 'being happy', for example. Substantively, the list of functions needs improvement, and ideally, should match those used for the study of the 'uses' of other institutions, such as the mass media (see Chapter Thirteen). Methodologically, it would have been better to ask respondents to 'evaluate the relevance of each function for each holiday, rather than asking which function is the 'most important' one.
7. Respondents who identified a given function as 'principal' were asked to signify which was 'next in importance'. Only respondents who said that the principal function of a holiday was to give them free time were not asked a second time.
8. A second question was asked, in fact, with respect to the same list of functions: 'What other things does this holiday give you?' The replies are not reported here because their distribution is easy to infer from the initial question concerning 'principal' meanings. The discussion which follows draws on both sets of replies. But more fundamental is the problem of how to probe this matter with the degree of subtlety that it requires. At very least, we erred by not asking for replies to *each* of the proposed lists of functions with respect to each holiday.
9. This is a good example of the problem of question-making. After the event, it is evident that 'to keep the tradition' and 'to have a religious experience' ought to have been treated separately. It may well be that 'tradition' is more closely related to the feeling of 'connection with generations past'. While these are basic methodological flaws, we take comfort in the fact that they are also problems which are built into Jewish tradition. The holidays have many different layers, and those that survive continue to collect new meanings. It makes discussion of secularization in Judaism particularly difficult. On the other hand, the separate dimensions of belief and practice in Judaism confound the definition of religiosity.
10. See footnote 8, above.
11. The December 1971 issue of the journal *Petahim* was devoted to their deliberations (in Hebrew). See also Hanoch Bartov, 'Back to Abnormal', *Commentary*, Vol. 57, March, 1974, on the changing meanings of Yom Kippur.
12. Throughout the study it is clear that the young are more present-oriented. They say so (in Chapter Fourteen) and act it.

PART THREE GOING OUT

CHAPTER SIX The Supply of Culture

There is little use studying the consumption of culture without a clear idea of what is available to be consumed. It is easy to build an elaborate theory as to why the residents of East London prefer football to playing golf, but it is no less important to note, at least for the record, that golf courses are not easily accessible – physically, economically or socially.[1]

Just as there are studies of consumption which overlook supply, so there are studies of supply which do not take account of actual use. Government year-books and UNESCO publications report on such things as number of theatres, number of cinema seats, number of radio receivers and the like. Useful as they are, one cannot infer much from these studies about the relationship between supply and demand. Ultimately, of course, one of the most interesting questions in the study of culture is the effect of supply on demand. Does the availability of good television programmes make a difference in the standards of taste? Does the availability of a theatre affect the rate of theatre-going?

In the present study, we have made an effort to take account of the supply of culture and to relate it to demand. In each of the fifty-six communities in which we carried out our survey of the population, we also attempted to audit the supply of culture that was being proffered at the time. After considering alternative ways of accomplishing this, we finally decided to base our analysis on the posters that publicized coming attractions. This is the accepted mode of publicizing local events of all kinds, and the municipalities levy a small tax for the privilege. At our request, they also kept a record of all such announcements for the focal period of our study, the month of June 1970.

Of course, there are drawbacks to this method of studying supply. For one thing, some of the smaller towns and rural areas do not have municipal notice-boards. In these cases, we interviewed the 'co-ordinators' of cultural events or a member of the local cultural committee to obtain the information we sought. Another problem arose when we realized that the posters sometimes referred to events that were scheduled to take place at a future time; we decided to include these, nevertheless, on the assumption that they would balance out announcements in the past which probably referred to events in the present. Still another problem arose from the fact that certain announcements referred to events which were scheduled to take place elsewhere. We decided to treat these as if they were taking place locally, thereby accepting the assumption of whoever took the trouble to distribute the announcement and pay the tax for posting it. Thus, if an event scheduled to take place in Haifa is publicized in ten towns and villages in the North, we counted the event as part of the cultural supply of all eleven places.

In general, posters refer to single events. Where a poster refers to more than one event, each was coded separately. On the other hand, when the same play or film is announced for a number of performances at the same place, we counted the 'programme' as one and recorded the number of 'performances' separately. Thus, 'events' or 'programmes' on the one hand, and 'performances' on the other, constitute our units of analysis.

In the case of films, we arbitrarily assumed that since most cinemas schedule their programmes on a weekly basis each theatre offered four different films during the course of the month. Some cinemas, of course, have a more rapid turnover, and others hold over a film for many weeks, but by and large, this short cut seemed legitimate to us. Again, each film is considered a 'programme' and each repeat screening a 'performance'.

Apart from the announcements of cultural events, the notices which we gathered included other kinds of events which are excluded from the analysis which follows. These refer to events specifically intended for children; 'public service' advertising (such as Government savings programmes, etc.); announcements by schools affiliated to the formal school system (we did, however, include announcement of private courses such as language courses, secretarial schools, etc.); and death notices.

Altogether, we recorded some 2,600 events that took place in the fifty-five communities (data for one community were unobtainable). These were then classified into 30 types of activity ranging from film and theatre to voluntary activities, studies, organized hikes, special prayer services, and so on. In addition to number of performances, each event or programme was further classified according to its location, price of admission, intended audience, attributes of its organizers (commercial, governmental, etc.) and whatever other salient characteristics could be inferred from a close reading of public announcements.

In spite of all the limitations of this method, it permits an estimate, albeit a very crude one, of the cultural menu which was offered to the population of Israeli cities, towns and villages, in the last month of the spring of 1970.

1. *Size of Settlement and the Supply of Culture*

Imagine a large billboard in the centre of a town square on which are posted all of the events scheduled for the whole of the forthcoming month. Imagine all of the adult residents of the town on an early evening promenade reviewing this listing of coming attractions. In principle, all of the events advertised are being proposed to each of the onlookers, and if there are 100 different events on the billboard, he is being invited – if he can manage it – to partake in all of them during the course of the month. In fact, of course, most people do not partake in most events: if they did, there would be many more events.

In Table 6.1 we group the fifty-five communities in the sample according to size in order to examine the relationship between community size and the number of events. It is clear from the table that there is a direct relationship between the two. As might be expected, the larger the town, the more events from which to choose. Thus, the average number of events in the four large cities is 233, whereas in cities whose population ranges between 50,000 and 100,000, the average number of events is 93, and so on.

TABLE 6.1 *Average Number of Cultural Events, and Average Number of Events* Per Capita, *by Type and Size of Settlement*

Type and size of settlement	Number of settlements in sample	Average number of events per settlement	Average number of events per settlement *per capita*
Large cities: 100,000 and over	4	233	1 : 977
Cities: 50,000–100,000	6	93	1 : 730
Cities: 20,000–50,000	14	47	1 : 610
All cities	**24**	**90**	**1 : 809**
Towns: 10,000–20,000	5	28	1 : 506
Towns: 2,000–10,000	5	18	1 : 361
All towns	**10**	**23**	**1 : 447**
Large village	1	6	1 : 392
Small village	2	20	1 : 54
Moshavim (co-operative)	10	7	1 : 60
Kibbutzim (collective)	8	16	1 : 23
All rural settlements	**21**	**12**	**1 : 48**

If these data reinforce the impression that big-city life is the locus of culture, the last column of the table gives a somewhat different perspective: the smaller the size of the town, the larger the number of events *per capita*. Thus, in the five towns of population 2,000–10,000 there is one event for each 361 persons whereas in the four largest cities, which are ten times larger than these towns, the ratio is one event per 1,000 persons. Examination of this column reveals that the growth in number of events with increasing city size consistently falls below the increase in number of people.

It is interesting to note the richness of cultural life in the kibbutzim, both in absolute numbers and in events *per capita*. The moshavim fall quite far behind. The average number of events in the kibbutz equals that of the towns (2,000–10,000) which are five times their size, while the ratio of events to people is forty times larger than that in the large cities. In this sense, the kibbutz member may be said to lead the richest cultural life in the country.

2. *New Towns and the Supply of Culture*

The supply of culture should also be examined in terms of the age of a town, not just size. Old, established communities might be expected to offer their residents a more elaborate cultural menu if it were not for the fact of extensive Government investment in the cultivation of the new towns, those in which new immigrants constitute a high proportion of the population.[2]

Comparing new and old towns of the same size, as Table 6.2 does, indicates some difference in favour of the veteran settlements. The gap appears both among the larger towns (only two 'new' towns are in the 50–100,000 class: Beersheba and Bat-Yam) and among the smaller ones.[3]

TABLE 6.2 *Average Number of Cultural Events, by Age of Settlement*

	Number of settlements in sample	Average population per settlement	Average number of events per settlement
Cities of 50,000–100,000			
Old-established	4	71,000	100
New	2	70,000	79
Cities of 20,000–50,000			
Old-established	6	32,000	62
New	8	26,000	36

Despite these differences in the overall averages, it is important to note that there are exceptions: there are 'new' towns that exceed 'old' ones of equal size; Ashdod, for example, offers a larger supply of cultural events than veteran Rehovot, and so on. On the other hand, certain new towns fall far behind old-established towns of equal size; curiously, these include the resort towns of Ashkelon and Tiberias both of which, ironically, are classed as 'new'. By the same token, 'new' moshavim – those settled by post-1948 immigrants – are far below the old-established moshavim in their supply of culture.

3. *Geographical Location and Culture Supply*

Still another factor which affects the number of cultural events in different cities is their relative proximity to, or isolation from, other cities. The obvious question is whether isolated towns are more self-sufficient, and thus provide a larger supply of events than towns of equal size which are located in the shadow of the metropolis. Actually, there are two questions here: (1) Is there a significant difference between the total supply of culture in more centrally located as opposed to more isolated places? and (2) Is the proportion of out-of-town events which are locally publicized greater in the former than in the latter?

Over the entire sample of fifty-five settlements, 77 per cent of all events take place locally. Thus Table 6.3 reveals that almost one in four events which are advertised locally take place elsewhere. This proportion is affected by city size, of course: while only 8 per cent of the events publicized in the four largest cities take place out of town, the comparable figure is 36 per cent for cities of 2–10,000 population. Moreover, the influence of city size is also reflected in the distance of these out-of-town events from the towns in which they are publicized: the smaller the settlement, the higher the proportion of far-away events which are included in its 'supply'.

But the relationship between city size and the proportion of out-of-town events is not altogether linear. The middle-sized cities (50–100,000 population), in particular, publicized a lower proportion of at-home events than would be expected, judging from their size alone. This suggests that other factors, such as a city's age or its relative isolation, ought to be taken into account. Table 6.4 does this.

Of the six cities in this group, four have veteran status and two are 'new'. In Beersheba, one of the two, virtually all publicized events take place within the city limits, whereas in Bat-Yam, the other 'new' city, only 6 in 10 of the locally publicized events actually take place locally. Judging from these few cases, there appears to be no relationship between age of city and the ratio of local to out-of-town events.

The geographic location of a city, however, *is* related: the three cities which are situated outside of the orbit of the metropolis have higher proportions of at-home events than the three cities in the Tel Aviv area. Beersheba, which is most distant of all, is also most obviously isolated culturally; the local advertising of out-of-town events is minimal. Bnei

TABLE 6.3 *Proportion of Locally Advertised Cultural Events Taking Place Locally or Elsewhere*

Type and size of settlement	Number of settlements in sample	Total advertised events (N = 100%)	Per cent taking place locally	Per cent taking place in nearby settlement	Per cent taking place in distant settlement
Large cities: 100,000 and over	4	(930)	92	3	5
Cities: 50,000–100,000	6	(557)	66	28	6
Cities: 20,000–50,000	14	(663)	76	16	8
All cities	**24**	**(2150)**	**80**	**14**	**6**
Towns: 10,000–20,000	5	(138)	72	17	11
Towns: 2,000–10,000	5	(90)	64	12	24
All towns	**10**	**(228)**	**69**	**15**	**16**
Large villages	1	(6)	50	0	50
Small villages	2	(40)	70	12	18
Moshavim (co-operative)	10	(72)	51	7	42
Kibbutzim (collective)	8	(127)	67	13	20
All rural settlements	**21**	**(245)**	**63**	**11**	**26**
All settlements	**55**	**(2623)**	**77**	**14**	**9**

Brak, at the other extreme, seems to be wholly dependent on events taking place outside. Given the concentration of orthodox groups in Bnei Brak, it appears likely that its idiosyncratic cultural events are not of the kind that need street notices. But for the kinds of events that do, Bnei Brak is not an autonomous community.

TABLE 6.4 *Proportion of Locally Advertised Events Taking Place Locally or Elsewhere, by City Size, Age and Geographical District (cities of 50,000–100,000 only)*

City	Age	District	Total advertised events (N=100%)	Per cent taking place locally	Per cent taking place in nearby settlement	Per cent taking place in distant settlement
Beersheba	New	Southern	(83)	93	0	7
Netanya	Old	Central	(84)	80	15	5
Petah Tikva	Old	Central	(136)	75	21	4
Holon	Old	Tel Aviv	(90)	72	22	6
Bat-Yam	New	Tel Aviv	(75)	61	31	8
Bnei Brak	Old	Tel Aviv	(92)	16	80	4
All cities 50–100,000			**(560)**	**66**	**28**	**6**

A different case again is that of Ramat-Gan, the fourth largest city in the country. The number of cultural events offered in Ramat-Gan are as many as Jerusalem or Haifa, even though the latter are twice its size. Moreover, the size of the supply cannot be explained by reference to the proportion of Tel Aviv events which are included on Ramat-Gan billboards. While such out-of-town events are certainly represented, the proportion of at-home events is high nevertheless. It almost seems as if Ramat-Gan is making a determined effort not to be swallowed, culturally, by the metropolis. But Ramat-Gan notwithstanding, the overall pattern appears to be that the more centrally located towns are more likely to refer their residents elsewhere for the consumption of culture than less centrally located towns of equal size. Furthermore, the total number of events publicized in the latter – that is, not just the number of at-home events – appears to be greater.

4. *Import-Export Ratios*

This kind of analysis can be applied to the cultural exchange within and among regions. Events in Jerusalem, for example, are widely advertised elsewhere, but Jerusalem residents are not much appealed to from elsewhere.[4] The six settlements of the Tel Aviv region, on the other hand, offer events which are widely advertised elsewhere (258 advertisements, or almost half of the total advertising for out-of-town events). Most of this advertising, however, is placed in other towns of the same region (84 per cent or 174 of the 208 advertisements). Thus, of an average 35 external events publicized in each of the towns of the Tel Aviv region, about 30 per cent are intra-regional.

The seven settlements of the Haifa region originated 72 announcements that were displayed elsewhere and publicized 66 announcements of the events of other settlements. Forty-three per cent of these latter related to intra-regional events. In this latter sense, the Haifa region stands second only to the Tel Aviv region. The other three regions are far behind in this respect. The twenty settlements of the Central Region, for example, displayed a total of 152 advertisements for out-of-town events, only 28 per cent of which referred to events taking place within the region itself. Their proximity to Tel Aviv makes them natural clients of the metropolis.

It is curious that the Southern Region is so low on the measure of intra-regional advertising (16 per cent). It suggests that the region's major city, Beersheba, is not serving as a focus for out-of-town events, in spite of the fact that no other major city is easily accessible to the settlements of the region. It is possible, of course, that the events of Beersheba are publicized in other ways, i.e. not by poster or through the local culture committees; all we can say is that the methods employed in the present study do not reveal such activity.

5. *Types of Events*

Eighty-five per cent of the events publicized in Israel in June 1970 could be classified into seven categories. These are recorded in Table 6.5, according to their frequency in each settlement type.

Cinema is the most popular event in urban settlements. Thirty to forty per cent of all advertised events referred to films. In rural areas, films drop to 15 per cent of all advertised events. It is interesting to observe that the relative importance of films is greatest in the largest cities, in spite of the fact that these cities have the largest number and greatest diversity of other kinds of offerings.[5]

Theatrical programmes account for some 10–15 per cent of all events. Again we encounter a curious phenomenon: the number of programmes is not greater in the larger cities. Two additional factors must be taken into account here, however. First of all, it should be remembered that we are tabulating *announcements*, and that some of these (as Table 6.3 shows) refer to events taking place elsewhere; thus, some of the publicity for theatre constitutes an invitation to the residents of Town X to

TABLE 6.5 *Frequency of Advertised Cultural Events, by Type and Size of Settlement*

Type of event	Average for 4 large cities 100,000+ population		Average for 6 cities 50–100,000 population		Average for 14 cities of 20–50,000 population		Average for 10 towns 2–20,000 population		Average for 21 rural settlements	
	N	%	N	%	N	%	N	%	N	%
Cinema	96	41	34	35	16	34	7	30	2	17
Theatre	35	15	8	9	6	12	3	11	1	8
Lectures, meetings, etc.	35	15	7	8	5	11	2	10	1	8
Celebrations	12	5	7	8	7	14	4	17	4	35
Courses, studies	13	6	18	20	5	11	4	17	1	8
Light entertainment	9	4	7	8	5	11	1	4	1	8
Other	33	14	12	12	3	7	2	9	2	17
All cultural events	**233**	**100%**	**93**	**100%**	**47**	**100%**	**23**	**100%**	**14**	**100%**

attend a performance in City Y. Secondly, we are here reporting on 'programmes' or productions, not performances. In the large cities a 'programme' may be given a number of performances. Indeed, in Tel Aviv – where this is particularly the case – we discovered that plays were presented an average of five times during the period of the research.[6] In the other cities, multiple performances are much less usual.

Lectures and voluntary activities of various kinds occupy another 10–15 per cent of the posters. Special celebrations – of holidays, jubilees and the like – are particularly characteristic of rural settlements while publicity for courses of all kinds seem rather more frequent in middle-sized cities. Light entertainment is equally frequent everywhere.

The remaining categories (15 per cent of the total publicity) cover such events as concerts, chess tournaments, night clubs and special prayers. No one of these residual categories accounts for more than 1 per cent of the total supply.

Altogether, it is the homogeneity of the distribution of the different types of events that seems noteworthy. The largest cities differ hardly at all from the smaller cities. Even the rural areas do not deviate very much from the overall pattern, except for the higher rate of celebrations and the lower rate of cinema.[7]

6. *Culture Suppliers*

Every announcement of a cultural event mentions the name of the individual or the organization offering the event. Sometimes there is more than one name mentioned. The supply of culture is obviously dependent on these impresarios, and we tried – within the limitations of our data – to identify them.

Most events were organized by a single individual or agency. This is particularly characteristic of large cities, on the one hand, and kibbutzim, on the other. In rural areas, however, several different groups are listed as co-sponsors of the event. Typically, these might involve a national organization (such as the Labour Federation) and a regional council.

This difference in sponsorship is reflected also in the distribution of commercial as opposed to public sponsorship. As Table 6.6 indicates, 6 in 10 big-city events are commercially sponsored. This proportion drops to 4 in 10 for the smaller towns and to less than 1 in 10 in rural areas. The public impresarios include municipalities, local and regional councils, the Labour Federation, the Education Ministry, political parties, and others. Public sponsorship typically involves more than one of these organizations.

The division of labour among commercial and public sponsors extends to types of events as well. Films and light entertainment are offered by commercial sponsors, and particularly in the cities. Theatre offerings and courses of all kinds also tend to be sponsored commercially in the big cities, and much less so in the towns. Public agencies are responsible for the organization of lectures and other meetings, and for other types of voluntary activities and sports. In the rural areas, public organizations are responsible for virtually every kind of activity except light entertainment. The low overheads involved in the movement of folk singers, jazz groups, etc., apparently make the organization of such events commercially viable almost anywhere.

TABLE 6.6 *Organization of Cultural Events, by Type and Size of Settlement*

	Number of settlements (N=100%)	Per cent commercially organized	Per cent non-commercially organized*
Cities (20,000+ population)	(24)	59	41
Towns (2–20,000 population)	(10)	42	58
Rural settlements	(21)	7	93

* Non-commercial includes local authorities, the Labour Federation, Government Ministries, political parties, etc.

In most cities and towns, the role of the municipal council in the organization of activities is rather low. An 'active' council, relatively speaking, is credited with having organized about 20 per cent of the events in its jurisdiction. The outstanding exception in this respect is the municipality of Ramat-Gan which participated in the sponsorship of over 40 per cent of the city's cultural activities. This would explain the city's exceptionally rich supply of culture grants as noted above.

7. *The Price of Admission in Time, Money and Energy*

Most of the events we are discussing are one-night stands. This holds true of light entertainment, lectures, concerts, theatre, trips – almost all types of events. The only exception to this rule are films which are one-time presentations in rural areas, but much longer lasting (four to seven days is the mode) in the cities.

Performances are held on weekday evenings. The only public activity that is characteristic of Friday night is light entertainment: performers and discotheques make their rounds on this night. Films are launched on Saturday night for the weekly cycle, and as we shall see in a later chapter, the habits of movie-goers are attuned accordingly. In the smaller cities, concerts are also given on Saturday night.

In the cities, there is an admission charge to most events: three-quarters of all advertised events listed the price of admission. This proportion drops to 59 per cent in the small towns and falls away almost completely (14 per cent) in the rural areas. It appears that most things are paid for collectively, or from the funds of the regional councils, in rural areas.

8. *Summary*

Unlike the rest of the book, the analysis of this chapter is based not on interviews but on the collection and analysis of announcements of public events during the month of June 1970. Information was collected from each of the fifty-five communities which constituted the basis for the survey of attitudes and behaviour; in the smaller communities which do not have municipal notice boards, the local co-ordinator of cultural activities was requested to provide the information. Events not made public in these ways were necessarily excluded from the analysis.

Despite these methodological problems, it seems clear that size of city is strongly related to the supply of culture, although the number of events *per capita* does not increase with size. In the smaller settlements – particularly in the kibbutzim – the *per capita* supply is very much higher than in the cities.

Holding city size constant, we found that new towns – those populated by new immigrants – offered fewer events than old-established ones. More centrally located cities advertise each other's events more than do more isolated cities of equal size. The four large cities, however, are essentially autonomous in their supply of culture: they rarely refer their residents elsewhere.

These four – Tel Aviv, Jerusalem, Haifa, Ramat-Gan – each offers its people some 200–300 different events during the course of a month. These are the cities in which cinemas and theatre give multiple performances. Other events are typically one-time events; that is, they were not repeated over the course of the month. In other communities – one would not be far wrong to say in all cities except Tel Aviv – virtually everything is offered in single performance, except for films.

The most frequently advertised event is cinema. Films constitute at least 35 per cent of the total supply of cultural events. Theatre, accounting for 10–15 per cent of all events, comes next, followed by lectures and meetings. The relative proportions of these events is rather stable in the most diverse kinds of communities.

Some 20 per cent of all advertisements refer to events taking place outside the boundaries of the community. We have assumed that such advertising indicates a genuine market potential and thus that the cities in the Tel Aviv area have a very active interchange. The Central district is also oriented to Tel Aviv. Communities in the Southern area, on the other hand, to which Beersheba might have expected to play host, do not seem to be especially attracted to their metropolis.

In the cities, cultural events arise from private and commercial initiative. In the rural areas, public initiative and organization are far more frequent, and most activities are available without charge. Events in the smaller cities are more mixed in this respect.

NOTES – CHAPTER SIX

1. In this connection, see Isabel Griffiths, 'Gentlemen Suppliers and With-it Consumers', *International Review of Sports Sociology*, Vol. 5 (1970), pp. 59–68.
2. Our classification follows that of the Central Bureau of Statistics whose 'new' settlements either were established after the declaration of statehood in 1948, *or* a majority of whose population are new (post-1948) immigrants. Thus, certain veteran towns are called 'new' – Tiberias, Naharia, Afula, for example – because of the high proportion of newcomers to old-timers.
3. Even if the number of expected events is adjusted to take account more precisely of differences in average size, the gap is quite apparent. Thus, applying the ratio of 62 events for an average old-town population of 32,000 to the new towns which average 26,000 gives an expected supply of 57 events. Only 36 events are 'observed'.
4. These figures may be misleading because they include nation-wide advertising, in the month of June, of summer camps for young adults in Jerusalem. Indeed, the advertising was so pervasive that the decision was made to 'assign' this event even to settlements in which it was not explicitly publicized and/or mentioned. We suspect that such events, which focus in Jerusalem, probably have parallels in other seasons of the year as well, but we cannot be certain. A similar situation applies to a summer camp in the North which was advertised throughout the Northern Region. Note, too, that the Jerusalem region is represented in the sample of settlements by the city of Jerusalem alone.
5. It is worth recalling here that our coding of announcements for films was based on the assumption of weekly changes of film in each cinema. Thus, the number of film events in a given settlement is equal to the number of cinema houses multiplied by four. This system of coding probably inflates the number of films in the large cities, where films are often held over for several weeks, and lowers the number of films in smaller settlements.
6. Compared with newspaper listings, our data for Tel Aviv, which are based exclusively on posters, appears to understate the number of theatrical events. The posters indicate some 40 different productions on the boards

during the month of June compared with 60–70 in the papers. For the sake of consistency we report only the data from our primary source, the posters, but it is important to note that these data apparently understate the case, especially in Tel Aviv.

7. The celebration rate may reflect the fact that sources of information for rural areas were informants rather than posters. A neighbourhood celebration in an urban area would be much more likely to go unrecorded, therefore.

CHAPTER SEVEN The Consumption of Culture: Going Out

Is supply a function of demand? Do the leisure offerings of Israeli cities and towns reflect the leisure interests of their citizens? Perhaps it is the other way round: perhaps demand is a function of supply, in the sense that the public may learn to like whatever it is offered. This is a perennial argument in the field of popular culture and mass communications, and there are no easy answers. One clutches eagerly at the scant evidence that publics *are* discriminating, and that efforts such as the Theatre for the People project of the Ministry of Education are actually creating audiences. One thing is clear, however: the public cannot know what it wants unless it is aware of, and has experienced, the alternatives which are available. Most publics in most places have little idea that alternatives exist. Given that governments are increasingly prepared to subsidize those institutions of culture which seem to it deserving, the question as a whole merits constant attention.[1]

This chapter, like its predecessor, deals with leisure *outside* the home. Here, we want to examine the extent of participation and appreciation shown by the public for the public institutions of leisure. We want to match demand with supply, wherever possible.

Nevertheless, it should be borne in mind that most of the time that is definable as leisure is spent *inside*, not outside the home. Thus, using time budgets as the measure, 'discretionary' time (excluding work, household, sleep, meals, prayer) totals just over thirty-one hours per week. Some 25–30 per cent of this time, overall, is spent outside the home, of which only a small proportion – 5 per cent – is spent in a cinema, theatre, coffee house, discotheque, etc. On the other hand, some three-quarters of this 'discretionary' time is spent inside the home – one's own or somebody else's. Half of the home-time, approximately, is spent in visiting and conversation, and the other half with the media of mass communication.

Table 7.1 gives a different perspective on the same problem. It shows that about one-quarter of the population goes out for the purpose of spending leisure at least three to four times per week. Some 40 per cent 'go out' once or twice a week; and about 10 per cent once or twice a month. Another quarter does not 'go out' almost at all!

The joint influence of both education and age is apparent in these statistics. Among the least educated at every age level, the proportion of those who almost never 'go out' reaches 60 per cent. This group (0–4 years of education), however, is almost non-existent among the young. A majority of all other groups 'goes out' once a week or more.

About 40 per cent of young people 'go out' to spend leisure three or four times per week, while another 40 per cent do so once or twice. The mode for the older groups is once or twice per week. The influence of education is particularly apparent in the oldest group: education counteracts some of the isolating effects of age. This is a finding which will recur repeatedly throughout the study.[2]

TABLE 7.1 *Frequency of 'Going Out' to spend Leisure, by Age and Education*

Per cent

	Total (N=100%)	Daily or 5–6 times per week	3–4 times per week	1–2 times per week	1–2 times per month	Less frequently or never
Age 18–29						
0–4 years education	(25)	(12)	(4)	(27)	(16)	(41)
5–10 years education	(227)	19	26	35	8	12
11+ years education	(318)	10	29	46	9	6
Age 30–50						
0–4 years education	(171)	5	6	23	8	58
5–10 years education	(424)	5	10	50	13	22
11+ years education	(325)	4	14	51	16	15
Age 50+						
0–4 years education	(119)	6	6	25	7	56
5–10 years education	(332)	8	10	38	12	32
11+ years education	(239)	8	17	47	13	15
TOTAL POPULATION	(2180)	8	15	42	11	24

But not all of those who are 'out' are at a theatre or public meeting or coffee house. Judging from the time budgets, again, about 8 per cent of the population patronizes some place of public entertainment on a weekday evening, and this rises to 12 per cent on Saturday nights. Putting all these figures together allows us to estimate that some 20–30 per cent are out of their homes on a weekday evening, and perhaps 30–40 per cent are 'out' on Saturday night. Of these, about one-third are patronizing a place of entertainment, mostly the cinema.

Is this a lot or a little? Our best guess – based on the comparative data available (which are inadequate to the purpose) – is that it is moderately high. But more important, perhaps, is that the overall rate of 'going out' has two components: (1) a high proportion of going out to visit or just to walk, and (2) a relatively low rate of consumption of paid entertainment or other formally organized public events. The one exception, as will be shown below, is going to the cinema.

1. *The Implications of 'Going Out' for Politics, Art and Education*

The fact that most leisure is spent at home, and that so much out-of-home leisure is spent visiting other homes is significant. This is apparent even from a cursory examination of writings on the functions of leisure in society. From ancient times onward, it has been emphasized that leisure is a prerequisite to democratic politics.[3] The forum of the Greek city state was dependent on the leisure of the citizen (whose leisure, in turn, was dependent on the work of his slaves). By the same token, leisure is seen by historians of culture as prerequisite to creativity in the arts.[4] Drama and music are created for people with time. But the assumption, both for politics and for art, is that leisure time is spent out of the home – in the forum or the theatre or the coffee house, with moderately large groups on an equal footing. If television has changed the relationship between time-in-public and artistic creativity by being able to serve a dispersed audience sitting at home, it has probably aggravated the problem of democratic politics, as critics of modern society have observed.[5] The voluntary association, the political party, the mass meeting or lecture are still highly dependent on time 'out'.

The same thing holds true for normative Judaism. Leisure in Judaism, as we have already noted, is preordained: it is a natural right. But much of it is to be spent in public. Prayer requires ten people, and it is taken for granted that study is to be carried on in groups. Place is not so important: prayer and study are appropriate almost anywhere. Neither preacher nor teacher is prerequisite. But other people are necessary.

These are the ideals – of democratic politics, of artistic creativity, of adult education, of normative Judaism. It is unlikely that they were realized anywhere or any place. Certain historical elites provide the models, but how applicable are they to egalitarian societies? What is the optimum toward which participatory democracy should strive?[6] Moreover, it may be an error to underrate 'visiting others' as a context for political, artistic and intellectual activity. Indeed, home study groups are very well known both in traditional Judaism and in adult education, and lately *hugei-bayit* – political circles in private homes – have become a major feature of election campaigns in Israel. Indeed, this line of thought calls the *salon* to mind – this was a kind of elite visiting, too, and it has an honoured place in the history of art and politics.[7] But we must know more about the 'content' of visiting to make a sound judgement. We did, in fact, inquire on this point – as will be reported below – and it does appear that a certain amount of time spent with friends *is* spent in 'political circles' or in group learning.[8] Certainly some of it is spent on discussion of politics. Perhaps a quarter of those reporting on activities with friends said they do such things at least 'occasionally'. But these seem essentially minority pursuits and do not provide enough basis for revising our image of the different social implications of spending time in public or private domains. Still, it is a fact worth reckoning with, and certainly a subject worth far more study, as is the content of informal conversation more generally. Perhaps we will be forced to surrender our historical images of the arenas for the conduct of public affairs, from the forum, the market-place, the theatre, the synagogue, the coffee house in favour of groups of family and friends equipped with two-way cable television.

Let us see, then, as best we can, how Israelis spend their time 'outside'.

2. *Frequency of Participation in Leisure Activities Outside the Home: the Non-Participants*

It is difficult to decide, as we have said, whether going to the theatre 'several times a year' is frequent theatre-going or not. Obviously devotees of the theatre will consider it far too little; those who live outside of the metropolis may consider it quite frequent.

Or, if a person goes to the movies once a month and goes to the theatre once a month, it is obviously correct to say that such a person goes to the theatre and the movies with equal frequency. Yet, many people would consider once-a-month movie-going as rather infrequent and once-a-month theatre-going as rather frequent.

While it is difficult to judge whether a given frequency of attendance is high or low, or whether a given frequency for one activity is 'more' or 'less' than for another, it *is* possible to rank activities in terms of the percentage of the population who *never* participate in them. Table 7.2 gives these percentages.

From this list of those who never participate in a given activity it is evident that the most popular activities are movies and excursions: 80 per cent of the adult population engages in these activities at least 'sometimes'. Museum-going and theatre-going are also high on the list, although about 40 per cent of the population never attends. Light entertainment is only slightly less popular.

The least popular activities by far are going to discotheques and night clubs; taking trips abroad; and going to concerts. These, as we shall see, are not so unpopular as they seem; rather, they attract specialized audiences.

From this point forward, we shall be dealing primarily with those who do participate in these activities, and shall report on the frequency of participation.

TABLE 7.2 *Popularity of Activities Measured by Level of Participation*

Leisure activity	Per cent who 'never' participate*
Community centre	83
Concert	81
Travel abroad	77
Night club, discotheque	77
Sport (active)	75
Studies	71
Voluntary organization	70
Sporting events (passive)	69
Light entertainment	50
Lecture, symposium, meeting	43
Public park	42
Museum	37
Theatre	36
Cinema	21
Excursion (pleasure, sightseeing)	20

* 'Never' in certain cases refers to non-participation in the past year.

3. *The Participants: Youth and Education*

A first sketch for a portrait of the participants in the several departments of public life is presented in Table 7.3. The table reports on the rate of participation of each of the nine age-and-education groups in 13 different activities. For the reason already mentioned, we have had to decide rather intuitively what rate to use for each activity although such decisions are necessarily bound by the norms of actual behaviour. Thus, in the case of going to the cinema, we chose the rate of once a week; the rate chosen for theatre-going is 'several times per year'.

It might be well to recall again, at this point, that the heart of the table is in the second and third rows of each age group. The youngest group (age 18–29) has virtually nobody with less than an elementary school education, and therefore the first row is effectively blank. The second row in each age group consists, roughly, of those with an elementary school education, and the third consists of those who have completed secondary school or more.[9]

Reading of the table will indicate that there are some cultural activities which are related to age, some to education and some both to age and education. Consider the first two columns of the table, for example: movies and theatre. Movie-going at the rate of once a week or more is strongly related to age, but not to education. The young – whatever their education – go to the movies once a week or more. The groups

TABLE 7.3 *Participation in Out-of-Home Activities, by Age and Education*

	N	Per cent attending **cinema** Once a week or more	Per cent attending **theatre** Several times per year	Per cent attending **concert** Within past 3 months	Per cent attending **museum** Within past 3 months	Per cent attending **light enter-tainment** Within past 3 months	Per cent attending **night club** Several times per year	Per cent attending **lecture** or **meeting** Within past month
Age 18–29								
0–4 years education	(48)	(25)	(19)	(–)	(9)	(24)	(6)	(11)
5–10 years education	(389)	57	47	1	31	50	33	12
11+ years education	(554)	52	64	9	42	55	38	30
Age 30–50								
0–4 years education	(272)	9	8	–	7	7	2	7
5–10 years education	(699)	23	37	3	22	24	7	19
11+ years education	(535)	15	56	16	42	26	12	24
Age 50+								
0–4 years education	(211)	7	12	–	9	4	1	10
5–10 years education	(533)	15	33	8	17	11	1	21
11+ years education	(430)	20	60	30	39	19	–	34
TOTAL POPULATION	(3671)	26	43	9	29	27	13	21

	N	Per cent attending **sporting events** Occasionally	Per cent actively participating in **sports** Once a week or more	Per cent actively **studying** On regular basis	Per cent going on **excursions, trips** Several times per year	Per cent attending **community centre** Occasionally	Per cent visiting **public parks** At least once a fortnight
Age 18–29							
0–4 years education	(48)	(9)	(2)	(11)	(21)	(12)	(20)
5–10 years education	(389)	41	25	17	59	10	39
11+ years education	(554)	48	31	53	82	19	34
Age 30–50							
0–4 years education	(272)	18	5	11	28	8	24
5–10 years education	(699)	35	13	19	52	15	43
11+ years education	(535)	35	26	49	74	21	40
Age 50 +							
0–4 years education	(211)	9	4	8	25	11	25
5–10 years education	(533)	18	9	14	36	18	39
11+ years education	(430)	23	20	38	63	30	36
TOTAL POPULATION	(3671)	32	19	29	57	18	36

over 30 go very much less. Among older people, some small influence of education on attendance may be discerned, particularly among the over-50 age group.

The statistics of theatre-going are very different from those of movie-going, as the table shows. Here, education is the key, while the role of age is rather unimportant. Within each age group, the higher the education, the higher the rate of theatre-going. Only about 10 per cent of the least educated go to theatre as often as 'several times a year' compared with 40 per cent of the elementary-education group and about 60 per cent of those with secondary-school education or more. Thus, unlike the cinema, age is all but irrelevant in determining who goes to the theatre.

Concerts combine both background factors. At each age level, the proportion of concert-goers increases sharply with education (virtually the only ones who go are those with secondary schooling or more). But the concentration of concert-goers is among the highly educated of the older age group. Thirty per cent of the best-educated group of 50 years or over went to a concert in the past three months. Is the price of admission a good explanation? Very unlikely; since peak income is reached in the 30–50 age range. Is there some other reason that associates age-plus-education with concert-going? The reader is referred to a later point in the discussion.

Continuing across the table, we find education to be the key factor in museum attendance, attendance at lectures and seminars, study in general, and even in going to the park: the higher the education the higher the participation. Age, on the other hand, is the key to light entertainment, discotheques and night clubs as it is to movie-going. For the elementary-educated group, age is an important factor in museum-going, too: young persons with 5–10 years of education were twice as likely to have been to a museum or exhibition in the past three months as were persons over 50 with the same education. But, for the well-educated group, we see (once again) that education eradicates the influence of age.

Both age and education affect participation in sports and membership in voluntary organizations and community centres. It is the better educated in each case who participate more. In the case of sports, it is the better educated young; in the case of community centres, however, it is the better educated old.

In short, as far as activity outside the home is concerned, the factors of age and education, in their several combinations, play important roles in affecting who will do what. Altogether, the table teaches two major lessons: (1) those with least education are excluded, in very high proportions, from almost everything – even from sports and public parks; (2) although there is a 'natural' tendency for older people to participate less, high education regularly overpowers it.

4. *Is Ethnic Origin Relevant to Participation?*

In a sense, these age-education groups may be considered 'sub-cultures' with their own patterns of activity. Most modern societies incorporate such sub-cultures based on age and education. But there are other factors to reckon with as well. Two of the most salient in Israeli life are religion and ethnic origin. As a general rule, we can say that religious persons participate less in public activities than non-religious people. In part, this is because the average education of religious persons is lower. But even comparing persons of equivalent educational level, the non-religious are more active in cultural and public events. Exceptions are study, and, of course, prayer, where religious persons are the more active. Below we consider the influence of religiosity on participation in the several activities.

What about differences based on country of origin? Here, too, as in the case of religion, it is important to distinguish between those that result from differences in educational level and those that persist even after education is held constant. Indeed, as a general rule, social research in Israel has shown that education supersedes ethnicity. In other words, what seems at first glance to be a large difference between Israelis of Western and Eastern origin, turns out to be a difference between persons of differing levels of educational achievement; that is, when equally educated members of the two groups are compared, the ostensible ethnic difference disappears. This suggests that education in Israel is a very powerful socializing and equalizing force. But until the large educational gap between the two groups is overcome, the differences remain – even when they are caused 'only' by education, and not by ethnicity.[10] It is a race against time.

In the present study, dealing as it does with patterns of consuming culture, there is some reason to believe that ethnic differences should be more in evidence than in other areas. Indeed, cultural activities is one of the areas where diversity is considered legitimate, often even desirable. Our respondents themselves express this in their affirmation of the desirability of perpetuating ethnic traditions in music and religious folkways, while – at the same time – disaffirming the desirability of ethnic organization on political (and to a lesser extent, economic) grounds.[11]

Table 7.4 reports on the relationship between ethnic background and participation in cultural activities. The tables hold education constant – in the sense that they permit comparisons of persons with different ethnicity but of the same educational background. And they go one step further. They compare the generation of immigrants (that is, members of both ethnic groups who were born outside Israel) with the generation born in Israel to immigrant parents.

TABLE 7.4 *Participation in Out-of-Home Activities, by Ethnic Origin, Generation and Education**

	Total population	Born in Asia–Africa	Born in Europe–America	Israel born; father born in Asia–Africa	Israel born; father born in Europe–America	Israel born; father born in Israel
A. *Per cent who go to cinema once a month or more*						
5–10 years education	57	60	52	70	59	68
11+ years education	66	67	77	80	76	64
B. *Per cent who go to theatre at least several times per year*						
5–10 years education	36	24	48	27	51	28
11+ years education	60	42	65	58	70	55
C. *Per cent who attended concert within past six months*						
5–10 years education	6	2	11	2	12	–
11+ years education	22	6	29	7	21	21
D. *Per cent who visited museum within past six months*						
5–10 years education	28	26	31	32	35	18
11+ years education	41	45	53	47	59	62

* Base figures for above percentages also give an approximate idea of the relative size of the groups:

5–10 years education	1546	646	687	108	66	39
11+ years education	1454	292	802	66	239	55

As far as movie-going is concerned, we find very little difference between ethnic groups in either the first or second generation.

Theatre-going is quite different again. Even after holding education constant, there are gaps in the frequency of theatre-going between Europeans and non-Europeans. Among those with 5–10 years of education, the Europeans go to the theatre twice as frequently as Orientals in *both* generations. Among the better educated, there is some evidence that the gap evident in the first generation has closed slightly in the second: 42 per cent of those of Eastern origin and 65 per cent of Europeans go to the theatre at least several times a year in the first generation (a difference of 23 per cent) compared with 58 per cent and 70 per cent (a 12 per cent difference) in the second.

Concert-going shows some of the same patterns (and some different ones) as theatre-going. Among the lower educated, six times as many Westerners attend concerts. Among the better educated, the gap in the first generation (a factor of 5) is narrowed in the second. But judging from what we know about concert-going, there is reason to believe that this gap will *widen* as the second generation grows older, since age will probably bring a higher proportion of better educated Westerners to the concert hall.

On the whole, however, it cannot be said that those of Eastern origin – even when they are well educated – have become acculturated to European patterns as far as theatre or concert music is concerned. Generations do not overcome the ethnic difference in museum-going either – but the difference between the groups is so small that it is not a matter of concern.

5. *City Size and the Consumption of Culture*

In the chapter on the supply of culture, we saw very large differences among cities and settlement types: the larger the settlement, the more cultural activity. Of course, we saw, too, that the smaller supply in smaller places nonetheless offered more activities *per person* than did larger places. Thus, while a resident of Jerusalem, say, has a choice of 200 activities per month, he has to 'share' these activities with 200,000 other adults, while the far fewer activities from which a resident of Dimona has to choose need be shared with far fewer people.

Depending on how one interprets these findings, therefore, one will be either surprised or reassured to learn that the extent of consumption of culture is essentially independent of city size (Table 7.5). Holding education constant, the frequency of attending the theatre, or going to a museum, is not really different in Jerusalem or Dimona, in Tel Aviv or in Kiryat Shmoneh. This means that persons of like education in large and small places tend to consume culture at much the same rates and in

TABLE 7.5 *Participation in Out-of-Home Activities, by Size and Age of Settlement and by Respondents' Education*

	Large cities	Cities: 50–100,000		Cities: 20–50,000		Urban settlements		Farms and moshavim	Kibbutzim
		Old	New	Old	New	Old	New		
A. *Per cent who go to cinema once a week or more*									
0–4 years education	9	6	12	10	15	4	11	6	(100)
5–10 years education	20	25	30	22	34	28	38	37	79
11+ years education	23	29	37	26	30	18	37	36	69
Total population	**20**	**25**	**32**	**22**	**28**	**20**	**30**	**27**	**72**
B. *Per cent who go to theatre at least several times per year*									
0–4 years education	16	–	20	12	17	13	10	5	(100)
5–10 years education	38	32	38	30	31	43	36	28	78
11+ years education	64	54	54	59	52	57	45	56	92
Total population	**50**	**37**	**43**	**40**	**35**	**46**	**30**	**28**	**89**
C. *Per cent who attended concert within past three months*									
0–4 years education	–	–	–	–	–	–	–	–	(–)
5–10 years education	7	4	4	3	3	7	1	–	9
11+ years education	23	11	4	19	11	8	7	4	31
Total population	**14**	**7**	**4**	**9**	**5**	**7**	**3**	**1**	**26**
D. *Per cent who visited museum within past three months*									
0–4 years education	11	4	–	4	11	10	7	9	–
5–10 years education	28	19	34	22	21	17	12	19	12
11+ years education	44	43	45	48	39	34	34	37	36
Total population	**37**	**28**	**35**	**31**	**24**	**24**	**18**	**21**	**29**

much the same forms. But note: the average level of education is higher in the big cities.

There are, perhaps, slight differences which ought to be mentioned. Persons in smaller places (always controlling for education) are more likely to partake of movies and light entertainment than persons of equal education in larger places. And, contrariwise, museum attendance (in particular), concert- and theatre-going are somewhat more frequent in larger places than in smaller ones. These differences, of course, reflect the state of supply. But they are *very small differences* compared with the very large differences evident in the supply.

Kibbutzim, as the table shows, are remarkably like big cities. Indeed they exceed large cities in movie-going and in theatre attendance, in reading and in museum-going. The consumption of culture in the kibbutz is nothing short of extraordinary. Of course, we also noted how the kibbutzim stand out in the supply of culture.

How does one explain these discrepancies between supply and consumption? There appear to be two possible explanations – and both are probably true. First of all, it is likely that the supply *per capita* does indeed 'satisfy' the persons in smaller places. The chances are that they attend whatever is brought to them – and thus manage to keep up with the average person of their own education in the larger cities. It may be that they would do more if more were available to them.

Secondly, there is good reason to believe that this homogenization of exposure to cultural events is also a product of the mobility of the population. We have already seen that travel is one of the most popular forms of leisure-time activity, and shall return to this subject below. But it is also likely that people from the smaller towns go to the bigger cities for the express purpose of spending their leisure. This is evident in Table 7.6. The proportion of village dwellers who say they 'prefer going elsewhere, at least occasionally, to spend leisure' is twice that of the big-city dwellers. The towns are in-between. And the kibbutzim, as usual, are an exception: like the big-city dwellers, only one-quarter of kibbutzniks say they prefer going outside their settlement to spend leisure.

The statistics, then, show that the consumption of culture is rather similar in otherwise very different kinds of settlements, for persons of similar educational attainments. At least this is true of most activities. But that does not mean, necessarily, that the people everywhere are equally satisfied with their ways of spending leisure. What is the *subjective* feeling of a secondary-school graduate who resides in a small town to whom the theatre comes three times a year or who makes the journey to Tel Aviv to see a play? Is he satisfied that he is fulfilling the same statistical quota as his ex-classmate who lives in Tel Aviv and goes to the theatre no more often, or does he feel relatively deprived?

TABLE 7.6 *Preference for Spending Leisure Out-of-Town ('Occasionally' or more often), by Size and Age of Settlement and by Education*

	Large cities	Cities: 50–100,000		Cities: 20–50,000		Urban settlements		Farms and moshavim	Kibbutzim
		old	new	old	new	old	new		
0–4 years education	9	15	25	32	20	40	24	26	–
5–10 years education	22	39	33	31	31	44	49	59	19
11+ years education	26	44	42	39	45	55	58	61	26
TOTAL POPULATION	24	38	37	36	32	49	45	52	25

Even if he were completely objective about it, there is no doubt that the choice of what to do is more limited in the smaller place, even when the individual does 'as much' as his big-city friend. Do people perceive these differences?

To find out, we looked again at the series of 'obstacles' to spending leisure which were discussed in Chapter Four – this time by city type and size. Two major complaints are related to city size: the 'lack of adequate opportunity' and the 'lack of suitable companionship'. Complaint about inadequate opportunity decreases with city size. Unaffected, however, are established middle-sized cities and kibbutzim: the level of dissatisfaction with leisure opportunities in both of these types of settlement is as low as that of big-city dwellers. Compared with the established cities, new cities of middle size are twice as dissatisfied with what is available to them. This difference between veteran settlements and new ones is evident – though less pronounced – for each of the other sizes as well, mirroring the differences in supply which were noted in Chapter Six. And the higher the respondent's education, the more keenly is this felt.

The other complaint – the lack of suitable companionship as an obstacle to spending leisure as one would like – divides the new and established cities even more sharply. This time, city size makes almost no difference; it is the newness, and perhaps the ethnic or socio-economic mix of the population. The low educated in new towns are at least as dissatisfied on this score as the well educated.

Policy-makers concerned with leisure and culture in the new towns cannot afford to limit their attention simply to the task of improving the supply of culture. This is the easier of the two problems. It is evident that social integration is a prerequisite for the enjoyment of leisure and culture. People in the new towns feel relatively deprived with respect to opportunities for spending leisure, but they seem to experience difficulty enjoying what they do have, for lack of a sense of society.[12]

6. *Summary*

Judging from the proportion of Israelis who 'ever' participate in them, the most popular out-of-home activities are pleasure trips and films, theatres and museums, public parks and public meetings, and light entertainment. Fifty per cent or more of the population are involved in these activities at least occasionally.

We have seen how age and education affect participation. Young people, to begin with, are outside the home much more frequently. Age is often more important than education in affecting participation: activities such as the cinema, the discotheque, light entertainment and museum-going are participated in extensively by young people, almost regardless of their educational level.

Just as youth overpowers educational disabilities for the young, education overpowers the disabilities of age for older people. While education is important at all age levels for certain activities – such as going to the theatre – it is of critical importance for the older age groups. Lack of any education is associated with virtual withdrawal from public activity and participation.

Certain ethnic differences remain even after educational levels are held constant. Frequency of cinema-going knows no difference between the ethnic groups. Museum-going is virtually unaffected. There is an ethnic difference in the rate of attending the theatre, but the difference is on the wane in the second generation. Only the concert hall shows no sign of yielding to ethnic integration.

The consumption of culture by persons of a given level of education is virtually uninfluenced by place of residence – in spite of the great variations in the supply of culture by city size. Nevertheless, residents of all but the largest cities and the kibbutzim *feel* deprived. They complain that their ability to spend leisure as they would like is impeded by the lack of adequate opportunities and facilities. Residents of new towns say that they lack suitable companionship for spending leisure.

NOTES – CHAPTER SEVEN

1. Recall Griffiths, op. cit., and Roberts, op. cit., pp. 79–85, for discussions of access to alternatives and of government as patron of the arts. The debate over paternalism and elitism vs. audience choice is also at issue here, since the evidence from broadcasting, for example, does not suggest that audiences freely choose 'better' things. But it is no less true that audiences are often unacquainted with the potential availability of 'better' or 'different' things.
2. Education may be confounding two things: occupation and broadened horizons. As was reported in Chapter Four, blue-collar workers say they are more tired, and older manual workers are presumably more tired still, whether from monotony or from hard work. This might explain their preference for spending leisure at home, and their expressed preference for resting and sleeping over other forms of recreation. But it seems to us that this is only half the story. The other half is that education helps even older people to remain connected with the cultural institutions of the society, and thus attracts them to participate, and, perhaps, even to feel less tired.
3. See, for example, G. Tarde, 'La Conversation', in *L'opinion et la foule*, Paris, 1922, 4th edition; Hans Speier, 'Historical Development of Public

Opinion', *American Journal of Sociology*, 55, 1950, pp. 376–88; John D. Photiadis, 'The Position of the Coffee House in the Social Structure of the Greek Village', *Sociologica Ruralis*, 5, 1965, pp. 45–54.

4. The influence of increased leisure among businessmen, women and servants has been much discussed in connection with the form (and content) of the eighteenth-century novel. See, for example, Ian Watt, *The Rise of the Novel*, Harmondsworth: Penguin, 1957, pp. 78–9. The rising 'visual literacy' of the twentieth century – particularly with respect to painting – is seen as paralleling the spread of reading by authors such as Kroeber, Toeffler and Rosenberg and Fliegel in the collection edited by M. Albrecht, J. H. Barnett and Mason Griff, *Sociology of Art and Literature*, New York: Praeger, 1970. The same set of influences has also spread musical enfranchisement, as noted by Paul Henry Lang in *Music in Western Civilization*, New York: Norton, 1971. Lang emphasizes not only the spread of participation in musical activity, but also the influence of the new middle-class audience on composers. Now, composers were not only given commissions to enrich the musical holdings of their patrons' libraries, but also hearings in concert halls. Looking further back, Sebastian de Grazia discusses the relationship between the ideals of leisure and creativity in ancient Greece, in his *Of Time, Work and Leisure*, op. cit.
5. 'It is from such perceptions that the critique of television developed by the New Left has sprung. They point to its manipulative power and to its reinforcement of that atomization of society into tiny family groups.' From Stuart Hood, 'The Politics of Television', in Denis McQuail, ed., *Sociology of Mass Communications*, Harmondsworth: Penguin, 1972.
6. Certain pessimistic theories of participation suggest that the free-discussion-of-everything-by-everybody is a paralyzing affair. See the discussion in Robert Crain, Elihu Katz and Donald Rosenthal, *The Politics of Community Conflict*, New York: Bobbs Merrill, 1965. See also Bernard R. Berelson, Paul F. Lazarzfeld and William N. McPhee, *Voting*, Chicago: The University of Chicago Press, 1954, Chapter 14.
7. Cf. Speier, op. cit.
8. We asked, 'When you meet with friends, how do you spend your time together?' The catch-all category, 'conversation', was how most people described their interaction but some specifically volunteered that they studied together, participated in political circles, etc.
9. This is a good place to point out that our three-way division of educational levels, and of age groups, is an optimum solution to the problem of grouping persons whose behaviour in the consumption of culture is essentially homogeneous. Other cutting points for age and education proved less successful than these. Of course, the need to create such groupings altogether is dictated by this style of data analysis.
10. To speak of two ethnic groups – Western and Eastern, or Ashkenazi and Oriental – as sociologists is to prejudge an important issue. Jews came to Israel from scores of different nations, speaking scores of different languages. Nor is it true that there are only two liturgical traditions, though admittedly the different liturgical traditions are not as numerous

as the different countries from which the immigrants came. The fact is that this dichotomy *emerged in Israel*, abetted – if only to a minor extent – by the sociologists and statisticians. The intermarriage rate among people of different national origin is far greater within the two 'groups' than between them. It is obviously far more problematic to have two large groups, with some tension between them, than to have seventy or so small groups.

11. Detailed discussion of this point is introduced in Chapter Fourteen, pp. 261–3. On the whole, there is a prevailing optimism concerning the future of ethnic relations in Israel, judging from this study and from others. A different kind of study – one more concerned with the ethnography of cultural traditions in Israel – would obviously give much more weight to differentiation along ethnic lines. Such studies are much needed, before these differences fade away.
12. This recalls Robert Merton's study of a new housing estate in the United States where people reported difficulty in finding baby-sitters for their children. The problem was not that teenagers were not available for the job, but that people did not have easy access and confidence in each other.

CHAPTER EIGHT The Popular Out-of-Home Activities

In this and the following chapters, we want to explore in greater detail the quality of participation in the various leisure activities. This chapter expands on the out-of-home activities. The chapter that follows will introduce activities inside the home. Separate chapters are then devoted to television, to other at-home pursuits and to books.

1. *The Four Most Popular Activities: Cinema, Excursions, Theatre and Museums*

These four – cinema, excursions, theatre, museums – are the most popular 'outdoor' activities, measured by proportion who 'ever' do them. Measured by frequency of participation, the median cinema-goer goes to the movies once a month; while the median for the other three activities is 'several times a year'. Once-a-month excursion-goers, however, are more numerous than once-a-month visitors to the theatre or to a museum. Table 8.1. outlines these data.

TABLE 8.1 *Out-of-Home Activities*

Per cent 'ever' participate	Night	Day
80–85	Cinema (M)	Excursions (Q)
65	Theatre (Q)	Museums (Q)
50–60	Lectures (community centres, etc.) (Q) Popular music (Q)	Parks (W)
20–30	Concerts (Q)	Sports (W)

Median participation (among participants):
(W) weekly; (M) monthly; (Q) quarterly, several times per year

The table makes clear that there are several activities in which about half the population participates; these are lectures, popular music and public parks. And then there are the minority activities, such as concert-going and active sports. Those who do go to parks and who do go in for sports, do so with much greater frequency than participants in the other activities.

Perhaps it is simply a statistical mirage, but these activities seem to come in couplets, a day-time activity and a night-time activity. Thus, the excursion and the cinema; the museum and the theatre; the park and the choice of lecture or rock group; the concert and sports. Whether there is any deeper semiotic significance to these couplets is a question worth exploring; at least it makes life outdoors seem more interesting.[1]

The day-time activities have an active aspect – the excursion, the museum, the park, sports – while the evening activities share the more passive attitudes of an audience. The day-time activities are largely visual experiences, rather than the audio-visual of the theatre and cinema or the predominantly audio of lecture and pop music. Indeed, the day-time activities invite conversation and commentary, and hence sociability, while the evening activities are more individuated in the sense that friends may go to the cinema together but are not supposed to talk.

The outdoor activities share an integrative attribute: they bring very diverse kinds of people together in shared experiences. The day-time activities, however, bring people into touch with the character of the country: its natural beauty, its historic monuments, its cultural treasures, its plastic arts. The evening activities are divided in this respect. The cinema tends to be quite remote from the Israeli reality or, often enough, from any reality; only about 5 per cent of films are Israeli-made. The theatre and popular music are quite ambivalent from this point of view: some performances reflect indigenous creativity; others, perhaps most, are imported. Lectures, alas, are almost always indigenous. On the whole, the evenings are more cosmopolitan. Add to this the proportion of imported programmes on television – something which will be discussed in Chapter Ten – and the idea of 'a culture in subtitles' presents itself. This is one of the dangers of culture in small nations: the 'free-flow of information', as someone has said, is mostly in one direction.

2. *Cinema and Excursions*

Cinema: Israelis seem addicted to the cinema. Whether this addiction will outlast television is still unclear, but the signs suggest that it may. According to the statistics, two years after the beginning of television broadcasting, Israelis were attending the cinema 18 times per year. By comparison, Americans were attending 7 times per year, British and French 4 times.

But there *has* been a decline in movie-going since television, and it will continue. Yet, for the time being, it is inescapable that movie-going is the most popular out-of-home activity. Young people go to the cinema with their friends; the correlation between the frequency of cinema-going and of visiting friends is high (0·52). Young persons are also more likely to know in advance something about the films they are going to see. Films are a frequent subject of conversation.

With age, the role of informed cinema-goer passes to women. Men above the age of thirty are far less likely than their wives to know in advance about the film they are going to see. They are also much less likely to show interest in film criticism in the newspapers. Women become 'culture brokers' for their husbands in this sense, and this is true not just for cinema but for the other arts as well.

Films are primarily in the English language. Most of these are American. Asked about the last film they attended, 60 per cent said that the film spoke English. Five per cent of 'last films' were in French, 3 per cent in another European language, and 6 per cent in Eastern languages.[2] These last are the Indian films, which are particularly attractive to cinema-goers of lower education and Eastern ethnicity. Films are not dubbed in Israel; they are subtitled. The audience is too small – commercially speaking – to warrant the expensive lip-synch dubbing that is now so popular elsewhere. So, the films are all subtitled in two languages (Hebrew and French in the case of English-language films) and, typically, they transport one very far from home.[3]

Ten per cent said that the last film they saw was in Hebrew. This is a new and very important development. The film industry in Israel may actually have reached a take-off point, a result of several factors: the boom in documentary film-making following the Six Day War; the contracts let by the newly established television service; and a very active policy of promoting foreign investment in film on the part of the Ministry of Commerce and Industry. The local film industry has increased its production of feature films from twelve in 1967 to twenty-seven in 1969, which was about 5 per cent of the total number of films (425) exhibited in Israel that year. So, although television and other causes have brought a decline in the number of imported films, a gradual closing of movie houses and a decline in total attendance at the cinema, the number of home-made films has increased.

Loyalty to the Israeli film is very high. Almost a third of movie-goers, particularly the less well educated, say they go to all or most Israeli films. But Israeli films, so far, are 'about' Israel only in so far as they speak in Hebrew and take place in Israel. But, for the most part, they are stereotyped stories based on international models of cops and robbers, inter-ethnic romance, and the war documentary. Yet, there are some promising signs, and it may be that film production in Israel will one day become a focal point for genuine creativity.

Excursions: Now, for contrast, let us look at the day-time counterpart of the film, the excursion or pleasure trip. The excursion used to be even more of a leveller and a mixer before the mass influx of private automobiles, just as the movies were before the coming of television.[4] More than one-fifth of all households owned a private car at the time of this survey, and as car owners all know, the world seems altogether more accessible ever after. The driver-member of the bus co-operatives used to be the heroes of Israeli society, and the bus was by far the most popular form of transportation for rich and poor alike. But that has changed.

Nevertheless, the family excursion, like the cinema, still brings almost everybody out at least several times a year. Those who stay home are primarily the uneducated (less than 5 years of schooling), and the group over 50 years of age with 5–10 years of education. Fifty to eighty per cent of all other groups go somewhere at least several times a year.

Where do they go? Some go abroad. Twenty-three per cent of all adult respondents said they had been on a trip abroad, and 10 per cent of these have been more than once. This number is very large considering the very high cost of travel relative to income. The cost per person for one month in Europe on a package tour equals half a year's net salary for the average Israeli. Most of those who have been abroad have been only once, and it is easy to see why.

In any case, the excursions that take place 'several times a year' are to places that are closer to home. Israel abounds in places to visit, and by virtue of the size of the country, these places are easily accessible. Moreover, the same places can be seen over and over again from different points of view: having seen Caesarea once as a Crusader, one can return to look at it again as a Patriarch, an early Christian, a Roman, a Zionist, or even as surf-diver or golfer. These historical 'strata' make for endless fascination. One of the successes of the Israeli school system is in instilling an interest in the country, as history and geography, which is expressed in constant travel and exploration. This early conditioning is regularly reinforced: in the youth movement, the Army, associations and organizations of all kinds, the mass media and even in institutions for the aged.

As part of the survey, we asked respondents to indicate whether or not they had ever visited each of eleven different sites. Almost everybody has been to the seashore; that comes as no surprise. But it is striking that 8 out of 10 Israelis have visited a kibbutz, and that 6 out of 10 have been to a development town. Moreover, the visit to a kibbutz or a development town probably implies knowing someone there:[5] only 3 per cent of the population lives on kibbutzim.

Two-thirds or more have visited Safed, the Negev desert, Hebron and Caesarea. These are extraordinary proportions. By Israeli standards, Safed and the Negev south of Beersheba are 'distant' from the concentrated urban population. And Hebron is a place that most people would have visited only since the Six Day War; that 7 of every 10 should have done so gives some insight into the character of domestic tourism in Israel, and some special insight into the passion that characterized travel in the occupied territories in 1967–8, immediately after the War.

About half the population has visited the two national museums in Jerusalem – the Israel Museum and the Yad Vashem Memorial to the extermination of the Jews in Europe. Equally large numbers have visited the historic site of Masada and the southernmost city of Eilat, on the Red Sea.

As we have seen already, education makes a great difference in determining who will go almost anywhere, and the same thing is true for travel destinations. Among these eleven sites, the historical and cultural ones – Masada, Caesarea, and the two museums – are three times more likely to have been visited by the best educated than the least well educated. The most egalitarian site is the beach: still, it is remarkable that 40 per cent of the unschooled who are 50 years or over have never been to the beach, and even more remarkable (though the proportion is unreliable due to the small base) is that this is true of more than 20 per cent of the uneducated young!

Hebron is another egalitarian site. The difference between persons of different educational attainment is very small here. The reason, apparently, has to do with the folk-religious importance of Hebron. This was the city of Abraham, and his presumed burial place. A settlement of religious Jews has been re-established in Hebron, earning the alternating opposition and support of the Government. And, indeed, if one examines the proportion of religious people visiting the different sites, this interpretation is confirmed. At each educational level, more religious than non-religious have visited Hebron. Something of the same phenomenon is to be seen at Safed, too, and for the same reason. Among those with less than five years of schooling, religious people visit Safed, city of mysticism and miracles, in greater proportions than the non-religious. Everywhere else, the opposite is true: non-religious persons, at each educational level, are more likely to have made the trip. Part of this difference is surely the result of religious restrictions on travel on the Sabbath and holidays; but, as we have seen, religious persons participate less in all the out-of-home activities.

While the well-educated young outdo their elders, this is sometimes not the case for the two groups with lesser education: the 30–50 group, or sometimes even the oldest group, have visited places which the youngest group of similar education have not seen. This holds true for the two museums, for Hebron, Safed, the kibbutz and elsewhere. While these differences, on the whole, are quite small, they are interesting because they reverse the trend which other out-of-home activities reveal. The activity of the 30–50 group, in particular, probably reflects the family-centred character of excursions.

Now that we have briefly surveyed these two most popular out-of-home activities, the differences and similarities between them may be more apparent. Education – which is to say, socio-economic status as well as learning – makes a difference in the rate of participation in both. But this does not hold for the youngest group in the case of the cinema: virtually all young people go with equal frequency. And it is not true for a few of the tourist sites, where people of all kinds congregate equally – at the seashore, for example.

The cinema separates the society according to age; the excursion does not. The peer group is the marching unit for the cinema; family or friends are equally likely on excursions.

The 'content' of the cinema is imported and subtitled. Excursion sites are obviously 'home-made'.

3. *Theatre and Museums*

Theatre: The professional theatre is based almost exclusively in Tel Aviv. Of the other cities, Haifa is the only one with a permanent theatre company and a theatre building. (Jerusalem has recently acquired a new and rather sophisticated theatre building but has yet to establish a theatre company to work in it.) But the theatres travel, either on their own or under the auspices of the Ministry of Education and Culture. And people travel to the theatre. Almost half the adults (43 per cent) go to the theatre at least 'several times per year', of whom 15 per cent go once a month. The frequency of theatre-going increases with educational level. With increasing age, the theatre-going rate of the less well educated declines, but once again, that is not the case with the well educated.

The four most popular stage forms – judging from respondents' last visit to the theatre – are musicals, evenings of short plays, drama and comedies. Musicals and musical skits were clearly preferred to drama and tragedy by the middle-educated group, while the upper-educated group chose between the two genres in rather equal numbers. The plays seen by the better educated are also evaluated as better plays by the critics.

More than the cinema, the theatre is Israeli. First there is a greater proportion of original plays than original films. Secondly, even the imported plays are presented in Hebrew. We asked respondents whether the last play they had seen was original or translated: about 17 per cent didn't know. Of those who did, almost 60 per cent said that the play they saw was an original Israeli play, and about 40 per cent said that it was not. Ninety per cent said that the language of the play was Hebrew

It would be wrong to say that the remaining 10 per cent heard 'foreign-language theatre', because almost all of the foreign language was Yiddish!

During the period of our survey, there were two plays on the boards which were based on Jewish ethnic traditions. One was a romantic and sensitive song-and-story evening by a blue-jeaned group that had discovered Hassidism, the folk movement of Eastern European Jewry. The other was based on the songs and stories of the Sephardi Jews who settled in the Balkan, Mediterranean and certain Southern European countries after the expulsion from Spain in 1492. The Hassidic play, *Ish Hasid Haya* (which later toured abroad as *Only Fools Are Wise*), had been seen by fully 25 per cent of our respondents; this is an extraordinarily large number. *Romanzcero Sephardi* had by then been seen by 2 per cent, no small proportion of a total population either. Both plays were popular, successful, and had won critical acclaim, at least by the middle-brow critics.

We asked our respondents what the two plays had 'given them'. Apart from being 'entertaining' – to which more than three-quarters agreed – sizeable proportions said that they had enjoyed the presentation of 'traditional content in a modern style' (66 per cent), and that it 'reminded me of the atmosphere of my father's house' (40 per cent).

Altogether, then, theatre-going is a popular activity and, compared with the cinema, both more indigenous and more 'festive'. It is not an every-night event like television, or an every-week event like a film, but a several-times-a-year event which seems to leave some trace. It is impossible, in a survey of this kind, to go very deeply into the nature of the experience of the arts, but clearly that deserves to be done.

Museum: Like the theatre, the museum is also a several-times-a-year experience. But it is a daylight activity and therefore rather more indigenous, more casual and more familial. Compared with the couplet cinema-excursion, which has the broadest popular appeal, the couplet, theatre-museum, is somewhat less popularly accessible. Museums and theatres are concentrated in the big cities. They generally charge admission. They may seem forbidding to those who have not been introduced to them early enough or been made to feel that they belong: three-quarters of those with less than five years' education never go. For all that, they attract about half the population at least once a year, and about four in ten people go several times a year.

What do the museum-goers see? In their last visit to a museum or an exhibition, 44 per cent named a specific exhibition of painting, sculpture or photography. About 10 per cent said they visited an archaeological exhibition. Another group – 11 per cent – simply gave the name of the museum (of whom 7 per cent named the Israel Museum). One-quarter of those responding said that the last exhibition they visited was of a commercial or informational nature.

Art exhibitions attract the better educated, the women, and, to a certain extent, the older people. Comparatively, commercial and informational exhibitions were disproportionately attractive to the less well educated, the men, and, to a certain extent, the younger people.

Ten per cent of the population buys art: the better educated (and thus better off) buy more. About half say they would be interested in buying but don't (or can't), thus implying a large potential market of art collectors if the conditions were right. The patrons (or those with the highest potential) are well-educated (11+ years) women in the 30–50 age group.

TABLE 8.2 *The Non-Participants*

	Per cent who NEVER participate			
	Cinema	Excursion	Theatre	Museum
Age 18–29				
0–4 years education	27	(54)	67	77
5–10 years education	6	18	41	40
11+ years education	4	6	15	18
Age 30–50				
0–4 years education	51	35	79	70
5–10 years education	16	19	39	40
11+ years education	9	8	15	18
Age 50+				
0–4 years education	64	50	76	76
5–10 years education	33	29	44	49
11+ years education	19	17	21	22

It is instructive to compare the two couplets of activities by examining the proportion of each age-education group who never participate in them (Table 8.2). Looked at in this way, the similarity between the two members of each pair is striking. Apart from being more popular activities, movie-going and travel are younger activities. The proportion of non-participants in cinema and excursions among the oldest age group is three times that of the youngest. No age difference at all is apparent among non-participants in theatre and museums. Only years of schooling make the difference.

There are, however, several important differences among museum-goers and theatre-goers which, although they have been mentioned in the previous chapter, are worth recalling here. Whereas both ethnicity and generation affect the rate of theatre-going, they are quite unimportant in museum-going (as they are in cinema-going). Again, whereas being religious reduces the rate of theatre-going (as it does cinema-going), it is less important in determining museum-going. In general, religiosity probably affects day-time activities less than night-time ones.

4. *Pop, Parks and Civic Participation*

The third couplet, ranked in terms of overall popularity, has parks as its day-time activity. Parks couple with popular entertainment for the young, and with lectures for the older groups.

More than a third of the population use the public parks regularly, that is, several times a month or more. On the other hand 54 per cent are non-participants, of whom 11 per cent say that there is no park in their vicinity (some of these may be rural residents).

Women are more frequent users of public parks than men, and, for both sexes, the age group 30–50 are the most frequent visitors. But altogether, neither age nor education much affects the use of public parks, apart from the usual drop in the participation of the least educated. This activity, like the other day-time activities, is influenced by the presence of children.

One-third of the users are satisfied with the parks. Two-thirds express criticism, saying either that there aren't enough parks, or that they are not well cared for, or both. In a related question, we asked respondents whether they would be willing to pay more taxes for their streets to be kept cleaner; about 40 per cent said yes and 60 per cent said no.

As night falls on this third set of activities, age takes over and differentiates. The young choose popular music. Light entertainment follows exactly the same demographic pattern as the cinema, except that the mode for film-going among young people is once a week or more while the mode for attending performances of light entertainment is once a month or less. Like cinema attendance, there is some evidence of higher rates of participating in popular music among those of Eastern ethnicity (though the ethnic difference disappears among the second generation with more than elementary-school education). Like cinema and theatre, light entertainment events are patronized less – at every age level – by the religious groups.

Light entertainment in Israel includes several distinctly different genres. One style is produced by electronic rock groups, of the type familiar throughout the Western (and not so Western) world. Another type has its roots in Army entertainment troupes, small groups of charming, choreographed boys and girls singing and pantomiming ballads and songs. A third type centres on a solo singer, often of considerable accomplishment, backed by a group of musicians and singers. Combinations of these three types are also found.

Light entertainment of this kind is popular for another reason as well, a reason which is one of the keys to the supply and distribution of culture in Israel: it is highly portable. Rock groups or Army performing troupes are designed to be wrapped up in a minibus or a truck and shipped to an outlying settlement. It is not expensive either. (The Israel Philharmonic Orchestra travels by bus, too, incidentally, but they, obviously, have very different requirements from a rock group or an Army troupe in such matters as space and acoustics.) Ease of mobility and staging is the prerequisite for successful theatre as well, since so much depends on subsidized one-night stands outside of Tel Aviv. A production such as *Ish Hasid Haya* (the Hassidic song-and-story performance discussed above) is a characteristic example.

Even more than performances of light entertainment, discotheques and night clubs stand out as youthful activity. Of those who go at all, half the group under 30 go once a month, typically. Other people go very rarely, if at all. Only about 20 per cent of the population have 'ever' been, compared with 50 per cent who go at least occasionally to hear performances of popular music and light entertainment.

As often as young people go to hear popular music or to a discotheque, the over-50 group go to a lecture. This is the *only* leisure activity in which those with least education participate as frequently as those with most education. Only the uneducated group of middle age falls slightly behind in 'ever' going, but the uneducated members of the youngest and oldest groups exceed those with an elementary-school education in the frequency of their attendance at lectures.

The question was this: 'Do you sometimes go to lectures, seminars or informational meetings on what is going on in the country?' Well over half the population say yes. Yet, although we know (see Chapter Thirteen) that the desire to understand what is going on in the country and the world occupies almost everybody (87 per cent), to our surprise only 24 per cent felt that the information in their possession was insufficient. Seventy per cent of the population say they have 'enough' information, and 4 per cent say they have 'too much', as if to comment on the never-a-dull-day character of domestic and international affairs in Israel. Apart from this surfeited group, Israelis say that the matters about which they would like to be better informed are politics and security; 54 per cent say this.[6] Eleven per cent mention social and educational problems, 5 per cent economic affairs and 2 per cent religious problems.

Altogether, the felt need of the population for more information does not appear to be satisfied by active participation in public affairs. Even if the public meeting is fairly well attended, the rate of membership and activity in voluntary organizations is remarkably low compared with other countries. Only 30 per cent say they are members of a voluntary organization of any kind – political, economic or welfare – compared with the United States, Sweden and Germany for which we have figures of 40–50 per cent. Here, too, participation increases with age: it is the senior citizens who are active in voluntary organizations. This is particularly true of the well educated, 55 per cent of whom said they were members of some organization, half of them describing themselves as 'active members'. This compares with 40 per cent and 25 per cent in the equally well-educated but younger group, even fewer of whom are active.

What is true of organizational participation is also true of community centres. About 30 per cent of the population go at least occasionally to the local community centre (14 per cent say there is no centre near them); and only about 10 per cent attend once a month or more.

In the entire area of organizational life, men are more active than women: in lecture-going (slightly), in membership and, particularly, in positions of leadership. Only in the organizations which deal with social welfare are women more active than men.

This difference in the rate of participation by men and women is reflected in answers to the question: 'Ought men (women) to give of their leisure time to public affairs?' With respect to men, 26 per cent say 'yes, he ought to', and 32 per cent say, 'it is desirable'. The corresponding percentages with respect to women are 17 and 29. It is the older people who are more affirmative in both cases. Curiously – and especially with respect to women – the young and better educated are *less* affirmative; or, if you will, less dogmatic. They do not insist that women, or even men, should give of their free time to public affairs, 'except if she (or he) wants to'.

On the other hand, the overall proportion of the population who agree to the norm of civic participation is well below the proportion of actual members. Overall, about 50 per cent affirm the idea of participation, but only about 30 per cent may be said to be active, even in the most minimal way.

It is sometimes said that membership in youth movements during adolescence is the proper kind of socialization for a society trying to accomplish things collectively, and the proper kind of assurance for public participation at a later age. Indeed, youth movements played a crucial role in the life of the Yishuv (the pre-State Jewish community in Palestine) as well as in the life of the Zionist movement in the diaspora. While the socialization function of these movements is still highly valued and is formally recognized by the educational institutions of the country, the centrality of their role as well as their membership is thought to have somewhat dwindled in recent years. But looking at youth movement membership by age and education, it is interesting to note that practically no change in the rate of membership characterizes the three generations. This is curious, but if one were to compare only the Israeli-born in each age group, it seems likely that these figures would reflect a lower rate of recent membership after the establishment of the State, as is commonly thought. It is also extremely interesting to note that movement membership in the old days was a more serious affair: the average period of active membership was considerably longer.

What is certain, on the other hand, and equally striking, is the different rate of participation characterizing the three educational strata. The largest difference is among the youngest group, the Israel-born. Only 20 per cent of those who continued to secondary school did not belong to a youth movement compared with half of those with an elementary education.

5. *Serious Music and Sports*

Our last couplet of outside-the-home activities comprises the 'minority' activities of concerts and sports. Only 20 per cent 'ever' go to concerts and, surprising as it seems at first, only 30 per cent 'ever' go to sporting events. Twenty-five per cent themselves engage in sport.

Spectator sports in Israel means European-style football (soccer) almost exclusively. Of the 31 per cent who attend, there are a few mentions of basket-ball and light athletics, but by and large it is football that attracts all the attention. More than in the other daylight activities, age is as important as education in the composition of the audience for sports.

The statistical picture of the sports audience takes on a wholly different aspect if its composition is examined according to sex. Women show interest in spectator sports only in the youngest age group (18–29), and this interest divides equally between football and basket-ball. Older women show no interest at all. If we compute the audience for spectator sports as a proportion of the male population, we find that it is no longer a minority activity. Approximately three-quarters of the men aged 18–29 participate at least occasionally as do about 6 in 10 of the 30–50 group, and 4 in 10 of the oldest group.

Sports lotteries – in which active interest in spectator sports can be parlayed into a cash prize – is a popular activity in Israel, along with other publicly managed lotteries. The most popular of all of these is the national lottery, *Payis*. Over 40 per cent of the population invest at least once a month in one or more of these lotteries. Younger people tend to do more of this sort of gambling, but it is remarkable – at each age level – how much this activity is concentrated among the middle education group, those with 5–10 years of schooling.

Active participation in sports is also a largely masculine activity. Altogether, only 26 per cent of the population engages in active sport, but those who do, do so weekly or even daily. In this sense, one might say that it is not a minority activity in terms of man-hours, compared with most other leisure activities, which are more sporadic.

Age, education and sex describe the sportsmen. They are, first of all, young. With age, education becomes increasingly important. Whereas the drop in the rate of weekly activity among the elementary-school educated is from a high of 25 per cent to 9 per cent as one goes from the youngest to the oldest group, the parallel decline among the best educated is from 31 to 20. At each age level, women are about one-third of the total.

The two popular sports are both individual rather than team activities, and are probably pursued for the sake of exercise. These are light athletics and swimming, and each engages about 30 per cent of athletes. Their popularity increases with education and age, and they are the favoured choice of most sportswomen.

Fifteen per cent of the active sports people play football. The large concentration of players is among young men with elementary-school education; more than 41 per cent of this group are active.

Basket-ball is the favourite of 7 per cent of young people, men and women. Smaller numbers choose other sports.

If sport is for the young and for the day-time, concerts are for the night and the old. It is a genuinely minority activity despite the very high level which the performance of serious music has reached in Israel. Cultivated by the German Jewish migrants to Israel in the 1930s, symphonic and chamber music in Israel quickly achieved international fame, and generated a myth that subscription tickets are obtainable only through inheritance. Nevertheless the fact is that concert audiences are old. Things may be changing; young conductors and imaginative impresarios are having their way in new and old musical organizations. But the changes, if there are any, do not yet show in the statistics for 1970. Fewer than 20 per cent of the population 'ever' go to concerts; only 12 per cent have been within the last six months. Of these, half were in the over-50 age group, and 80 per cent of these were well educated.

We have already noted that this is one of the areas in which both the ethnic gap and the generation gap is very large. The repertoire is exclusively European, with an occasional Israeli composition.

6. *Summary*

This is the out-of-home Israeli scene, by day and night. The out-of-home leisure activities have been presented in pairs according to their relative popularity (in terms of proportion 'ever' doing them), together with cognate activities with which they are associated.

It is important to point out that this is only one of many possible ways in which such material might be presented. Even in terms of other measures of popularity, the order of presentation could be different. Thus, the criterion of proportion of population engaging in an activity during an average week would order the activities as follows: cinema (30 per cent), active sport (28 per cent), public parks (25 per cent), excursions (11 per cent), theatre and museum (6–7 per cent), lectures and popular music (5–6 per cent) and concert (2 per cent). Frequency data are not available for spectator sports. Or, if the activities were ordered according to the modal frequency-of-use by those engaged in the activity, the order would be active sport and park (weekly), cinema (monthly), concerts, museums, popular music, lectures, excursions, theatre (quarterly). These criteria obviously cast quite a different light. Their import is to throw films, parks and active sports together, apparently because of their ready accessibility as to time and place, and, on the other hand, to group the more formal activities of theatre, museum, concert, lecture and popular music, all of which are bound by time and place. Notice that the minority activities of sport and concerts are pursued at considerable frequency by those engaged in them.

The day-time activities, at any rate, are generally distinguishable from the night-time ones by accessibility and flexibility as to time and place; being located in the open air; by their more active character; by their permitting conversation; by their low cost; by their emphasis on the visual. As far as participants are concerned, the day-time activities are more sexually differentiated, are generally biased toward the better educated and are rather egalitarian as to age.

The night-time activities, on the other hand, while somewhat favouring the better educated, are based primarily on the criterion of age. The young, we have seen, go out much more than their elders. Moreover, they choose different activities – the cinema and popular music – from their elders. When 'older' people go out, they choose 'their' activities – lectures and concerts, for example – proportionately more. Night-time activities are engaged in by couples or groups of peers of both sexes. They take place in special places of assembly. They are organized typically for attentive audiences who pay admission, and their content – on the whole – is cosmopolitan or international rather than local or indigenous. While this is the modern, middle-class pattern of the West, other societies organize the night-time differently. Differentiation as to sex, rather than age, characterizes many societies at night: the men go out, the ('good') women stay in.

Considering the ubiquity, accessibility and activity-level associated with the day-time activities, on the one hand, and the fact that night-time activities cost money, it is curious that education should be the key factor in affecting participation in day-time activities, and that age should be the key factor at night.

Referring back to Table 8.1, there is another thing to note about the four pairs of activities. The first two of the popular activities (movies and excursions) are characterized by informality and ubiquitousness. They are everywhere, and you don't dress up to go. The second pair – theatres and museums – are formal and require specialized facilities. Similarly, for the minority activities: the first two are informal and everywhere; the second are for dressing up and specialized places, such as concert halls and swimming pools.

Missing from all of this are two out-of-home activities whose importance we seriously underestimated and thus did not inquire about in depth. Their importance is revealed in the time-budget data (cf. Table 3.5): one is the coffee house, the other the walk, the passegiata. Both of these are important night-time activities, though they have many of the attributes of day-time: ubiquity, accessibility, low cost, active and conversation-linked. They are, of course, also popular in the day-time, and we cannot with the data at hand say more than this, just in case there remains any doubt that the ordering of activities in this chapter is a tentative one.

NOTES – CHAPTER EIGHT

1. Other things might have been included – coffee houses, for example – but our data on frequency of participation are too crude. They might also have upset the analysis which follows, which – we warn again – is a groping effort to organize a large mass of material in meaningful, or at least readable, form.
2. An increasing number of Arabic films are being imported according to official statistics, but their proportion (12 per cent) in the total number of films imported is far greater than their proportion among the total of last films seen by a sample of all Israelis.
3. The functions of the cinema and other media are the subject of Chapter Thirteen. It might be noted that 'escape' is not a keenly felt need among Israelis, although the need 'to be entertained' is considered important.
4. This analogy – what television is to film, the private car is to the bus excursion – was suggested by James Curran at a seminar of the Mass Communications Study Group of the British Sociological Association in February 1973, where some of the ideas in this chapter were discussed.
5. This is a guess.
6. The preoccupation with security problems is evident in newspaper

reading as well. It is not surprising that this is the pervasive concern. In the present instance, respondents were asked to name the single subject on which they most wanted information. In the case of newspaper reading, respondents could say yes to a large diversity of topics, and so, indeed, they do.

PART FOUR MASS MEDIA AND HOME CULTURE

CHAPTER NINE The Consumption of Culture: At Home

Seventy-five per cent of Israeli adults, we estimated, are at home on an average weekday evening. Of the 25 per cent (35 per cent on Saturday nights) who are out, about a third have paid the price of admission to some public entertainment. By far the favourite out-of-home activity of the Israelis, however, is visiting somebody else's home! On an average weekday evening, half or more of those who are outside their own homes are inside someone else's home.

Looking down the street in this particular way reveals that fully 90 per cent of adults are in a home, their own or someone else's, during an average weekday evening. For most people the evening is for the kinds of activities that go on inside houses: conversation, study, hobbies and mass media, especially television. In 1970, when almost 6 in 10 Israelis owned a television set, 53 per cent of the population spent an evening viewing. The other media, too, especially the reading of newspapers and books, occupy people in the evenings. It is this kind of house-slippered leisure with which we shall be dealing in this chapter and in the two chapters which follow.

1. *The Popular In-Home Activities*

As we did in the case of out-of-home activities, let us begin with a quick glance at in-home activities according to their popularity, measured by the proportion who 'never' engaged in them.

The list ranges from the 71 per cent who 'never' study to the 2 per cent who never listen to the radio and the 1 per cent who never visit their parents. Strictly speaking, neither meeting friends, nor study, nor hobbies need be carried on at home; in fact we shall show in Chapter Twelve exactly how much study goes on at home and how much in formal, institutionalized settings. But it is convenient, and largely justified, to consider these as in-home activities, just as it was right to treat sports, which includes some degree of in-home exercising, as an out-of-home activity. While only 30 per cent study, about 60 per cent have a hobby.

If 'never' reading a newspaper is a measure of functional illiteracy as far as one's role as citizen is concerned, then about 15 per cent of the population are illiterate. The proportion who 'never' read books is somewhat higher (22 per cent). On the other hand, there is virtually nobody who 'never' listens to the radio or views television. There is no doubt that the electronic media connect some people to the society who would otherwise remain unconnected, except, perhaps, through word-of-mouth.

The other universal activity – in which virtually nobody 'never' participates – is visiting family. Friendship is less widespread; 11 per cent 'never' meet friends.

2. *A Map of Cultural Activity: Home vs. Outside and Serious vs. Popular*

Before continuing with a detailed report on the quality of these at-home pursuits, it will be of some use to see how all of them – inside and outside – relate to each other. In other words, we are interested in the correlations among activities. Is frequency of reading books, for example, positively or negatively related to frequency of viewing television? Do people who engage in certain forms of cultural activity at home find related things to do outside or is location (in or out of the home) a more important predictor than content?

Overall, our expectation is that activities might cluster together (that is, they will be intercorrelated) for one or more of several reasons: (1) because of location – they take place outside the home, or inside it; (2) because they are performed alone or in the company of others; (3) because they depend on different kinds of media such as print, electronics, or live encounters; and (4) because they belong to the same 'brow' level – serious vs. folk or popular.

These relationships can be examined by means of a new computer method which maps all the items in relationship to each other, such that the distance between any item and all the others is an expression of the magnitude of their interrelationships.[1] The map (Figure 9.1) gives the distance between any two activities as an inverse function of the size of the correlation between them: the larger the correlation, the closer together. Thus, to the activities discussed so far, we now add activities such as listening to the radio, watching television, reading newspapers, visiting friends, and the like.

Looking at the map itself suggests that two of these four dimensions are, indeed, relevant for grouping the cultural activities. The first of these is whether an activity takes place inside or outside the home; the other is whether or not an activity is 'highbrow' or 'popular'. Thus, in the upper right-hand sector of the map are the concerts, theatres, lectures, voluntary associations – in other words, out-of-home and highbrow. The fact that they are clustered together means that people who engage in one of these activities with a particular degree of frequency engage in the others with a like degree of frequency.[2]

Below the cluster of activities which are out-of-home is a second 'highbrow' cluster of indoor activities: studies, book-reading, gramophone records and the like. Following the map clockwise, the next stop is at the 'popular' out-of-home sector featuring night clubs, singers and dancers. Finally, the upper left-hand sector of the map includes the popular in-home activities such as newspaper-reading and television-viewing.

FIGURE 9.1 *SSA–1 Map of Leisure Activities*
(Two dimensions; coefficient of alienation 0.2)

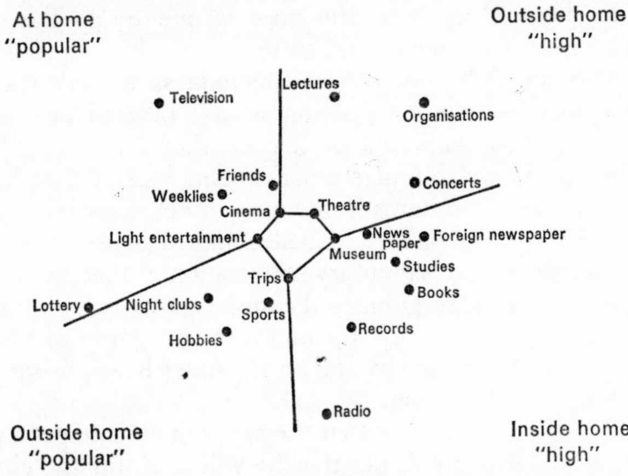

The combination of whether an activity takes place inside or outside home, and whether it is serious or not appears to be the optimal way of accounting for the groupings of most of these activities. The highbrow-popular dimension cuts the map down the middle and is the stronger of the two dimensions. Thus a person who goes to concerts, for example, is also likely to attend the theatre or to be a member of a voluntary association – because they are both out-of-home and serious. But the concert-goer is also a consumer of highbrow activities inside the home – for example reading a foreign-language weekly or participating in some form of study; and he is far less likely to go to night clubs, for example.

3. *The Circle of Popular Activities*

Looking at the map in another way reveals a circle of activities at its centre. This ring has an interesting statistical characteristic. It is called a circumplex because each item in the set is most closely correlated with the two items adjacent to it, and when presented graphically a kind of circle results.[3] Movie-going, for example, is most highly correlated with theatre-going, on the one side, and with popular music events, on the other. Theatre is closest to cinema and museum; museum to theatre and excursions. And so on.

It will be noted that the items that compose this circumplex are the out-of-home activities, including the most popular among them: films, theatre, museums, excursions and popular music events. Each of them – as art form – includes great variations in content, and this, of course, enables individuals with widely differing tastes to partake in them. The important thing is that individuals with widely differing tastes do participate in them. A person who goes frequently to the cinema is likely to go often to the theatre and so on.

Still, in spite of the high interconnectedness among these major activities, the serious-popular division is still in evidence. Note that theatres and museums cluster together on the right side of the circumplex while films and popular music events cluster together on the other side. In a sense, the items in the circumplex constitute 'gateways' to the rest of the cultural sphere. Theatre and museums point the way to concerts, lectures and voluntary associations; that is to say, the correlation between theatre-going and concert-going is higher than, say, that between going to a popular music event and going to a concert of serious music. Popular music events, on the other hand, bring people to discotheques, sports and so on.

It is almost as if one could say that the key to it all is to get a person to 'go out'. Once out, it is a safe bet that he will head for the cinema: we know this from the high frequency of cinema-going. Emerging from the movies, he has a crucial choice to make: should his next trip be the theatre or to a popular music event? If he opts for the theatre, he has increased his chances of going to a concert next time. If he opts for a popular music event, his next outing will more likely be to a discotheque.

The activities in the circumplex are highly integrative from a sociological point of view. We know from the extent of their popularity that they take people out of their homes and bring them together. And far more important than their differences on the highbrow-lowbrow dimension is the fact that, as a group, they stand midway between the markedly highbrow and the markedly lowbrow activities. In other words, both highbrows and lowbrows meet at the movies and at the theatre, at museums and on the road.

Still, having said this, it is equally clear that the map reflects the different patterns of activity of the old and the young, and of the better and less well educated. Simply looking at the out-of-home places and events on the map reminds us that virtually all of them are more frequented by the better educated. The less well educated are much more likely to be at home. Parenthetically, however, we might note that if a less well-educated person *does* go out, he is more likely to do 'everything' than the better-educated person.[4]

But the map reminds us that age is an important factor, too. Indeed, the difference between the two clusters of out-of-home activities, the one labelled serious and the other popular, is primarily a question of age. The highbrow activities that go on outside the home reflect not only education but older age. Attendance at concerts and membership in voluntary organizations, it will be recalled, are clearly associated with older age. By the same token, the outdoor activities which have been labelled popular in the map are essentially young persons' activities. Indeed, they all imply active effort, whether it be in excursions, sports, hobbies or discotheques.

4. *The Indoor Activities*

But we have yet to examine the indoor activities in detail; the map redirects us to these.

TABLE 9.1 *The Non-Participants: Those Who 'Never' Engage in In-Home Activities*

	Per cent who 'never'
Visit parents*	1
Visit siblings*	2
Visit other kin*	3
Listen to radio	2
View television†	4
Meet friends	11
Read newspapers	15
Read books	22
Have hobbies	39
Read magazines	45
Buy gramophone records	50
Study	71

* Among those who have such kin.
† Over 40 per cent did not own a set at the time of the survey.

From Table 9.1 it is clear that everybody has the opportunity – at least on occasion – to listen to radio and to view television. Although only about 60 per cent of respondents owned television sets when the survey was conducted, all obviously spend some time with the new medium. The map shows that viewing television is not closely related to other activities, but it does fall on a level with the activities of older people such as lectures and organizations. Frequency of radio-listening, in this sense, is a younger activity as the map implies, and Chapters Ten and Eleven will confirm.

As has been noted, 15 per cent never read newspapers and one-fifth never read books. This is almost certainly a reflection of the scope of functional illiteracy: while there isn't much of it in Israel, it is there. Reading books is closely connected with study, as the map shows. But while four-fifths of the population read books, only 30 per cent are actively engaged in study. As we shall see, however, the rate of reading is high compared with most other nations.

Sixty per cent of the population have a hobby. The location of hobbies on the map implies that these are outdoor rather than in-home activities. This is partly the case – as we shall see below – but rather less so than one might have expected from its location.

Notice from the map, too, that getting together with friends is just on the border between indoor and outdoor – just where it should be.

Table 9.2 looks at these activities from the point of view of the age-education groups. There is one very important difference between this table and Table 7.3, which related age and education to out-of-home activities. Whereas age and education proved equally important – perhaps age had a slight edge – in public activity, it is education, not age, which is important within the home. Consumption of the mass media, hobbies – virtually everything – increases with education. Even friendships and conversation, as we shall soon see, are influenced by education.

'Active reading' (that is, having read a book in the last month) is very strongly related to education and remarkably little to age: the youngest age group is only slightly ahead. At the level of highest education, about 6 persons in 10 have read a book in the past month. That is twice the rate of those with 5–10 years of schooling.

Still, those with 5 years of schooling read newspapers: 9 out of 10 read daily newspapers regularly. This is not true, however, for those with less than 5 years of schooling. Only 4 out of 10 persons in this group read a daily newspaper, and virtually none read books. They listen to the radio regularly, and watch television almost as often as the better-educated groups. But it is important to note that they are somewhat behind the other groups even with respect to broadcasting. Putting these figures together with the relatively high non-participation of the lowest-educated group in out-of-home activities indicates that there are pockets of genuine social isolation among these people. Moreover, this isolation is not limited to the aged; it is evident among part of the uneducated younger groups as well.

Television peaks among the 30–50-year-olds, as family and household obligations conspire to keep people at home. That this is the case seems

TABLE 9.2 *Participation in At-Home Activities, by Age and Education*

	Total (N=100%)	Per cent reading books	Per cent book readers (*One book per month or more*)	Per cent reading newspapers	Per cent viewing television	Per cent owning gramophone records	Per cent having hobby	Per cent listen to radio (*Two hours or more*)
Age 18–29								
0–4 years education	(48)	38	12	(36)	(50)	(47)	(61)	87
5–10 years education	(389)	80	30	93	50	46	69	90
11+ years education	(554)	95	67	98	36	60	79	92
Age 30–50								
0–4 years education	(272)	32	3	40	46	34	37	80
5–10 years education	(699)	76	23	92	66	48	62	90
11+ years education	(535)	97	57	97	59	74	70	89
Age 50+								
0–4 years education	(211)	33	5	37	41	27	35	72
5–10 years education	(533)	71	25	89	52	40	47	84
11+ years education	(430)	92	55	98	52	56	60	85
TOTAL POPULATION	(3671)	78	37	86	52	51	61	87

evident from the relatively lower-viewing rates not only among the younger group, but among those who are older as well. But it also probably reflects the pressure to buy a TV set exerted by the younger children of the 30–50-year-olds on their parents. Those of middle education, like those of middle age, are the most ardent television fans. Television and books will be discussed at length in later chapters.

Hobbies and record-collecting are also associated with education in the usual way. Records, like television, peak in the middle-aged group; hobbies are most popular among the young.

5. *Seeing Family and Friends*

But there is more to being at home than attending to the mass media. Interpersonal relations are still very much alive. Research on informal social relations elsewhere generally finds that the institution of friendship, and the number of friends, is more important in the modern, rather than the traditional, sectors of society. It is more prominent among young people and among those with higher education. For young people, it has been argued, the peer group is the social context in which one learns to sever family ties and to assume adult roles; friendship is at once a society for mutual protection and a society in which the individual is required to stand on his own feet.[5] Lest we stray too far from common sense, it should not be overlooked that young adults are also courting. For persons of higher status, friendship is an institution which cuts through some, but not all, of the day-time boundaries which divide people. It does not generally cut through class boundaries, for example.

The lower classes, many studies have found, rely much more on family. They see more of their families than do the middle classes; and they live closer to them. They don't 'leave home' very readily, or very far behind.

We wanted to see whether these generalizations hold true for Israel. Table 9.3 presents the data.

As far as friendship is concerned, the pattern is clear. At each level of education, the likelihood of frequent meeting with friends increases; thus, the higher the socio-economic status (measured crudely by education), the more likely one is to meet with friends at least weekly. Still, half of those with least education meet their friends at least weekly.

Age, too, makes a difference. Among young people, more than 80 per cent see their friends weekly, regardless of educational level. Indeed, almost half of this group see their friends daily. Only those with no schooling at all – an insignificant number in the present generation – are less likely to see friends or not to have any. While the percentage is unreliable because of the small base, note that it is on a level (about 50

TABLE 9.3 *Meeting Friends and Visiting Family*

	Per cent who meet friends weekly or more often	Per cent who see parents weekly or more often*	Per cent who see married children weekly or more	Per cent who see parents of spouse weekly or more	Per cent who see siblings weekly or more often	Per cent who see aunts, uncles, cousins weekly or more
Age 18–29						
0–4 years education	(54)	(70)	†	(58)	(46)	(25)
5–10 years education	81	88	†	69	75	21
11+ years education	87	82	†	68	74	18
Age 30–50						
0–4 years education	52	52	60	53	41	14
5–10 years education	68	68	63	55	50	11
11+ years education	75	70	66	58	48	13
Age 50+						
0–4 years education	48	†	80	†	30	10
5–10 years education	61	†	73	†	35	13
11+ years education	71	†	66	†	40	9
TOTAL POPULATION	70	72‡	69‡	59	52	14

* For those who have such kin.
† There are, of course, few appropriate kin in these categories.
‡ Includes aged 18–29 and over–50 having appropriate kin.

per cent) with older people with equally low education. Close to 30 per cent of this least educated group have no friends at all. The relative isolation of the least educated is visible here again, indicating that their isolation is not only from public gatherings and from the media that connect one with the outside world, but from people, from non-kin who connect outside.

It is of interest that the youngest group is not only most active in visiting friends, it is also most active in visiting family. Some of these young people, of course, still live with their parents. But most do not. Parents are not cast off in favour of friends.

The rate of visiting parents falls off with increasing age and increasing responsibility for one's own nuclear family. That may not be surprising. But what is surprising is that even the frequency of seeing family is positively related to educational level. The higher the education, the *greater* the likelihood of seeing one's parents once a week or more. Note that the rate of seeing friends and the rate of seeing parents (and married children) is almost precisely parallel within each of the six age-education groups from 18–50 years.

The situation is different for the oldest age group, those of 50 years or more. While friendship increases with education, as in the other groups, visiting married children appears to decrease. The change is not evident in the upper-educated group who neither gain nor lose the companionship of either children or friends, but rather in the two lesser-educated groups who see a little less of their friends but very much more of their children.

The findings hint that older people rely relatively more on family than on friends, but the picture is not clear-cut: the well-educated group does not fit for one thing.

Men spend more time with friends. At each age level, the rate of interaction with non-work-related comrades is higher for men than for women, while women spend somewhat more time with family relations and much more of their time with children. Recall the time budgets of men and women in this respect. The data reveal that up to age 45, men give their friends twice as much time as do women, while women give their time to the children. The crisis of age 45 is made very vivid by these data: there is a sudden drop for the men in amount of time spent with friends, and, for the women, in amount of time spent with children. There is some evidence (among the women) of a compensating increase in interaction with family relations (married children?), but the major increase in the allocation of time to others is in time spent with spouse alone. At age 45, husband and wife begin to spend two hours a day just with each other. Ten years later there is a corresponding increase in time spent with self alone. Even at age 55, however, women are still spending five times as much time with children than are men.

Adding all this together suggests that friendship is an institution which belongs to the young, educated and unmarried more than to any other group. With age, friendship remains more important for men, though there is also some decline with age in the amount of time spent with friends. The proportion who say that they have no friends at all also somewhat increases with age. Increasing age finds husband and wife spending more time with each other and more time by themselves. Age 25–45 is prime time for the nuclear family: women are with spouse and/or family 6·5 hours on an average weekday, and men 3·5 hours.

TABLE 9.4 *Time Spent with Friends, Family Relations and Children**

	Men					Women				
	18–24	25–34	35–44	45–54	55+	18–24	25–34	35–44	45–54	55+
With non-work friends (without spouse)	3·4	1·8	1·3	0·7	1·0	1·5	0·7	0·6	0·7	1·0
With neighbours	–	0·1	0·1	0·1	0·3	0·1	0·2	0·3	0·5	0·3
With spouse together with others (children and/or kin and/or friends)	0·6	1·2	2·1	1·5	0·8	0·7	1·8	1·7	1·2	0·9
Children (without spouse)	0·1	0·5	0·6	0·3	0·2	1·6	3·3	3·1	1·7	1·1
With family relations (other than spouse and children)	1·2	0·6	0·6	0·5	0·4	1·4	0·7	0·6	1·0	0·7
With spouse alone	0·9	1·6	1·1	1·7	2·5	1·5	1·5	1·2	2·0	2·4
Self alone	13·4	12·8	13·0	13·6	15·4	14·3	14·8	15·2	15·4	16·7

* As noted in Chapter Three, these data have been weighted so that the various demographic groups are represented in the proportions given in the *Statistical Yearbook*. Moreover, it should be noted that the reporting on 'with whom' one spent each period of time is incomplete, and from 3 to 4 hours of the day typically remain unaccounted for. The time that was reported by each age-sex group in the present table was therefore 'stretched' to equal 24 hours, by proportionate weighting of the time-with-others that was reported.

Respondents were asked what things they 'generally' do together with their friends. Overwhelmingly, they said that they 'sit around' – in conversation, in watching television, even in study. Young people said they often go to the cinema together or on excursions or to a café; far fewer said they go to dances or to discotheques. The middle-aged and middle-educated sometimes play cards, and the older and better educated sometimes go to lectures together. But, by and large – and perhaps apart from the very young – friendship is more an indoor than an outdoor 'activity'.

So, we have found that friendship is important – but there is very little evidence, even for those for whom it is most important, that it displaces family ties. Even the most modern sectors of Israeli society are highly oriented to family.

6. *Closeness to Family of Orientation*

We have been examining three different groups of intimates: one's own spouse and children, or the so-called family of procreation; one's parents and other relatives in the family of orientation; and friends. Measured in terms of frequency of contact each of these institutions is of great and continuing importance to the Israelis.

While the family of orientation commands less attention as one grows older and founds a family of one's own, the frequency of visiting parents and other relatives continues to be high. Indeed, it is higher than any of the comparative statistics we have been able to find. Young and Wilmott, for example, in their study of lower-class families in East London report that about 40 per cent of married men and women had seen their parents within the past twenty-four hours and 40 per cent had seen siblings within the past week; our study gives higher figures.[6] This is all the more remarkable in that the London figures are considered to be unusually high, describing, as they do, families huddled together in a depressed urban area.

Our figures are also higher than those reported by Adams in his study of family visiting patterns in a town in North Carolina.[7] Sixty per cent of adults in Greensboro visit their parents more than once a week when the parents also live in Greensboro; 87 per cent of Israeli adults visit their parents that frequently when both live in the same town. The frequencies for visiting siblings and other relatives are also higher in Israel.

Indeed, the centrality of family could hardly be otherwise in Israel, despite the importance of peer groups, youth movements, Army and other social and ideological efforts to mobilize youth. This is surely an example of continuity with the closely knit family of Jewish tradition but also the response of a society half of whose members witnessed the destruction of their closest kin. It is as if the strengthening of family ties in Israel were an attempt to spit back at the tidal wave of disaster. Indeed, the story of the response of Israeli families to 'distant' relatives is yet untold. The readiness to play surrogate parents and grandparents for cousins and second cousins and their children is a heroic tale. We have no hard data to document this point in the present study, but there is an echo clearly heard in the repeated affirmation of the centrality of the family throughout the data. The 'need to spend time with my family' is high on everybody's list. Evidence of the narrowness of the generation gap is introduced in Chapter Fourteen. The only direct measure of family continuity comes from the following question: 'How familiar are you with the customs and atmosphere of the home in which your father grew up (that is, in your grandfather's home, when your father was a boy)?' The same question was repeated for mother's parents' home. The distribution of replies to the two questions is identical: 41 per cent say they know much, 31 per cent say they know a little; 25 per cent say they know nothing. These figures mean very little, of course, until the day when somebody compares them with the second generation of immigrants in other societies. One has the sense that among American Jews, for example, most of whom come from the same backgrounds as the European Jews who came to Israel, the feelings of familiarity and continuity with the culture of grandparents would be considerably lower.

Altogether 97 per cent of respondents say that they have some relative living in Israel, and 73 per cent have a relative living in the same city.

7. *The Mass Media and Other In-Home Activities*

This, then, is the context in which the mass media are consumed. The overwhelming majority of people are at home in the evenings, and most of those who are not in their own homes are in the homes of friends or relatives. We have noted that more than half the population watches television in the evenings – although when the study was conducted only 60 per cent owned a set.

Taking the population as a whole, and disregarding the fact that television ownership was not yet universal, we have also noted that the average adult spends over an hour a day watching television. When time spent on television is added to time spent with the other media – radio, newspaper, books – one-half of all leisure time is accounted for.

The following chapter examines the response to the introduction of television. A chapter on radio-listening, newspaper-reading and other in-home activities examines these activities in the light of the influence of the introduction of television. Then, we turn to consider the state of the book in Israel, and the nature of its relationship to its ancient partner, study.

8. *Summary*

The map of intercorrelations certifies the validity of our division of activities into those that take place inside and outside the home. It also underlines the importance of age and education as organizing principles for the analysis of leisure pursuits. We know that young people are the heaviest patrons of out-of-home activities although certain serious 'outdoor' activities are sought out by older people.

Inside the home, education is the most important determinant of pursuing almost any sort of leisure activity – from hobbies to reading to conversations with friends and, curiously, even including the extent of family visiting. The visiting rate is also remarkably high.

NOTES – CHAPTER NINE

1. An exposition of the method and its underlying principles is to be found in Louis Guttman, 'A General Nonmetric Technique for Finding the Smallest Coordinate Space for a Configuration of Points', *Psychometrika* 33, 1968, pp. 469–506.
2. The categories of frequency vary by activity. However, the tables and the text in these chapters dealing with the different activities give a fair picture of the categories.
3. This is one of several graphic structures noted by Professor Guttman in his work with smallest space analysis (see Note 1, above). Other forms include the simplex, radex, multiplex.
4. This conclusion is based on an examination of the data of Figure 9.1 separately for respondents of each of three levels of education. To our surprise, we found that the size of the correlations were quite different within each education group. Among the *least* educated, the correlations stand up very well – and, indeed, many of them become stronger. Now, as we know, lower-educated people are less likely to go out. This means that *if they do go out* engaging in one kind of activity is quite predictive of engaging in another. This generalization is less true for middle education, and even less so for those with 11+ years of education. In other words, it is more difficult to predict for the best-educated group that if they engage in activity A they also engage in B and C.

   In any case, the moral of the story is that while educated people do more of almost everything, the lower educated are more 'consistent' or less selective. If they do anything, they do everything. Ironically, the slogan 'the more the more' is applied to well-educated and young people erroneously: the correlations among their activities are weak even though they do do everything in higher proportion. It is the least well educated to whom the slogan is most applicable.
5. Cf. S. N. Eisenstadt, *From Generation to Generation*, New York: Free Press of Glencoe, 1956; also see Elihu Katz and Avraham Zloczower, 'Ethnic Continuity in an Israeli Town, II. Relations with Peers', *Human Relations*, 44, 1961, pp. 309–27.
6. See Michael Young and Peter Wilmott, *Family and Kinship in East*

London, Harmondsworth: Penguin, 1968. We have averaged the figures in this study which are reported separately for men and women and for visiting father and visiting mother. To be on the safe side, we compared their married population only with those of our respondents who are over thirty; had we carried it out on the entire married population our figures would be appreciably higher.

7. See Bert Adams, *Kinship in an Urban Setting*, Markham, 1968. Adam's young adults are somewhat older: their median age is 33; ours are 18–29. Comparison with our 30–50 group would also show our figures to be higher. Adams also analyzes men and women separately (finding, as do Young and Wilmott, that females visit their relatives more frequently). We have recomputed his figures to make them comparable to ours.

CHAPTER TEN Television: The Newest Medium

Television came to Israel in 1968, after more than a decade of debate over whether it should be introduced at all. Its opponents said that it would debase the effort to revive Hebraic culture; that it would impose criteria of personality and charisma on the conduct of politics; that it would replace the goals of productivity with the values of leisure and consumerism; that it would make people passive. Its advocates insisted that, properly employed, it could contribute – as had radio – to the renaissance of Jewish culture; that it would integrate far-flung settlements in the national communion; that it would promote the social and economic goals of nation-building. It was not until Ben-Gurion stepped down from the premiership and a new government came to power that a faint green light began to flash, and preparations for the introduction of television were begun. The Six Day War of 1967 gave impetus to the decision, challenging television to lead the way to a deepening of communication with the Arabs.

Fifty-eight per cent of Israeli adults had television in their homes by June of 1970 and 83 per cent were regular viewers at least several nights per week. Four years earlier, when we studied the uses of leisure in Haifa and Ashdod, only 6–7 per cent owned a set, although 50 per cent had seen television somewhere before – abroad, or at an exhibition, or on a visit to a café or a home with a set tuned to Beirut, Damascus or Cairo.[1]

Despite the very high cost of buying a television set – three months of the average worker's take-home pay! – the rate of acquisition of television receivers in Israel is one of the steepest in the world.[2] About the same proportion own a washing-machine; a somewhat smaller proportion have a telephone and fewer (24 per cent of our sample) own a car. While set ownership is widespread, it is related to income: the bottom third of the income ladder, earning less than IL600 per month (about £60), is substantially below the national average in set ownership. The best educated lag a little, but not very much; on the whole, set ownership increases both with income and education. Those aged 30–50 own proportionately more sets than the younger and older groups.

During the period of our study, Israel television was on the air four hours nightly; like radio, it was operating under the aegis of a BBC-like Broadcasting Authority. It was (and still is) supported by the payment of a licence fee by set owners, and it does not carry advertising. An

FIGURE 10.1 *Ownership of TV Sets from 1965 to 1970 (%)**

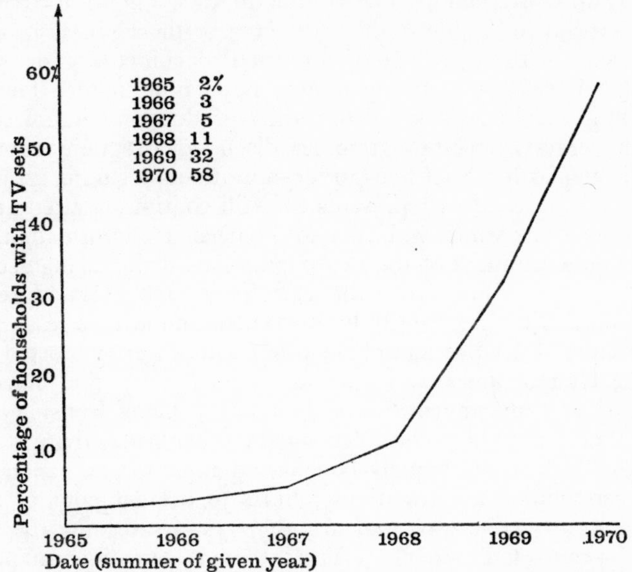

* Figures from 1965 to 1969 based upon data from *Statistical Abstract for Israel*, No. 21, Central Bureau of Statistics, Jerusalem; 1970 data collected in the present study.

TABLE 10.1 *Ownership of a Television Set, by Age and Education (June 1970)*

	Total (N = 100%)	Per cent who own a set
Age 18–29		
0–4 years education	(48)	50
5–10 years education	(390)	51
11+ years education	(552)	56
Age 30–50		
0–4 years education	(270)	49
5–10 years education	(693)	72
11+ years education	(532)	69
Age 50+		
0–4 years education	(210)	35
5–10 years education	(535)	52
11+ years education	(428)	56
TOTAL POPULATION	(3658)	58

average evening would consist of a children's programme from 6 to 6.30 p.m., a feature programme, a news bulletin, then a political commentary and discussion in Arabic, until 7.30. At 7.30 the Hebrew programme would start with a half-hour imported documentary or situation comedy, followed by a twenty-minute news programme. The rest of the evening would be devoted to locally produced or imported documentaries, entertainment programmes, discussion programmes or feature films, closing with a brief five- to ten-minute news summary.

This nightly schedule represents the still-continuing attempt to find a programme mix which will cater to the needs for information, education and entertainment of the two populations while taking account of the constraints arising from the extremely high costs of television production and the necessarily limited talent and artistic resources of a small country. Fifty per cent of the programmes were imported, mostly from the United States, and a world traveller would find himself able to keep up with the adventures of the Saint or Chief Ironside in Israel just as almost anywhere else. Yet, on the other hand, there were programmes which were uniquely Israeli – attempts to find expression for Jewish ceremonies and traditions, efforts to present popular Hebrew songs in an attractive way, and to find ways of satisfying the Israeli's hunger for more and more news. Yet, if there is something unique about Israel's television service, it is the programming in Arabic. Here is an attempt to combine politics, entertainment and information for presentation to Israeli Arabs and to the one million Arabs in the territories occupied by Israel. To do this, without estranging the Jews (who had waited so long for television), the Arabs (who can tune in on the Arab stations if they like) or both, is a difficult steering job.

When we turn, therefore, to ask how people feel about television and what effects its introduction has had on Israeli leisure and culture, we shall not expect the answers to be simple and clear-cut. Indeed, even in more simple and clear-cut situations, in other nations and other times, the assessment of the effects of a new medium of communication is not simple. We are *not* asking the question whether television is more or less effective than, say, radio or films, in changing people's attitudes or directing their actions; at any rate, that is a different (and, most researchers would agree, an unrewarding) question. We are not asking whether the life styles presented on television have affected viewers' own behaviour or aspirations; this has yet to be done. Nor are we asking Marshall McLuhan's question whether the new medium has affected the ways in which Israelis organize their perceptions, although it is not an irrelevant question to put to the People of the Book.

What we *did* ask – just two years after the introduction of television – is how patterns of spending time have been affected, how tastes have been moulded or changed, what people have learned to expect of the new medium, but primarily what they do 'with' television, how television serves them (rather than what it does 'to' them). In answering these questions, we shall be assisted by the pre-television data collected four years earlier and by data from the Continuing Survey.[3] Since the opportunity to conduct 'before and after' studies has been missed so regularly in so many countries, such comparative data are unusual, even if they fall short, in the ways just specified, of asking some of the important questions.

1. *How Do People Feel about Television?*

As we have noted, television now consumes more than one-quarter of the 'discretionary' leisure time available to adults in this society. The average person views for over one hour, but the average also includes those who don't own sets or, for other reasons, don't view. The time spent viewing by owners of sets is close to two hours, which is not very different from the sixteen to seventeen hours per head per week of the British viewer. Indeed, viewing time is not much affected by increase in the number of hours of transmission provided the peak 7–11 p.m. hours are accounted for; the number of hours of broadcasting at other times and on multiple channels simply tend to fractionate the audience.[4] In any case, the heaviest viewers – in terms of number of hours spent with television – are middle-aged (30–50), middle-educated (five to ten years of schooling) women. But the differences among social groups are altogether quite small, and it is only the relative absence of young people from the daily television audience that deserves attention; the lesser participation of the least educated groups is already familiar.

As far as the rest of the population is concerned, television is their evening 'out'. And their reactions to the medium are very mixed, even contradictory. First of all, they view. Secondly, they complain: 6 in 10 say that television is *less* interesting than they had expected.[5] Thirdly, they do not relate the time they spend viewing to their evaluation of the medium; the heavy viewers say that television is 'less interesting' in the same proportion as the light viewers. Finally, very few people are willing to lose out on any amount of television viewing time. We asked respondents if they would agree to give up one evening of television if it meant getting better programmes; only one quarter, at most, can be said to be willing.

Is it the medium or the message that is less interesting than expected? Perhaps it is the medium: add together the years of talk about it, plus the great expectations that life would be different thereafter, plus the heavy price of buying a set, and perhaps let-down is a normal reaction. Or perhaps it is the message: perhaps people expected something different from what they are getting.

2. *Attitudes Toward Content*

Despite their disappointment, it is very rare for people to say that they would like 'less' of a particular kind of programme. This type of question has been put to respondents repeatedly in a variety of studies, and if one takes the results at face value, one is forced to the conclusion that most people are satisfied with anything (or everything) and call for 'more' or 'the same amount'. At least, they are reluctant to vote 'less' as if they were hurting someone's feelings. At first glance, then, people seem to be satisfied with the message, whatever it happens to be. This jibes very well with Americans' attitudes toward their television programmes. 'The verdict is clear', says Steiner. 'For most people, "most programmes" are not great, but are clearly a cut above satisfactory.'[6] This is very much the situation in Israel, if it were not for the undertone of 'less interesting than I expected'. It is almost as if there were some barometer against which people measure the overall performance of the new medium, and another easily shifting standard which allows one to find any given programme reasonably acceptable. Perhaps there is a 'tribal memory' which the People of the Book can call upon when asked to make a sweeping generalization, and yet another standard which they find more appropriate to the assessment of their liking for *Mission Impossible* or *Hawaii Five-O*.

Like its predecessors, the present study found the appreciation for most programmes quite high. Each of the seven very different types of programmes about which we inquired was sufficiently disliked by 10–20 per cent for them to say that they would like to see 'less' of it. But the large majority, considering each programme in turn, said that they would like to see this type of programme broadcast 'more' frequently or about the 'same'. There is some variation in enthusiasm for the several types of programme which constituted the standard fare of Israel television at the time.

If we are to take the list seriously, light entertainment is at the top, imported and Israeli. Full-length feature films are about as popular. Lower down are the imported series – the Western and the action shows – and the serious discussion formats which, of course, are locally produced. It is instructive that the much-vaunted *Mission Impossible* is the kind of programme which more people than any other have had enough of: 22 per cent call for 'less' of its kind!

Of course, preferences differ among viewers. The less well educated and the young prefer light entertainment and the imported action films; men like both of these more than women do. On the other hand, the current affairs and documentary programmes are better liked by better-educated, older persons and by men more than women. Again, as in newspaper-reading, the young emerge as far less politically minded than their parents.

If we recall that, by and large, entertainment is the category that gets most votes when the current line-up of programmes was considered, we shall have another seeming contradiction with which to contend. We asked viewers about their expectations of television: 'What do you look for in particular on television? Entertainment and amusement; culture and education; or news and information? Please rank these according to their importance for you.' In ranking these traditional content categories of entertainment, information and education, over half named information and current affairs as the most important content type. About a third ranked entertainment in first place and 12 per cent said that their prime expectation was for programmes of education and culture.

Is this a contradiction? Perhaps so. News is one of the central features of Israeli culture, and it may be simply a reaffirmation of national solidarity to say so. Or perhaps Israelis feel that current affairs really *is* most important, but that it is in good supply, whereas light entertainment is what one needs 'more' of. Indeed, some critics have said that light entertainment *is* in short supply on Israel television. We tend to believe in the latter interpretation, that news, information and current affairs really come first.

This request – to rank the three categories of content – has been put to respondents several times over the last few years, beginning in February 1968, i.e. three months before Israel Television first went on the air. Examining Table 10.2, which presents these data, reveals how information and entertainment have vied with each other, with the gradual ascendancy of information. Thus, the expectation that television will provide information above all has been with us from the very first. This expectation is expressed with almost equal frequency among the various subgroups of the population; there is almost no difference among education groups, although older persons and men preferred current affairs to entertainment more than younger persons and women.

Much more interesting, however, is the steady decline in the proportion giving culture first place – from 24 per cent of the population in February 1968 to 12 per cent in the summer of 1970. This trend is particularly important because it appears to be an example of a genuine 'effect' of television on attitudes; more specifically, it seems to be an effect of 'supply' on 'demand'. Prior to the beginning of television broadcasting, about one-quarter of the population said that what they were seeking in the new medium primarily was 'culture and education'. But as time goes by, and as the content of the medium coincides with the expectations of the majority for information and entertainment, this minority expectation gives way and 'adjusts' to the idea that among the three, 'culture' comes last.

Moreover, it is interesting to consider this process in the light of the finding that most people think *other* people want more popular programmes, while they, themselves, are quite tolerant of the idea of 'highbrow' programming. About one-fifth thought that the public prefers high-level programmes, while almost half agreed (for the question was intentionally loaded) that the public actually prefers programmes of a lower level. The remainder said either 'both' or that they 'don't know'.

TABLE 10.2 *Audience Expectation for Entertainment, Information and Culture on Television – Comparison over Time*
Per cent

Rank order of expectations	Feb. '68		April '68		Oct. '69		Summer '70	
Entertainment, culture, information	21		28		16		13	
Entertainment, information, culture	14		18		24		20	
Entertainment as first choice		**35**		**46**		**40**		**33**
Culture, information, entertainment	14		10		10		8	
Culture, entertainment, information	10		7		7		4	
Culture as first choice		**24**		**17**		**17**		**12**
Information, entertainment, culture	20		21		25		39	
Information, culture, entertainment	21		16		18		16	
Information as first choice		**41**		**37**		**43**		**55**
TOTAL	100%		100%		100%		100%	

Despite the distribution of opinions concerning the public's taste a third of the population would 'certainly' approve and an additional 18 per cent would be 'likely' to approve highbrow programmes, even if the audience for these programmes were smaller. Only one-fifth said that such programmes should definitely not be shown. Considering the proprietary interest which most viewers seem to feel about the regular time they set aside for viewing, together with the fact that all have paid the licence fee in order to be equally served, this seems remarkable. It may even imply that a great number of these viewers would like to keep their options open for viewing high-level programming themselves. For the fact is that everybody watches everything.[7]

Beyond these considerations, it seems to us that these attitudes also reflect the deference towards elitist cultural values inherent in the Jewish tradition, and the consequent wish to see television in Israel as a medium of some cultural worth, even if its peaks sometimes soar over the heads of the bulk of its audience. In this connection, it is interesting that older people, far more than younger ones, feel that others want high-quality programming. And indeed they do, judging from older persons' greater appreciation of current affairs programmes, their liking for classical music, and so on. The question is whether the younger generation will inherit them?

There is, finally, one more aspect of general programming into which we inquired: the preference for home-made vs. imported programmes. In the listing of favourite programmes, there was no discernible difference: light entertainment was equally preferred, whether domestic or imported, and among the less liked programmes, there were some that were imported and some that were home-made, although it is true that the action-adventure programmes which a large minority wants 'less' of were all imported.

The issue of home-made vs. imported goes to the very heart of the problem of television in small nations, and even in many large ones. The conflict is between the desire both to employ television as a medium for the promotion of indigenous culture and, on the other hand, to respond to public demand for longer viewing hours, which can be satisfied, it appears, only by filling the screen with financially cheap, imported series and serials.

Viewers were asked: 'To what extent do you agree with the ratio of imported programmes (produced abroad) and original programmes produced at home?' About one-quarter said they approve of the existing schedule (which is based on importing approximately half the programme hours), whereas one-third would like to see more locally produced programmes and 15 per cent want more imported programmes. About one-quarter had no opinion.[8] In other words, among those who want to see changes introduced, over two-thirds prefer local rather than imported programmes. Moreover, this preference is equally clear at all educational levels (Table 10.3).

The tendency of the majority of people to acquiesce in whatever television provides has already been emphasized and needs no further elaboration here. It is therefore significant to notice that nearly half the population are alive to the possibility of change and have opinions about it. Among them, twice as many would like to see more programmes which are locally produced rather than more imported ones. Those who feel that change is desirable are opting for a medium which is more reflective of indigenous culture. This preference is all the more striking when one contrasts, on the screen, the relative homeliness of domestic programming as against the dazzle and technological sophistication of the imported programmes. These are also the people who say that 'public opinion' deserves a larger voice in determining programme schedules.

To sum up the attitudes toward programming on Israeli television, it appears that there is some tension between norms and expectations of the medium on the one hand, and satisfaction with specific programmes on the other. A majority of the population is satisfied with most of the programmes. Judging from expressed preferences light entertainment is preferred to other categories of programming and no clear preference emerges as between home-made and imported programmes. In discussing the medium *in general*, however, a majority says that television is less interesting than they expected, that current affairs and information programmes are the type of programming most sought, and that the ratio of imported to home-made programmes should be revised in favour of the home-made. We have argued that these seeming contradictions are not necessarily so, and, in any case, that they can coexist; the fact is, of course, that they do. We have also emphasized that over the long run, there is some suggestion that norms and expectations expressive of demand adjust themselves to what is being supplied.

TABLE 10.3 *Attitudes Toward Ratio of Local and Imported Programmes*

		Per cent who say				
	Total (N=100%)	More Israeli programmes	More imported programmes	All right as is	No opinion	
Age 18–29						
0–4 years education	(37)	16	27	22	35	100%
5–10 years education	(338)	28	23	32	17	100%
11+ years education	(496)	37	17	26	20	100%
Age 30–50						
0–4 years education	(197)	28	10	26	36	100%
5–10 years education	(640)	32	17	32	19	100%
11+ years education	(462)	38	15	27	20	100%
Age 50+						
0–4 years education	(138)	21	7	33	38	100%
5–10 years education	(437)	32	11	30	27	100%
11+ years education	(346)	39	11	25	25	100%
TOTAL POPULATION	(3091)	33	15	28	24	100%

3. *Attitudes Toward News*

News, we have seen, is given first place in the assessment of what people want from television. This expectation fits very well with the image of Israel as a news-hungry country. Its security problems, and the chronic possibilities of military incidents, result in a situation in which news bulletins have a larger audience than any other single type of programme, and a very large number of people tune in to radio news almost every hour on the clock – especially in times of crisis. The speed with which radio can provide news bulletins thus gives radio a predominant place as the major source of news dissemination. Yet, despite the fact that radio still provides the most up-to-date and continuous news service, 62 per cent of the respondents in our sample reported that they prefer television news to radio news. This seems even more surprising when we consider the fact that television provides only one extended news programme during the evening, and that the visual element in television news was still rather underdeveloped.

Nevertheless, news-listening habits created by the characteristics of radio news bulletins continue to impose themselves on the preferences for the patterns of news presentation over television. In response to a question concerning the character of news presentation, 41 per cent of the respondents said they would rather have 'short items on lots of topics, as in radio news', compared with 31 per cent who would rather have 'long items on fewer topics, as in the radio's news magazine'. The preference for the former alternative, however, can also be seen as preference for the *status quo*, since not only our respondents, but television's news directors also opt for the staccato presentation of news established by radio rather than for the lengthier treatment of a smaller number of the day's events, a pattern in which television could perhaps excel and more fully differentiate its news presentation from that of radio.

Another issue concerning news presentation involves the balance between world and Israeli affairs. Preoccupation with news concerning one's own country is not, of course, unique to Israel, and the 'crisis mentality' of many Israelis reinforces the natural tendency to concentrate on information which might be immediately relevant to the audience, at the expense of a more balanced news diet. This had occasionally given rise to criticisms that an unbalanced news diet in favour of Israeli affairs exacerbates the ethnocentricity of many Israelis and leads to a state of mind which will tend to reject uncomplimentary or critical views of Israeli affairs by outsiders. This criticism seems unjustified, since our findings indicate that the Israeli media present a balance of local and foreign news which is similar to that of the *New York Times* or the BBC World Service. And, indeed, the majority of Israelis are satisfied with this balance: six in ten respondents agreed with the present pattern, while the rest were equally divided between those who favoured a more even balance and those who would like to get even more news of Israel and less about non-Israeli affairs.

Exposure to certain foreign media – the BBC, the Voice of America, and various Eastern European stations – is to some extent related to a desire to see more international coverage on Israeli television. Whereas the percentage of those who are critical of the dosage of Israeli affairs is

13 per cent in the total population, it reaches 20 per cent among those exposed to foreign media. (However, among those who attend to broadcasts from other Arab countries and from Cyprus, the percentage critical in that way is equal to that in the general population.) One might speculate whether these respondents turned to foreign sources because they sensed inadequate coverage in the local media – or whether their feeling that local coverage is inadequate developed as a result of their additional exposure. Both presumably reinforce each other. But one must bear in mind that it is the better educated who are both critical of what they consider the over-emphasis on domestic news and who attend to foreign media. Strictly speaking, there is no 'causal relationship' here.

4. *Programmes in Arabic*

Out of a total of about four and a half hours of television broadcasting per evening, approximately one and a half hours are in the Arabic language. Although these broadcasts are designed primarily for the Arab residents of Israel, including those in the territories currently administered by Israel, a large proportion of the audience for these shows is Jewish.[9] Moreover, the possibility of picking up programmes originating in the neighbouring Arab countries has probably conditioned some Israeli viewers to watch certain programmes without even understanding the language. Indeed, some programmes – the musical variety shows, for example – do not necessarily require an understanding of the language in order to be enjoyed. Others (the children's or women's programmes, for example) have no counterpart in the Hebrew schedule. Altogether, then, the programmes in Arabic could command a large Jewish audience, including both speakers and non-speakers of the language.

The most widely watched Arabic programme is the musical entertainment show, watched more or less regularly by 39 per cent of the Jewish population, and the extremely successful Arabic children's programme, *Sammy and Susu*, watched regularly by 37 per cent. While the wide appeal of musical entertainment programmes is understandable, the success story of *Sammy and Susu* deserves special mention. Its very wide appeal is attested by the fact that our respondents are all adults. While some of these, to be sure, are parents who view with their children (the programme has Hebrew subtitles which require a parent to read them aloud to younger children), others presumably watch it for their own enjoyment. Although the respondents were not asked about other programmes for children, it is our impression that this is the most popular one among adult viewers. Our data also indicate that the percentage of viewers of this programme does not decline with age: as many older people watch the programme as young adults and middle-aged respondents. Furthermore, in ranking the Arabic programmes according to the proportion of non-Arabic speakers in the audience, we find that *Sammy and Susu* has the largest proportion, presumably because of the Hebrew subtitles (which, at the time of the study, were not given for most other Arabic programmes) as well as the interest value of the programme itself. Whatever the reason, it appears that the programmes in Arabic constitute an integral part of the television fare of a large number of Jewish viewers, notwithstanding the language barrier.

As has been indicated, approximately 25–30 per cent of total television hours per evening are given to Arabic programmes. When asked whether this amount should be reduced in order to make room for more Hebrew broadcasts, over half of the viewers said they were satisfied to leave the schedule as it is, while one-quarter agreed that there should be fewer programmes in Arabic. A small part of the audience suggested increasing the Arabic schedule.

The better-educated viewers are most in favour of maintaining the Arabic service intact. This is certainly not because they are heavier viewers of the programmes in Arabic but rather because they are presumably affirming the validity of the idea of Israel broadcasting in Arabic, whether for reasons of civility and service, propaganda and persuasion, or dialogue.

Country of origin and knowledge of Arabic also affect attitudes to Arabic broadcasts on Israel television. Immigrants from Asia and North Africa are known to be less tolerant toward Arabs than other groups, despite (or perhaps because of) the obvious affinity between at least some part of their cultural heritage and that of the Arabs.[10] Table 10.4 reflects these orientations. The Europeans and native Israelis are more accepting of the balance between the two languages of broadcasting. Some of those who know the Arabic language – about 15 per cent of Arabic speakers in each of the ethnic groups – favour increasing the programme time allotted to the Arabic service.[11]

An examination of attitudes toward the potential utilization of television for teaching Hebrew to Arabs and Arabic to Jews sheds light on the complexity of Israeli attitudes toward the Arabs. Basing one's expectations in this area on one set of historical precedents, it might have been expected that – since Israelis conceive of themselves as being in a dominant position *vis-à-vis* the Arabs – they would, like other 'dominant cultures' before, be keen on spreading their own language and culture. At the same time, they might also be expected to interest themselves in the other culture, albeit to a lesser extent and not as a matter of course. Responses to the suggestion that television be used to teach these two languages suggest, however, that the reverse of these expectations is instead the case. Many more people think that it is

TABLE 10.4 *Attitudes Toward Ratio of Hebrew to Arabic Programmes, by Knowledge of Arabic and Ethnicity*
Per cent

Knowledge of Arabic and ethnicity	Total (N=100%)	Decrease broadcasts	Remain as is	Increase broadcasts	No opinion	
Asia, North Africa						
Know Arabic*	(452)	29	46	13	12	100%
Do not know Arabic	(116)	34	44	3	19	100%
Europe, America						
Know Arabic*	(61)	16	62	15	7	100%
Do not know Arabic	(562)	25	57	3	15	100%
Native Israelis						
Know Arabic*	(111)	22	59	12	7	100%
Do not know Arabic	(139)	14	73	4	9	100%
TOTAL POPULATION	(1441)	25	55	8	12	100%

* Speaks, reads or writes Arabic.

important to teach Arabic to Jews than think that it is important to teach Hebrew to Arabs. Table 10.5 presents this picture.

While feeling against Arabs underlies some of the resistance to using television to teach them Hebrew, it is also important to note the correlations between attitudes toward teaching Hebrew to Arabs and Arabic to Jews. About 60 per cent have the same opinion about both languages. This may simply reflect a negative attitude toward use of the medium for language teaching or a more deep-rooted feeling that the two cultures ought not to be drawn closer.

TABLE 10.5 *Comparison of Attitudes on the Desirability of Teaching Hebrew to Arabs and Arabic to Jews on Television*
Per cent

	Use television to teach Hebrew to Arabs?	Use television to teach Arabic to Jews?
Highly desirable	17	40
Desirable	31	36
Possibly desirable	15	10
Not desirable	20	9
Highly undesirable	10	2
No opinion	7	3
TOTAL	100%	100%
N	(1579)	(1592)

5. *Television and the Sabbath*

The issues raised by the broadcast of television programmes on the Sabbath reveal, perhaps in their clearest form, the controversial aspects of the role and place of television within the larger framework of Israeli culture. The essence of the public controversy which preceded the introduction of television in Israel had to do with considerations regarding the role and the effects of the new medium upon the development and dissemination of a genuine Israeli culture. During the first year or so of broadcasting, while its schedule was still limited to three, and then four, evenings a week, the Sabbath still remained – in the eyes of the religious sectors of the population as well as of other 'cultural traditionalists' – a religious and cultural 'reservation', still free from the encroachment of the new medium. The real significance of the introduction of television broadcasting on the Sabbath lay, therefore, in the perceived threat of this action for the religious, as well as the cultural and social, contents of Friday night, and its meaning in Israeli life.[12]

Religious considerations aside, the introduction of television broadcasts on Friday night can be seen as a test-case of the ability of a well-established pattern of cultural heritage and social activities to withstand the pressures of change emanating from the introduction of new leisure-time opportunities. Looked at in this way, the established patterns of Friday night activities certainly seem to have been seriously affected. Our data indicate that television viewing has become one of the most popular Friday night activities, much like the role it has assumed in the leisure pursuits of regular weekdays.

In time-budget data which were collected concerning that evening, half the respondents mentioned having watched television which makes it the single most frequently cited activity. In second place is visiting or hosting one's friends or relatives, which is now the second most popular activity since the introduction of television on Friday night. Social visiting, it might be added, used to be the single most frequently cited activity on Friday night, according to time-budget data which we collected in 1966, and participation in this activity has subsequently gone down. Indeed, considering the fact that the content of these visits may, for some, now be an evening of viewing, this further highlights the centrality of television in the Friday evening pattern of activities.

The above generalizations, however, somewhat exaggerate the capacity of television to erode established patterns of social and cultural behaviour. It seems that when the commitment or the motivation to preserve the traditional pattern of activities is strong enough, the effective lure of television is quite small. Thus, among respondents who describe themselves as religious, only a very small fraction report watching television on Friday night.

TABLE 10.6 *Participation in Various Leisure Activities on Friday Evening**

	Per cent
Mass media	
1. Television	50
2. Radio	27
3. Newspapers	24
4. Books	8
5. Gramophone records	3
6. Periodicals	2
Social life	
7. Conversation	20
8. Visiting	18
9. Hosting	14
10. Parties, dances	5
11. Games	4
Non-home recreation	
12. Cinema	2
13. Night club, discotheque	2
14. Coffee house	1
15. Light entertainment	1
16. Theatre	1
17. Museum, exhibitions	0
18. Concert	0
Other leisure activity	
19. Walking (in town)	8
20. Excursions	1
21. Hobbies	1
22. Public lecture	1
23. Clubs, organizations	0
24. Sports	0
25. Creative activity	0
26. Letter-writing	0
N	(320)

* These figures represent the percentage of respondents who mentioned each activity at least once on their time-budget records between 7 p.m. and midnight on Friday evening, either as a primary or a secondary activity. Since most people were engaged in more than one activity, the percentages add up to more than 100 per cent. (See Chapter Three for details.)

Respondents have been weighted by sex, age and education in order to be representative of the population as a whole.

While the religious opponents of television on Friday night fought in the name of the illegitimacy of Sabbath broadcasting *per se*, the 'cultural traditionalists' questioned the ability of television to provide an evening of viewing whose contents would be commensurate with the traditional and cultural heritage of the Sabbath. They felt that television was bound to broadcast programmes which are less meaningful culturally than those activities which it would be replacing.

The broadcasting authorities clearly realized the challenge which Sabbath broadcasting presented, and they attempted to create a viewing schedule which would do justice to the special character of that evening. By June 1970, when this survey was conducted, the typical schedule for a Friday evening included three central features: (1) an extended news programme, *The Weekly Newsreel*, based on in-depth reporting and news features (re-broadcast on Saturday night, for the benefit of those viewers who refrained from watching on the Sabbath); (2) a programme of 'Israeli entertainment' featuring an Israeli artist; and (3) an imported 'quality' programme, usually a series, such as Shakespearian plays, or *Daniel Deronda* or *The Forsyte Saga*. While judgements may vary as to the true cultural significance of this schedule, it does represent an attempt to aim a cut higher than the common weekday fare.

The single most popular programme is the news magazine, pulling about 62 per cent of the population, or almost all Friday viewers with access to a set. This is not surprising in light of what has already been said about the attraction of news programmes in general in this country. In second place is 'Israeli entertainment', which is a programme of proven popularity, with 57 per cent of the sample viewing. The imported 'quality' programme attracted a much smaller audience, ranging from a low of 24 per cent for the series of Shakespeare plays to approximately one-third of the population for *Buddenbrooks* and *Daniel Deronda*. In this respect *The Forsyte Saga* was much more successful. The first instalment was broadcast on Friday night and was seen by half the population.

Altogether, then, the alternative which television offered for the traditional 'culture of the Sabbath' represents a fairly routine sample of fare, and the audience's preferences indicate that these offerings were quite acceptable.

A direct question concerning preferences for various kinds of content was put to the respondents. They were asked whether, in their opinion, an effort should be made to orient the content of Friday night programmes to the special character of that evening. About half of the respondents felt that programmes on the Sabbath should in some way be appropriate, while 28 per cent did not see any need for special, 'more appropriate', programmes, and 18 per cent objected altogether to television being broadcast on that evening. There were considerable differences, however, in what people perceived as 'appropriate'. The proportion of respondents, for example, suggesting that the 'appropriate' programmes should be connected with Jewish tradition was equal to that of those whose conception of 'appropriateness' led them to favour light entertainment programmes. One might find in this almost-even split an indication of the dual meaning of Friday night for the population: while for some this meaning is rooted in tradition, others see it simply as the main free evening of the week.

TABLE 10.7 *Expectations of Television Programming for the Sabbath Eve*

'In your opinion should an effort be made to make the Friday night programmes particularly appropriate for the Sabbath?'

	Per cent who say
No, I oppose television broadcasting on Friday night	18
No, they need not be particularly appropriate	28
Yes, programmes should be related to Jewish tradition	18
Yes, there should be more serious programmes than on weekdays	5
Yes, there should be light entertainment programmes	17
Yes, a review of the news	–
Yes, more than one of the above categories	6
No opinion	8
TOTAL	100%
N	(1591)

A more significant effect of the intrusion of television into the Sabbath eve lies, perhaps, not so much in the nature of the content to which it exposed the population, but rather in its impact on the reshaping of that evening's activities. Since television-viewing can, in some ways, be seen as more directly competitive with the other media, it is interesting to note that, apart from radio-listening (which constitutes its most similar alternative), television-viewing affected social activities somewhat more than it affected other media-consumption activities. The impact of television on the social character of Friday night is, therefore, more significant than its effect on reading which, in any case, can be taken up at another time when there are no broadcasts. Moreover, it should be noted that other evidence (see Chapter Twelve, on reading) suggests that respondents may be exaggerating the influence of television on other leisure activities.

An examination of these data by the respondents' age and level of education reveals that changes have been greatest among the heaviest viewers, those of middle age and middle education. It seems again that the attraction of television as an alternative to other activities is smallest

TABLE 10.8 *Effect of Television on Other Friday Night Activities, by Age and Education*

		Per cent who say they do less*						
	Total (N=100%)	Radio-listening	Visiting or entertaining	Strolling	Listening to records	Book-reading	Newspaper-reading	Games, chess, cards, etc.
Age 18–29								
0–4 years education	(36)	36	14	28	25	8	11	6
5–10 years education	(346)	39	22	28	22	22	15	14
11+ years education	(497)	36	16	18	16	16	10	6
Age 30–50								
0–4 years education	(210)	25	17	19	12	7	5	9
5–10 years education	(638)	48	25	33	27	25	19	23
11+ years education	(471)	53	25	18	31	25	15	12
Age 50+								
0–4 years education	(158)	23	16	14	8	6	6	4
5–10 years education	(448)	37	25	25	17	18	11	15
11+ years education	(354)	44	26	20	23	21	11	14
TOTAL POPULATION	(3158)	41	24	23	22	19	13	13

* It should be borne in mind that some activities are intrinsically more popular than others. Thus, 26 per cent did not stroll on Friday evenings before television; 50 per cent never played cards, chess, etc.; compared with only 9 per cent who never visited; 9 per cent who never read the newspapers, etc.

when the motivation to maintain these other activities is strongest (as seems to be true for the young).

Two additional activities of some significance in the traditional framework of Friday night – eating and sleeping – also did not escape the pervasive impact of television. A fifth of the respondents, for example, reported that they often watch Friday television while having their meal (although we have no way of knowing to what extent these people indeed regarded the Sabbath meal as an occasion of traditional significance). Likewise 13 per cent of the respondents favoured beginning Friday night's television broadcasts at an earlier hour, implying, also, that they do not consider television viewing an infringement on the traditional Sabbath institution of the festive family dinner.[13] As for sleep, a fifth of the respondents reported that they go to bed later, now that television is broadcast on Friday night.

What, then, can we say about the effects of television on the 'culture of the Sabbath'? There is hardly any doubt that television has affected the entire range of activities and time budgeting of a great number of people on an evening which has a special familial, social and cultural flavour. At the same time, there is no basis for assuming that it has seriously changed the character or detracted from the significance of the evening. It can hardly be claimed that the replacement of radio-listening or newspaper-reading by television in any way alters the cultural content of the Sabbath eve. The certain diminution in the amount of time devoted to social activities is rather more significant.

Thus, the prevalence and amount of viewing on Friday night is quite ironic in the Israeli context. It can be explained by reference to the fact that, for some, television indeed provides the only recreational facility on a Friday night and, perhaps, the only alternative to loneliness as well. On an evening in which a high normative premium is placed on cultural uplift and social recreation – and yet most means of public entertainment are closed down – the opportunities afforded by television should not be discounted. Television undoubtedly fills a certain void for those to whom the absence of social contact on this evening could otherwise be threatening. And, if it is granted that one of the unique characteristics of Friday night in Israel is its home-centred quality, then this has surely not been eroded by the introduction of television on that evening.

6. *Conclusion*

The fieldwork for this study was concluded approximately two years after the introduction of television. On the basis of its evidence one is forced to conclude that television has not lived up to the expectations held out for it by most Israelis. No doubt, the long wait for it inflated expectations. But it did not turn out to be as evil as the fearful feared, or as good as the hopefuls hoped. In short, it is certainly not the powerful means of communication that Israelis anticipated.

But the fact is that the problem of Israeli Television is not so different from the problem of television in many other new and small nations. The budget required is enormous; the demand for talent is unrelenting. Countries larger than Israel have found themselves overcommitted.

Unless some new forms of television are created, especially tailored to the capabilities of small countries, there seems little choice other than to import 50–60 per cent of programming. This, obviously, hardly satisfies the expectation that television will contribute to the renaissance of indigenous culture. And if television broadcasts are on the air every day of the year, it is obviously not sufficient to note that special holiday programmes or coverage of special events are, on the whole, of high quality.

Only if one believes that television will impress itself on people's minds in some deep, McLuhanesque way is there any basis for treating the introduction of television as revolutionary. Apart from this possibility – which remains unstudied here – the most that can be said is that the new medium is taking its place gradually alongside the other institutions of Israeli leisure, making it just a little more attractive to stay home.

NOTES – CHAPTER TEN

1. The place where people first saw television is based on our surmise; we did not collect data on this. The figures for Haifa are certainly higher than the national average, since it has good reception of Lebanon's television stations. Also, Haifa has an Arab community living on good terms with the Jews and many Arabs owned sets in 1966. The present study is limited to Jewish respondents, but we are assuming that they have had contact with their neighbours.
2. Steeper than Australia, Belgium, Austria and Brazil, and equalling that of Sweden. From research on the diffusion of innovation, it is well known that 'late' adopters of many innovations adopt on a larger scale, thus benefiting from the venturesomeness of the pioneers and early adopters. Something like it may have been at work here.
3. Here, as elsewhere, the Continuing Survey is a reference to the trimestrial inquiry conducted jointly by The Communications Institute of the Hebrew University and the Israel Institute of Applied Social Research.
4. See the article by Brian Emmett on radio and television audiences in D. McQuail, ed., *Sociology of Mass Communications*, Harmondsworth: Penguin, 1972.

5. Complaining that television is less interesting than anticipated is more characteristic of the better educated. These, incidentally, are also the groups who *view more*. As has been found elsewhere, the evaluation of television is not a very good indicator of the amount of time spent sitting in front of it.
6. Gary Steiner, *The People Look at Television*, New York: Knopf, 1963.
7. Many people saw their first symphony concert ever when Israel Television broadcast the festive programme of the Israel Philharmonic with Leonard Bernstein conducting. Almost 90 per cent of the population viewed enthusiastically – although only about one-third owned a set at the time.
8. Perhaps people are not even aware of what is and is not imported: this is an interesting question which we neglected to ask.
9. It is appropriate to recall here that only the Jewish population of Israel is surveyed here. Nevertheless, it is interesting to note that Israel television was begun after the Six Day War, at least in part as a response to the threat, then the opportunity, of communication across the borders. Ironically, the number of television sets in the hands of Arabs in Israel and within range of Israeli transmitters is far smaller than originally estimated. Israel radio – it should also be noted – devotes considerable time to broadcasting in Arabic, on a separate channel, and its reputation in the area is that of a reliable source of information.
10. But not less prejudiced, either. See the data on befriending Arabs in Chapter Fourteen, pp. 263–5.
11. Note that speakers of Arabic among the native Israelis – most of whom are the children of immigrants from the Near Eastern countries – are *less* favourable to the *status quo* than native Israelis who do not know the language: more of the former favour decreasing broadcasting time in Arabic (though 15 per cent of them also favour increasing it). It is a fair guess that they are more negative in their attitudes to Arabic culture than their parents are.
12. For a fuller discussion of this issue, see Michael Gurevitch and Gila Schwartz, 'Television and the Sabbath Culture in Israel', in *Jewish Journal of Sociology*, June 1971.
13. It will be recalled that the starting time for Hebrew programmes on Friday evening is later than on weekdays in order not to compete with the festive family dinner.

CHAPTER ELEVEN Other Leisure Activities and the Influence of Television

Television takes time. Two hours represents about half the time available for 'discretionary' leisure on an average weekday. In 1970, Israeli society was devoting this amount of time to the mass media. The population as a whole – including viewers and non-viewers – was devoting an average of one hour per person to viewing television. The viewers were obviously devoting more.[1] Where is this time coming from?

A very rough answer to this question was given in Table 3.8 which matches the time budgets for the Jewish population of Haifa in 1966 and in 1970. Since the methods used for compiling these data were not exactly similar, and notwithstanding the effort which was made to make them comparable in presentation, caution must be exercised in interpreting them.

The differences noted are in time spent resting, eating, sightseeing and in radio-listening and cinema-going. But which of these differences is attributable to television? After all, four years is a long time and a lot of other things happened in Israel during this period, apart from the introduction of television.

The increase in time spent on excursions cannot, obviously, be explained by reference to television. (The burst of sightseeing in the occupied territories seems a more likely explanation.) On the other hand, the reduced time spent at meals may very well be attributable to television, either as a result of eating-while-viewing or because meals are aimed to start at the beginning of programmes. Cinema-going has surely been seriously affected by television, but since it is not a daily activity it has not given television much of its time. Unsurprisingly, radio is the chief source of television time, yet the story is not as simple as it looks at first glance.

1. *Radio*

Whereas 12 minutes were spent on television in Haifa in 1966 (viewing broadcasts from Beirut), 60 minutes is the rule in 1970, and that figure will increase soon to 2 hours or more. Listening to radio as a 'primary' activity – that is, the time during which radio was the main focus of attention – dropped from 54 minutes to 18 minutes per person per day.

Other data from the same two studies, however, suggest that the amount of radio-listening has actually *increased* in recent years. The explanation lies in the differences between the methods in which the data were collected and computed. In the 1966 survey we did not differentiate between primary and secondary activities, i.e. there was not separate calculation of the time devoted to activities which are performed simultaneously with other activities. Thus, the frequency of radio-listening – which is an outstanding example of an activity which serves as background for other activities – is understated for 1966. In 1970, on the other hand, simultaneous activities were computed separately, and the data on radio-listening as a secondary activity indicate that 2·5 hours of radio-listening as a secondary activity can be added to the figure of 0·3 hour. The time-budget data, then, do *not* indicate that radio-listening has fallen off in the period between the two surveys.

The change which television has brought to patterns of radio-listening concerns the timing of this activity. In the chapter on time budgeting, we see that the peak hours of radio-listening in 1966 – the evening hours – became, in 1970, the peak hours of viewing. On the other hand, data here indicate that the audience for radio actually grew during the morning and afternoon hours. In 1970, there was a higher percentage of respondents who listened to the radio during the day than there had been in 1966, and the increase more than makes up for the smaller percentage now tuned in during the evening.

Thus, there is evidence from three sources that there was a rise in radio-listening between 1966 and 1970: (1) in 1970 more than double the percentage of respondents reported that they listen to the radio 6 hours a day or more;[2] (2) radio-listening as a secondary activity reaches an average of 2·5 hours a day in 1970, which probably more than offset the underestimated figure of 0·9 hour in 1966; and (3) a profile of media activity during the day indicates a drop in evening radio-listening, but a steeper rise in the day-time audience.

It seems, then, that predictions about the decline of radio following the emergence of television did not immediately materialize in Israel. Radio has not yet experienced a loss in the total amount of listening hours, and has even gained in its day-time audience together with the rise of television. There seem to be several reasons for this. First, the limited schedule of television broadcasting means that television could displace radio only during the three hours of its broadcasts; this it has done to a large extent. That leaves radio with many hours of monopoly, during which there has actually been a rise in listening.[3]

Charting the proportion of radio listeners throughout an average weekday shows that 23 per cent have their radios tuned in between 6 and 7 a.m. This figure rises to 36 per cent between 7 and 8 a.m. and reaches another peak at 1 p.m. when 30 per cent are listening. During all other hours of the day, except during the afternoon rest hours between 2 and 5 p.m., radio-listening does not drop below 20 per cent. Only at the peak television hours, 8 to 10 p.m., does radio drop to 12 per cent. There is a brief recovery just after television signs off, and then a gradual falling away until radio shuts down around 1 a.m. This is the situation of 1970, when set ownership stood at 58 per cent, and the peak television audience, between 8 and 10 p.m., comprised 43 per cent of the population during the whole of those two hours! These figures will probably change slightly as television ownership becomes universal, but not too much, because the rapt attention of the early years will slacken somewhat. In Britain, for example, the viewing audience during the prime time of an average weekday evening reaches 63–65 per cent of the population.[4]

Radio in Israel is very closely tied to the need to be on the alert. Before the recent advent of day-time television in Britain, radio-listening in Israel outdistanced radio-listening in Britain by 15 per cent or more at any hour of an average day.[5] A rise in tension in the country is immediately reflected in a rise in attention to radio news bulletins. Altogether, the radio is experienced as an important link between the individual and the nerve centre of the society. It is not surprising that information programmes have the highest proportion of regular listeners; two daily news-magazines, at noon and in the evening, lead the list.

Radio has another function, too. It provides background and diversion for a number of different types of listeners. Young people listen many hours a day, mostly for the music. As Table 11.1 indicates, young people with 5–10 years of education listen most of all. Housewives have their favourite day-time programmes, and women generally are more likely to listen to classical music. As is the case with concert-going, age and education appear to be qualifications for listening to classical music even on radio. Cantorial music is a favourite of older people.

In general, the Light Programme (Channel B of Israel Broadcasting) and the Army-operated station, *Galei Zahal*, vie with each other for popularity, and particularly for the attention of young people. Overall, two-thirds listen 'a lot' to Channel B and over half to the Army station, but the proportion of young people who listen at least occasionally is equally high for both. The competition between the stations is based largely on popular music, imported and domestic, but many people feel that the competition has led to interesting innovations in the use of radio in the era of television. Only 30 per cent listen 'a lot' to Programme A, which carries the more weighty words and music.[6] Listening to Channel A increases with age and education; only 20 per cent of young people listen, compared with 51 per cent of the old and well educated.

Everybody (98 per cent) listens to broadcasting in Hebrew. But, in addition, foreign-language broadcasting on radio is extremely popular. One-fifth listen to programmes in Yiddish, and a like number to programmes in Arabic. Ten per cent each listen to French and English, and smaller proportions listen in other languages.

TABLE 11.1 *Hours of Radio-Listening, by Age and Education*

	Total (N = 100%)	Per cent who listen 4 hours or more per day
Age 18–29		
0–4 years education	(47)	63
5–10 years education	(389)	67
11 + years education	(549)	68
Age 30–50		
0–4 years education	(270)	47
5–10 years education	(692)	65
11 + years education	(524)	59
Age 50 +		
0–4 years education	(203)	19
5–10 years education	(522)	32
11 + years education	(423)	23
TOTAL POPULATION	(3619)	58

Some people feel that foreign-language broadcasting is legitimate only for reaching foreign audiences in neighbouring countries and overseas or for helping immigrants to Israel overcome the early difficulties in the process of absorption. Other foreign-language broadcasting is to be discouraged, they feel; and the predominance of the Hebrew language in Israel ought to remain unchallenged. Others feel quite the opposite. Precisely because Hebrew is triumphant – indeed, this revival of the language is probably one of Israel's most dramatic achievements – people ought not to be cut off from their connection with other cultures. That 20 per cent listen to programmes in Yiddish in spite of the fact that they understand the Hebrew language, simply means that they feel more comfortable and enjoy the connection with Yiddish language and culture. The size of the audiences for these programmes is nothing to belittle either: 10–20 per cent of the listening audience is extremely high, as radio ratings go.

Sizeable audiences listen to foreign stations, as well. While only 6 per cent say they listen 'a lot' to foreign broadcasts, as many as 16 per cent listen 'sometimes' to Arabic stations, 14 per cent listen to the BBC,

8 per cent listen to the Voice of America and 7 per cent to Radio Cyprus. A variety of European countries are also received. Listening to the BBC is concentrated among the well educated and reaches a peak among the young-and-educated. Arabic stations are heard by the less well educated. Among listeners to foreign stations, half listen to the news and to information programmes. These listeners are spread almost equally among all age-education groups. Half listen to light music, but these are concentrated among the young and among those, within each age group, who have had an elementary-school education, rather than among those with more or less education.

2. *Newspapers*

Even more than radio, newspapers are considered a tool for daily living – by citizens and by consumers. Eighty-five per cent read a newspaper though only about two-thirds read one daily. Not a small proportion read more than one daily paper: almost half of the readers read two or more. Television has not cut into the number of newspaper readers; in fact, they have increased, as Table 11.2 suggests. It may have reduced the amount of *time* spent reading newspapers, however. From a comparison of the time-budget data in Table 3.8, in fact, there appears to be a small decrease in the actual amount of time spent reading the newspaper. Both these findings – that more people read newspapers, but that slightly less time is spent doing so – are confirmed by an overall picture of newspaper-reading at each hour of the day in these two years as seen in Figure 11.1. Here, we find that evening newspaper-reading has gone down – making room for television, it seems – and that there has not been a concomitant increase during other hours of the day (as there had been in radio-listening). Thus, in brief, 7 per cent more respondents read a daily newspaper and yet slightly less time is spent in reading by the average person. While the rise in newspaper readership is probably unrelated to the effects of television-viewing, the decrease in time spent reading the newspaper may be more easily attributable to the emergence of an alternative leisure medium.

Despite the increased readership, the daily newspaper scene in Israel is strewn with dead or dying papers. The number of newspapers is decreasing; the 24 daily newspapers of 1967 were 20 in 1971, and are even fewer today.[7] The circulation of the two evening newspapers has risen steadily in this same period, so that the proportion who read only an evening newspaper (45 per cent) is almost three times as large as the proportion reading only a morning paper (17 per cent). One-quarter of all newspaper readers read both kinds.

Historically, most of the Hebrew morning newspapers were essentially party papers, in the sense that they were affiliated ideologically and

TABLE 11.2 *Newspaper Reading in Haifa, 1966 and 1970*
Per cent

	1966	1970
Daily	81	88
Several times per week	13	10
Only on Sabbath	5	1
Less frequently	1	0
TOTAL	100%	100%
N	(900)	(355)

FIGURE 11.1 *Percentage of Respondents Exposed to Newspapers,* Books,* Radio,* or Television* at each Hour of an Average Weekday (weighted; N = 1614)*

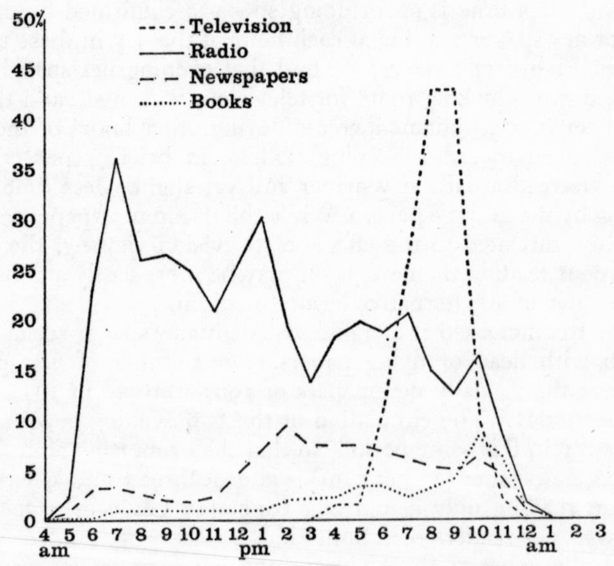

* As a primary or a secondary activity.

fiscally to a political party. There was nothing secret about this: they were the organs of the parties. The main exception was and is the independent *Ha'aretz*. About one-fifth of all newspaper-readers take it.[8] With the re-consolidation of the Labour Party and the realignment of most of the large and small splinters, *Davar* stands almost alone as Labour's newspaper, with about 10 per cent of the readership, though the left-wing, kibbutz-based *Al Hamishmar* has also survived. The religious groups, however, still support three different newspapers of their own, with a combined readership of less than 3 per cent of all readers, reflecting the kind of situation that once characterized the whole of the morning press in Israel. There are also a number of foreign language newspapers which have a combined readership of perhaps 15 per cent of all readers; most of these are also subsidized by Labour. Among these, *The Jerusalem Post* continues to play an important role as a source of news for foreign correspondents and for diplomats, tourists, English-speaking Arabs and others. There are also two papers in Hebrew – for beginners. Like the morning papers, the two evening papers are also national. There are no local dailies at all.

The two evening papers, *Maariv* and *Yediot Aharonot*, are tabloid in format, though rather serious in content. Well over half of the adult population see *Maariv* rather regularly and almost half see *Yediot*. Unlike the morning papers which are delivered to homes and sold on news-stands, enterprising newsboys (children and old men) of the evening papers seek out their customers on the streets, in shops and in offices. They are also sold on newsstands but are not delivered to homes. Properly speaking, they are not evening newspapers at all; they are not even afternoon papers. Their closing time is 8–9 a.m., and they are out on the street of Tel Aviv as early as 10–11 a.m. They are, in effect, late-morning newspapers. By contrast, the morning newspapers close just after midnight, and are not effectively available until their readers rise in the morning, somewhere between 6–7 o'clock.

Readers who take only morning papers are concentrated in the over-50 age group, while evening-only readers are strongly weighted by youth and middle-education (5–10 years of school). Our data also show that the readers who take both morning and afternoon papers are concentrated among the well educated and that the proportion of well educated increases with age. Considering the relevance of age and education, it is no surprise that Europeans (who are older and better educated) far exceed Israelis of Eastern origin in their readership of morning newspapers. Nevertheless, the greatest difference between the two ethnic groups is to be found in the first generation and among those with lesser education. First-generation Easterners prefer afternoon newspapers far more than their Western counterparts at the equivalent educational level. One wonders how many of the immigrants, and how many of their parents, were accustomed to reading a newspaper in their countries of origin; but we do not have such information, unfortunately.

Those who read only evening newspapers say that they do not read a morning paper because they have no time in the morning to read it; 6 in 10 give this as a reason. Other reasons offered were that the evening newspaper has the same news as the morning papers (16 per cent) and that the morning papers were too difficult (8 per cent).

In the face of all these difficulties, why do the morning papers continue to appear in the mornings? Why don't they come out in the 'evening' – which is, as we have noted, a euphemism for noon? The answer is bound up with tradition, of course, but it is also closely linked to the behaviour of the decision-making elites for whom the morning paper is a basis for action: the businessman, the civil servant, the Minister, all need briefing on what is going on, and feedback on what they have (or think they have) done. The editors and publishers of the morning newspapers are keenly aware of this, and some are even willing to lose money at it (not just in Israel). Their influence is tied, in no small measure, to the notion that they are somehow spokesmen for public opinion, or, at least, of the opinion of important sectors of the society. But the afternoon newspapers have overtaken them in this respect – at least as far as broadly based public opinion is concerned; the morning papers represent better-educated, more politically committed publics. Thus, the fate of the morning newspapers depends on whether they succeed in maintaining their hold on the better-educated sectors of the population, and whether they succeed in attracting young people to adopt their parents' habits as they grow older. Their key appeal, one suspects, is that they share with their readers the feeling of being closely involved in decision-making at high levels.

Support for the notion that morning newspapers are read by people who are more interested in politics comes from an analysis of the popularity of different departments of the paper. Thus, interest in politics, editorial opinion, economic affairs and related matters all increase with age as well as education – the identifying attributes of the readers of morning papers. Young people, especially the well educated, also find these topics interesting, but less often than their elders. For example, among those with elementary-school education, twice as many people over 50 say they find leading articles and commentators 'very interesting' as do those aged 18–29. Similarly, twice as many well-educated people over 50 find newspaper coverage of economic affairs 'very interesting' as compared with the youngest age group. Altogether, the youth – at any level of education – is far less interested in civic affairs than their elders.[9]

Matters which interest young people more than their elders are sports, stories about crime, satirical features and entertaining features, such as horoscopes, crossword puzzles and fashion. Young people are more interested in movie and television criticism, and in news of the world of entertainment; older persons are more interested in book reviews. Science and medicine interest the older and the better educated.

There are also pronounced differences in what men and women find 'very interesting' in the newspaper. Women are much more interested than men in the world of culture and the arts – mass media, film and theatre, literary supplements, light entertainment. They are more interested in medicine than men, a finding which we know from many other studies.[10] They are more interested in the horoscope. The men unsurprisingly are more interested in politics, sports and science. The division of interest between the sexes is still highly conventional in this society, except for security matters: everybody in Israel – regardless of age, education, sex or ethnicity – is 'very interested' in news of the national security.

The newspapers are not perceived by most readers as especially critical of the Government, nor do most readers think that they ought to be more critical. Thus, 6 in 10 persons say yes, the newspaper they read is generally supportive of Government policy; 30 per cent say sometimes yes and sometimes no; and only 3 per cent say that their newspaper generally 'objects' to Government policy.[11] Nine per cent, mostly unschooled readers, have no opinion. One wonders whether the newspaper editors would agree with this assessment.

Most readers do not feel that the press ought to pursue a more critical role. Only 4 in 10 say yes, and, interestingly, more young people feel this way than do older people. This is interesting, first, because young people are less likely to read the more political morning press; second, because they claim less interest in the political content of the paper; third, because they already consider the press less supportive of the Government than their elders.

This feeling, that the press is critical 'enough' and that the newspapers are performing creditably and credibly, is the product of long tri-cornered experience among Government, press and public. The problems of maintaining a reasonably free press in a country under siege are on constant view in Israel. Nor is the public – as we have seen – altogether sympathetic to the journalist's professional norm of trying to maximize the critical function of the press. Too much is at stake from the point of view of the national security, the public feels. And this feeling may be particularly true of old-timers who participated in the struggle for the establishment of a state – a struggle in which the Hebrew press played an integral and disciplined part.[12]

3. *Periodicals, Domestic and Imported*

Unlike the newspapers which seek to cover the widest possible range of interests, the periodical press is aimed at much more specialized audiences. There are no 'family' magazines, and no domestic news-magazines. Rather, there are a handful of women's magazines, movie magazines, magazines devoted to scandal in politics and sex and a handful of religious magazines, literary magazines, magazines of science and other professional fields.

Altogether, 53 per cent of the population see one or more of these, though only about one-third do so regularly. The most popular is the women's magazine, *La'isha*. Its readership is very widespread, with concentration among younger women. *Bamahane*, a weekly published by the Army, with strong emphasis on military affairs, is also very popular. Its coverage of economic and social problems and of the arts, and its human interest features, try to encompass the range of interests of young people and to attract other family members as well. More than the Army radio station, which is the sister-enterprise, *Bamahane* attracts attention from all age and education groups. The weekly *Ha'olam Haze*, whose swinging editor heads a one-seat parliamentary party, is also fairly popular. It has its own unique mix of news and gossip from the worlds of politics and entertainment together with a large dose of political and social criticism.

These two, *Bamahane* and *Ha'olam Haze*, for all of their differences in character, have in common an interest in politics and current affairs. This abiding interest – served primarily by the daily newspapers – is augmented not so much by the local periodical press, but by subscription to foreign news-magazines. The popularity in Israel of *Time*, *Newsweek*, *New Statesman*, *L'Express* and *Stern* is very high. About one-fifth of Israelis read an imported magazine with some regularity. Indeed, the popularity of these professionally produced periodicals as well as their competitive price may be part of the reason why no local publisher has attempted to compete. This, plus the short weekend plus the popular supplements to Friday's papers, may explain the dearth of a periodical press in Israel.[13]

We questioned the entire population, not just the readers themselves, about the reasons for the popularity of these overseas periodicals. Overwhelmingly, the public rejects the thesis that it has to do with inadequacies of the daily Hebrew press. Only small proportions think that foreign journals are read to compensate for inadequacies of the Israeli press. Nor does the public believe that periodicals from abroad are on a 'higher level' than the Israeli press. Rather, foreign periodicals are seen as complementary to, not competitive with, the Israeli press. The two predominant motives ascribed to their readers are that the

TABLE 11.3 *Reasons for Reading Imported Periodicals*

	Total (N = 100%)	Per cent who say reason is 'very important' Language of foreign periodical is easier	To know what people think about us in the world	Not enough world news in Israeli press
Non-readers	(399)	48	38	15
Readers	(1292)	42	50	21
TOTAL POPULATION	(1691)	47	41	27

	Total (N=100%)	To learn the language in which the periodical is written	To learn about the country in which periodical is printed	Foreign periodical is on higher level than Israeli newspapers	Not enough Israeli news in Israeli press	These subjects are discussed by my friends	In order to read stories about famous people	To be entertained	To get practical advice
Non-readers	(399)	21	17	10	10	9	10	9	8
Readers	(1292)	16	25	19	13	15	13	15	11
TOTAL POPULATION	(1691)	20	19	12	11	11	11	10	9

latter find them easier to read than Hebrew-language journals, and that they want to find out 'what people abroad are thinking about us'.

The readers themselves agree with these major motives. They agree that the language is easier for them, and – even more than the non-readers believe about them – they say that their major motive is to find out what others are thinking 'about us'. Readers, more than non-readers, assert that their imported journal is on a higher level than the local press and that they do learn more about what is going on abroad.

4. *Hobbies*

Unlike visiting or even television viewing, hobbies are solo activities, generally pursued by and for the individual. When hobbies are grouped together with reading, as they sometimes are, this is the justification: like books, hobbies are individual activities.[14] Even more than books, hobbies represent communities of interest which unite large numbers of individuals at least in the awareness that there are many others like themselves. Thus, stamp-collecting, or gardening, or raising a pet, or cooking all have well-developed commercial markets in which trading and pricing go on, and in which there may be considerable interaction and discussion among fellow-hobbyists. Of course, this is at the highly sophisticated and cosmopolitan scale of hobbying; most people who say that cooking is their hobby do no more than exchange recipes now and then, much in the way that book-readers exchange opinions about books or the books themselves. But this, too, represents a community of interest, and of connoisseurship.

Hobbies are pursued to a greater or lesser extent by about 6 in 10 Israelis. Having a hobby is linked to education: the more, the more. It is linked to age: the younger, the more. And hobbies are highly differentiated as to sex: handiwork, cooking and baking are women's hobbies, while collecting, sports, chess, raising pets are men's hobbies. Art and music, curiously, are claimed as hobbies somewhat more by men than by women.

The two most popular hobbies, by far, are handicrafts and the arts. The former – knitting, sewing, etc. – are particularly popular among younger and middle-aged women: it is the hobby of 22 per cent of the population, and of nearly half the women. It is obviously an extension of women's traditional domestic role, and it appears to be a case of learning 'to want to do what you have to do'.

The arts constitute the second most popular group of hobbies; 14 per cent of the population name them. Since the interview did not linger on this question, we cannot be certain that it does not also include music and art appreciation; our instruction to the interviewers was intended to limit this category only to those who were actively engaged in creativity in music, plastic arts, photography or writing. The fact that 23 per cent of the population own a musical instrument confirms the high interest in musical expression.

Six per cent of Israelis collect something; this is a rather smaller proportion than one would have thought, judging from the seemingly high interest in stamps and coins in the press and in the stores. Similarly surprising is that only 2 per cent have 'games' as their hobby, in a country where chess-fever is said to run very high. Slightly more people (3 per cent) raise pets or cook as a hobby. Collecting tends to be a hobby of the better educated; games are equally popular among each of the age-education groups; house pets are a little more popular among the elderly; and cooking is twice as popular among the uneducated as among the educated.

The whole question of hobbies is one that deserves further thought. While the data presented here are clearly inadequate, they do reinforce the image of the homespun character of Israeli society, and perhaps of a society which is artistically inclined. Other images are not reinforced at all: the image of the emancipated Israeli woman is surely not to be seen here; the image of the cerebral preoccupations, whose stereotyped representative is chess, is not much in evidence; the image of the outdoor, physically fit Israeli is only dimly in view. Instead, women are knitting; men are engaged in sports, games and collecting; and many more of both sexes than we supposed are involved with the arts.

NOTES – CHAPTER ELEVEN

1. *The Statistical Abstract of Israel* for 1972 gives the following distribution of viewing time for television viewers in the Jewish population of 14 years and over: 22 per cent up to 1 hour; 28 per cent 1–2 hours; 28 per cent 2–3 hours; 22 per cent 3+ hours.
2. 'Listening' here implies, of course, merely that the radio set was 'on', and not necessarily that the listener was actually listening attentively.
3. The number of day-time listening hours rose in Britain, too, after the introduction of television. See Brian Emmett in D. McQuail, op. cit.
4. From *Midlands Activities Survey*, London: ATV Network. Using a different method Emmett, op. cit., reports the viewing peak of 45 per cent at 8 p.m. on weekdays.
5. Cf. Emmett, ibid.
6. Our figure is considerably higher than the figure (about 11 per cent) of the Jewish population who listened to Channel A during the January–March 1972 survey period of the Central Bureau of Statistics. Cf. *Statistical Abstract of Israel 1972*, op. cit.

7. Including foreign-language newspapers printed in Israel.
8. Figures in this paragraph refer to estimated proportion of all readers of newspapers who read a given newspaper, regardless of what other papers they read and regardless of frequency of reading.
9. Again, one must conjecture as to whether this represents a social change which will grow up together with young people, or whether the youth will change as they grow older. We think the latter is more likely.
10. See Jacob J. Feldman, *The Dissemination of Health Information: A Case Study in Adult Learning*, Chicago: Aldine, 1966.
11. Readers of *Haaretz* are least likely (38 per cent) to say that their newspaper supports the Government unequivocally. *Davar* – the Labour newspaper – is at the other extreme (82 per cent). About 60 per cent of the readership of the two evening newspapers – which are politically independent – say that their paper usually supports the Government. *Jerusalem Post* readers see their newspaper as even more affirmative, while readers of the religious press and of the far-Left *Al Hamishmar* think otherwise, but less than *Haaretz* readers.
12. See Dina Goren, *Secrecy and the Right to Know*, London: Croom and Helm, (in Press).
13. For comparison with Britain, see the article by Winston Fletcher in J. Tunstall, ed., *Media Sociology*, London: Constable, 1970, pp. 83–6. The weekly periodical press is especially vigorous in England; women's magazines, in particular, have extraordinarily high readership. And the political weeklies, of course, are highly prestigious.
14. Associated Television's *Midlands' Activities Survey* lumps reading and knitting together in one category!

CHAPTER TWELVE The Oldest Medium: The Book

Reading and study were among the central values of traditional Jewish society. Indeed, it is impossible to explain the continuity of the Jewish people without reference to the unique status of the book. Any analysis of contemporary Israeli culture, therefore, must look to the fate of the book as it is affected by the weight of tradition and the temptations of modernity. This task is attempted here.

1. *The Place of the Book in Traditional Jewish Culture*

In traditional Jewish society, *the* Book refers, of course, to the Old Testament, that is, the Holy Scriptures and the body of rabbinic literature that was built upon it throughout the ages.[1] The Jews came to be called the 'People of the Book' by virtue of living according to the rules of *the* Book with which they were so preoccupied.

The commandment to devote time to study is indicative of this preoccupation. Jewish tradition did not leave leisure time – or, for that matter, any part of the rest of the round of life – to the discretion of the individual. As Katz points out, 'the ideal of studying Torah demanded the exclusive employment of one's time as a matter of principle: every free moment that remained after fulfilling religious obligations, making a living, and taking care of other essential needs, was to be devoted to the study of Torah.'[2] If only a minority could devote themselves entirely to the study of the Torah, anyone who lived in this society was aware of the normative requirement of setting time aside for study and of justifying time spent otherwise. The daily prayers include lessons from scripture and rabbinic writings in order further to inculcate habits of study and to strengthen the appreciation of books.

Two major social functions were fulfilled by the popular study of *the* Book. For one thing, this literature was the source of supreme authority concerning values and conduct. Its interpreters – the rabbis and the scholars – were at the apex of the system of social stratification.[3] Secondly, the continuous exposure – through perusal and study – to the ideas and images that are incorporated in this literature gave rise to a shared frame of reference, a shared set of symbolic experiences. Here is the key to the feeling of collective national identity which permeated the dispersed Jewish communities and which connected the present with the generations of the past.

The widespread literacy of Jewish society was unique, and differs from what occurred in other historical societies. In other societies literacy was limited to groups of the social elite, to the aristocracy or to the clergy.[4] (This was particularly the case in Catholic countries.) In traditional Jewish society, on the other hand, literacy was everyone's legacy. Some believe that this high degree of literacy among the Jews in the Middle Ages enabled them to fulfil specialized roles in European society, such as in commerce, and won for them the protection of the political authorities and, at times, even that of the Church.

If we accept McLuhan's assumption about the influence of print on personality, it is possible that precisely this preoccupation with study and reading have shaped a type of rational and disciplined personality that is particularly suited to modern urban society. The taboo on representation in the visual arts, in deference to the word, may have made it easier to think abstractly.

2. *The Secular Transformation of the Values of Reading and Study*

Two crises challenged the social and cultural order of traditional Jewish society, Hasidism and Haskalah (Enlightenment).[5] The expressionism of the one, and the rationalism of the other, affected the traditional concepts of study and of the book. Hasidism heightened the value of religious experience and by placing emphasis on charismatic leadership correspondingly diminished the value of disciplined self-study and the unmediated authority of the book. By contrast, the movement for Enlightenment (Haskalah) sought to open Jewish society to modernizing influences. In doing so, great importance was attributed to the values of study and reading, but the *meaning* of these activities was drastically changed.

The Haskalah marked the beginning of the secularization of the book. Study and reading became secular activities both from the point of view of their source of legitimacy and from the point of view of their content. Study is no longer founded in national-religious values but in individualistic ones which emphasize the development of the individual personality according to its particular inclinations. As a result, reading and study become either career-oriented activities or voluntary leisure activities rather than the normatively prescribed activity which was pursued 'for its own sake'. As for content, study and learning are no longer limited to a well-defined corpus of scriptural and rabbinic writings; on the contrary, emphasis is now placed on a wide range of secular subjects and on the reader's personal choice, according to his interests and inclinations. Obviously the shared frame of reference which arose from continuous exposure to the *same* sources, during the traditional era, is seriously threatened by these developments. The

People of *the* Book are beginning to be transformed into the people of books, or the people of reading.

This process of secularization, it is important to emphasize, does not mean that books and study became marginal values; on the contrary, they played a central role in the system of values of the Emancipation, and later, of the Zionist movement. Indeed, one of the fundamental assumptions of Zionist ideology was that the national revival of the Jewish people in the Land of Israel would encompass all areas of culture, including its traditional and modern elements, and that this cultural activity would encompass all groups of the population. The notion of 'spiritual centre' became one of the basic ideals for the Jewish state, in which the writing and reading of books would play a major role. In fact, in the period preceding the establishment of the State, the implementation of this ideal began to take form.[6] This was the period of the dramatic revival of Hebrew as a spoken language, of the establishment of institutions of science and art, of the founding of publishing houses and the undertaking of such literary enterprises as the translation of classic world literature into Hebrew. The underlying assumption in all of this was that the traditional values of reading and study would persist in the modern Jewish state, after undergoing secular transformation.

3. *The Value Attributed to Books, Reading and Study by Israelis*

A quarter of a century after the establishment of the State of Israel, and after the massive influx of Jewish immigrants from all over the world, we set out to examine the extent to which books, reading and study are significant both as valued concepts and as time-consuming behaviour.

We looked, first, at the salience of the concept 'People of the Book' for contemporary Israelis. As will be elaborated in the following chapter, respondents were asked to indicate the extent to which each of a series of national characteristics that has been attributed at various times to the Jewish people is descriptive of the 'people of Israel' today.[7] A substantial proportion (72 per cent) of the population affirmed that 'People of the Book' is still a central national characteristic. It is important to note, however, that younger people and better-educated people consider this characterization less appropriate than do older and less well-educated persons. Nor is it near the top of the list of characteristics, despite the high proportion of people endorsing it.

Our inference that the attitude to books is a central one in Israel rests not only on the fact that 7 in 10 Israelis say so, but on the fact that it is as highly correlated with religious values as with ethical-humanistic ones. As we shall see in Chapter Fourteen, orthodox observance and belief form one cluster of national characteristics while values associated with social justice form another. Subscribers to both clusters are equally likely to affirm that 'People of the Book' describes the people of Israel today. The representation of the interrelations among these values which appears as Figure 14.1 in Chapter 14 graphically demonstrates the 'centrality' of this concept standing, as it does, midway between a set of religious characteristics and a set of secular humanistic ideals.

The notion of 'spiritual centre' also finds expression in the interviews. When people are asked whether cultural and educational activity in Israel should be more intensive than in other countries, 70 per cent answer affirmatively. Here there are no differences among the generations or among different educational groups; nor are there differences among groups of different ethnic origin. The desire for Israeli superiority in this field, however, may be a component of the religious mission-consciousness: the more religious the person (the factor of education remaining constant), the more he tends to express his desire for Israeli leadership in this field.

Further evidence of the value attributed to reading is evident in the replies to the question: 'If there were another day of rest, what thing(s) would you like to do?' As reported in Chapter Four, most people say they would spend the extra time with the family, going on excursions, just resting, or arranging the house. But among all of the media and the arts, whether at home or outside, reading is easily the most attractive. Fifteen per cent say they would read books if they had this extra time; this contrasts with those naming theatre (6 per cent), newspaper-reading (4 per cent), television (2 per cent) and radio (1 per cent).[8]

Supply as well as demand underlines the continuing importance of books. In Escarpit's analysis of UNESCO figures for 1962, Israel stands first in number of books (different titles) published *per capita*. Recomputing the UNESCO data for 1968 in the same way, we found that Israel has slipped behind Switzerland (just barely) and Denmark, but still stands among the highest in the world, as Table 12.1 reveals. It should be noted, however, that this is, at least in part, a function of the degree of cultural heterogeneity of different societies. Escarpit,[9] for example, argues that the greater the cultural heterogeneity, the greater the need for publishing a larger number of titles, in order to cater to a wider spectrum of tastes, interests and even language preferences.

The data indicate that study, too, is highly valued. A majority of the population says that 'to study and advance myself' is 'important'. Eleven per cent say they would study if they had an extra day. Moreover, a large proportion of the population indicated interest in the possibility of formal study – not necessarily toward a degree – by means of radio and television, even if that required the substitution of some instructional programming for general programming during peak viewing hours. This will be detailed below.

On the whole, it appears that the values of the book, reading and study are still central to the Jewish community in Israel. There is evidence that the secular transformation of these traditional values actually 'took'.

TABLE 12.1 *Ranking of Selected Nations by Books Published* Per Capita*

	Number of titles published	Population in thousands	Number of titles per million population
Denmark	4972	4870	1243
Switzerland	6228	6147	1038
Israel	3075	3000	1025
Holland	11174	12743	859
Czechoslovakia	8103	14362	578
Great Britain	31372	55283	570
Belgium	4843	9619	538
France	18646	49920	373
USSR	75723	237808	318
Japan	31086	101090	311
Poland	9361	32207	292
Lebanon	543	2580	272
United States	59247	201152	246
Italy	8868	52750	171
Iraq	473	8634	59
Algeria (1967)	258	12540	22

* Based on UNESCO *Statistical Yearbook*, 1969. Book production by U.D.C. classes (number of titles), p. 529 and population area-density, 1968, p. 15. Israeli data are from a supplement to *Monthly Bulletin*, Nos. 2 and 4, April 1970, of Israel's Central Bureau of Statistics, and population estimates on p. 15 and p. 20 of the Israel *Statistical Yearbook*, 1969.

4. *Patterns of Reading and Study*

Even if the potential is there, the questions remain as to how much of it is expressed in actual behaviour and what is the extent of reading and study.

The most general finding in the field of reading behaviour is that in Israel there is a high degree of 'literacy' – in the sense of actual reading – as compared with various European countries.[10] More than three-quarters of the Israeli population reads books[11] and 65 per cent of the entire population reports that it reads the Bible at least occasionally.

Although the amount of reading varies among the readers from one book a year to more than fifty books a year, it is important to emphasize that 77 per cent of the entire population read at least one book in the last year, and that this is a high percentage in comparison to Western European countries. The percentage of 'active' readers – those who read at least eight books during the last year – is also higher in Israel than in those countries.

TABLE 12.2 *Readers of Books and Readers of More than Eight Books a Year – in Israel and in European Countries**

	Readers of at least one book in the last year (*Per cent of total population*)	Readers of eight books or more a year	
		(*Per cent of total population*)	(*Per cent among all readers*)
Israel	77	42	55
France	56	33	59
England	63	39	61
Italy	24	9	38
West Germany	52	17	32
Switzerland	69	23	33
Austria	54	14	26
Denmark	67	39	58
Holland	66	35	53
Belgium	42	21	49
Portugal	28	15	53

* *Survey of Europe Today*, London: Reader's Digest Association, 1970, pp. 120–1, is the source used for all countries except Israel. It is based on national sample surveys rather similar in method to ours.

As for Eastern Europe, we only have partial data, but there is some evidence to indicate that the urban population of the Soviet Union devotes more time to reading than the parallel population in other countries. The comparative data on 'time budgets' (see Chapter Three, p. 50) shows Israel second only to Russia (42 minutes and 48 minutes respectively) in the amount of time devoted daily to reading of books and newspapers.

However, we should not indulge in overly optimistic evaluations. Comparison of the reading publics in different countries shows that the proportion of 'active readers' *expressed as a percentage of all readers of books* is lower in Israel than in France, Denmark and England. A comparison with data of studies carried out in the United States also shows that the habits of the reading public in Israel and the United States are very similar.[12]

It seems, then, that although Israel has more people who sometimes read, the amount of 'active' reading is not remarkable. The rate of 'active readers' among the readers is not much different from that of other countries, and in some cases it is even lower. Thus, what is noteworthy in Israel is the living evidence of the tradition of Jewish literacy, even in the lowest classes. But the implicit potential is not expressed in a more active readership than is to be found in certain of the countries of Western Europe.[13]

Almost all homes have books – only 4 per cent have not – but these home libraries are not especially large. Two-thirds of homes have less than 100 books, and the modal home (30 per cent) contains between 10 and 50 books. About one in five homes have over 200 books. Still, by comparison with similar statistics from Dumazedier's study of a French town, it appears that Israelis have many more books in their homes.[14]

We inquired specifically about the presence of certain books. Ninety-three per cent of all homes own the Bible, and over 8 in 10 have a prayer book. Three in four have a picture album on the Six Day War, a subject to which we shall return in this chapter. Surprisingly high proportions (almost half the population) own a book of the Talmud, a copy of the *Book of Aggadah* by Bialik and Ravnitski, or an album devoted to art.[15]

5. *Who Reads?*

These data are all based on self-estimates, of course, but there is good reason to believe that estimates of this kind are reliable. We can even 'prove' it. In the present study, we asked two different questions, the answers to which could be checked against each other. One question asked: 'About how many books do you read in a year?' and the respondent was asked to choose among pre-coded categories: 1–5, 6–10, etc., up to 50+. The other question was: 'How long is it since you finished reading the book you read last?' and the respondent could answer 'this week', 'this month', etc. The two questions are totally independent of each other – and it is unlikely that respondents made the effort, even if they were able, to be consistent. Yet, the fact is that the distribution of the two sets of replies are consistent with each other. Thus, given the distribution of number of books read in a year, it is possible to calculate the probability of completing a book 'this week' and the results compare very favourably with the 37 per cent who said they finished reading one 'this week'. And so on. Moreover, American research on the validity of self-estimates of reading books reports that mis-estimates, when they occur, err on the side of modesty, and thus that the fear of exaggerated self-reports is misplaced.[16]

As in other countries, formal education is the most decisive factor in determining the reading habits of individuals. Age is all but irrelevant as a determining factor. In this last, Israel differs from the United States which shows a decreasing rate of readership with increasing age; this decline is particularly marked among those of middle or low education levels and beginning with age 35.

TABLE 12.3 *Reading Books by Age and Education*
Per cent

	Total (N = 100%)	1–5 Books	6–10 Books	11–20 Books	21–50 Books	50+ Books	
Age 18–29							
0–4 years education	(17)	(58)	(6)	(24)	(6)	(6)	100%
5–10 years education	(308)	42	20	17	12	9	100%
11+ years education	(531)	17	16	24	25	18	100%
Age 30–50							
0–4 years education	(82)	78	12	6	4	–	100%
5–10 years education	(513)	46	23	13	11	7	100%
11+ years education	(501)	22	17	27	21	13	100%
Age 50+							
0–4 years education	(58)	57	24	14	3	2	100%
5–10 years education	(376)	43	22	15	14	6	100%
11+ years education	(394)	19	21	25	19	16	100%
TOTAL POPULATION	(2780)	33	19	19	17	12	100%

That reading in Israel does not decline with age may well be further evidence of the vitality of the Jewish tradition of literacy. If so, we thought this might register in a comparison of the reading habits of the observant and the non-observant. But no such difference is apparent. (Indeed, there is even a drop in the number of books read by the well-educated-and-religious group, suggesting that this group may not treat the study of religious texts as reading. As we shall see below, this group has the highest proportion engaged in study.) It is likely that book-reading is a heritage which has been evenly spread throughout the nation in its secularized form.

Further evidence of both the heritage and its secular transformation is implicit in two further facts. Holding education constant, there is no ethnic difference in reading habits. Unlike attendance at the theatre or at concerts – with which book-reading is correlated and which reflect strong differences among Israelis from different countries of origin – reading is not affected by ethnicity. For example, among those with 9–10 years of schooling, 40 per cent of readers read a book per month or more. This is equally true of immigrants from the East (37 per cent) as from the West (44 per cent) and of their children (40 per cent and 38 per cent respectively).

Ostensibly, the tradition also appears to explain the fact that there are proportionately more women than men – although the difference is small – who do not read at all. However, if this is the traditional fact, the secular one is that *among readers* women read more than men. This is true at every age level except the busy-mother years of 25–34 when the reading rate for women equals that of men. As we shall see below, women exceed men particularly in the reading of fiction.

6. *Other Factors Associated with Reading*

Apart from educational level, however, none of the other factors – ethnicity, religiosity, even age and sex – makes much difference in the rate of reading. Nonetheless, we tried to go deeper to see whether variation in reading habits might be associated with factors such as childhood socialization, crowded living conditions and other patterns of spending leisure.

It is often alleged that the socialization of children affects their habits of study and reading, and that these habits carry over into adulthood. As an elementary test of parental influence, we asked all of our respondent readers whether their parents customarily read books. Half said that both their parents were accustomed readers; about a quarter said that neither were; and another quarter said only one parent read (18 per cent just father, 6 per cent just mother). Thus, quite a substantial proportion of today's readers say that one or both of their parents were not regular readers.[17]

There is a clear relationship between parental reading habits and those of their children, our respondents. Regardless of the educational level of the respondent, his reading habits were moulded, in part, by his parents' example. Table 12.4 shows this. Among those with 5–10 years of schooling, for example, there is a small but steady increase in the proportion of 'active readers' as one moves from respondents neither of whose parents were accustomed to reading to those who come from reading families. And the same sort of influence is apparent among the better-educated group. It is also an interesting example of how informal tradition and formal education go hand in hand.

As a second environmental measure – equally applicable to contemporary conditions as to the period of socialization – we correlated the rate of reading with the density of living conditions in respondents' homes. It has often been said that privacy and quiet are prerequisite physical conditions for reading, and that crowding militates against it. Our data do not support this assertion, however.

TABLE 12.4 *Reading Books by Parental Reading Habits*

	Per cent of readers who read at least one book per month			
	Neither parent customarily read books	One parent customarily read books: Just father	One parent customarily read books: Just mother	Both parents customarily read books
5–10 years education	29	30	35	39
11+ years education	49	52	56	67

Similarly, size of city makes no difference in the rate of reading. After education is held constant, city size has virtually no influence except, again, for a glimmer of a difference favouring kibbutzim and small, established cities.

Does television make a difference? Many people, including the respondents, think so. Almost half of the daily viewers say that they read less since television came. And the number is proportionately smaller for the less frequent viewers and for the non-owners of sets. But despite this widespread belief, the behavioural data – also based on the self-reports of the same respondents – fail to reveal any significant difference between owners and non-owners or between those who view frequently or infrequently. If there may be said to be any trend at all it moves in opposite directions at different educational levels: among those with 5–10 years of formal education frequent viewers read more, following the principle of 'the more, the more'; among the best-educated group, the most frequent viewers apparently read slightly less.[18]

Reading (it will also be recalled from Figure 9.1) is associated with theatre, concert and museum and with others of the 'serious' activities both in and out of the home.[19] At each educational level, there is a strong relationship to study. Ostensibly, this relationship appears to underline the traditional connection, but that is only part of it. As we shall see, the activities of reading and study both have secular as well as sacred aspects: they serve careers instrumentally; they serve the individual affectively; and they serve God and the Jewish people. The two are interconnected in all three ways.

7. *What Books?*

Respondents were asked to give us full particulars on the last book that they read. We successfully identified 600 different titles, showing, from the start, what a diversified activity modern reading is.[20]

We asked first about language: 'What was the language of the last book you read?' Seven in ten respondents told us that the last book they read was written in Hebrew! The success of the Hebrew language in Israel – in a nation of mostly first- and second-generation immigrants – is remarkable. Only 100 years ago, Hebrew was used almost exclusively for rabbinic writings.

Seven per cent read a book which was written in English and 5 per cent read their last book in French. One to three per cent read in German, Rumanian, Yiddish, Russian, Polish, Spanish, etc. About 1 per cent read a book in Arabic. Readers of non-Hebrew books are older, of course, and reading in Hebrew is strongly related to age. Only English and French survive into the second generation, and only the well educated read in these languages. Yiddish, German, Russian, Polish – what must have been the mother tongue of the parents of the 18–29-year-olds – are not read at all by the young.

Although most reading is in Hebrew, the books most frequently read are translations into Hebrew. The reading of books originally written in Hebrew is much less frequent than the reading of translations. Ironically, the translations are from the very languages that 'might have been' the mother tongues of the Hebrew readers.

Half the books read were categorized by their readers as fiction. Large proportions (15 per cent each) classified their last books as reportage (current affairs) or serious non-fiction (history, biography, etc.). Much smaller proportions (about 5 per cent each) read in Judaica, crime and detective or vocational categories. Non-fiction and Judaica are specialities of older people; vocational literature interests the well educated; detective and crime are liked by the middle-educated young. But the two major categories of fiction and reportage are virtually invariant with education or age.

A rough classification of the 600 titles indicates – with no presumption of statistical precision – that the books being read in Israel in the spring of 1970 fell into four general categories: one category had to do with Jewish and Israeli subjects such as the Six Day War or the Holocaust; a second category were international best sellers then current such as Solzhenitsyn or Philip Roth; late nineteenth-century and early twentieth-century classics constitute the third category with Tolstoy, Victor Hugo, Dumas, Balzac, A. J. Cronin and Garcia Lorca; while the fourth category comprises a mixed bag of best sellers of the last fifty years such as Hemingway, Pearl Buck, Ayn Rand, Alistair MacLean, Kazantzakis, Harold Robbins and others.

Fewer respondents mentioned modern writers such as Bellow, Sartre, Nabokov, Camus, and the detective writer, Erle Stanley Gardner. And, interestingly, as has happened everywhere else in the world, *The Forsyte Saga* – which had been recently shown on television – was singled out for mention by a number of respondents.

Altogether, though, it must be remembered that most books were mentioned by one person only. Only very few books were mentioned more than once.

We paid particular attention to the books which were originally written in Hebrew. Among them, there were two distinct best sellers: 28 persons named Tevet's *Hasufim Batsariah* (published in English as *The Tanks of Tamuz*) as the last book they had read.[21] Almost an equal number named the biography of the Israeli espionage agent, *Eli Cohen: Our Man in Damascus* by Eli Ben-Hanan. About ten other works by Israeli authors were mentioned by 4–7 readers. About a dozen people named assorted works by Agnon, Israel's Nobel Prize winner. Altogether there were 200 original Hebrew titles named by 300 readers among the 600 titles.

From a comparison of readership figures for some of these books with publishers' sales we estimate an average of 5 readers for each copy. This is a high ratio of readers-per-copy.[22]

Indeed, asked where they obtained the book they read last, one-third said they bought it, one-third said they borrowed it from friends and a fifth borrowed it from a library. About 1 in 10 received it as a present. This suggests that the 5-per-copy ratio which applies to Israeli authors is lower for other categories. For the original Hebrew books, we also are able to infer what seems commonsensical, that the proportion of buyers is inversely related to price while the proportion of borrowers is positively related: a word to the wise publisher.

Israelis are not frequent users of libraries, however. This is probably due as much to lack of habit as to the failure, thus far, to develop a nationwide public library system. Israelis know the location of the public library: 8 in 10 respondents were able to identify one nearby. But only 10 per cent of the adult population (16 per cent of readers) are registered with a public library, a figure which falls far below that of Britain (25–30 per cent) or the United States (25 per cent).[23] Interestingly the rate of enrolment in public libraries is much higher in smaller places, and particularly in rural areas and in new towns. The kibbutzim, as usual, surpass everybody else in this respect. But the importance of the public library in the new town – particularly to its better-educated citizens – is very marked in these data.

8. *Functions of the Book for Self and Society*

As has been emphasized, one aspect of the traditional idea of the 'People of the Book' implies the exposure of an entire nation to an identical system of ideas and symbols. The image and values of the nation have been shaped by means of this common exposure, as well as its way of comprehending the world that surrounds it. Here lies the importance of *the* Book and of the exegetic literature as a source and focus of national identity that unified it in its geographical dispersion throughout history. On the other hand, the meaning of the secular concept of the 'People of the Book' as a nation that studies and reads books is entirely different from, even contradictory to, the traditional concept. Not only is reading, in the secular sense, an individual activity which physically isolates the person from his social environment; it also neutralizes his exposure to any system of identical symbols and ideas, since the variety of ideas to which the book-reading public exposes itself is far larger than any variety of ideas offered by any other mass medium. The number of different books mentioned by respondents as the book last read is immense, and the book mentioned most frequently as 'the book read last' was mentioned by only 28 respondents, even though, as has been noted, this particular book stood out as a 'best seller' at the time of the study.

Beyond the fleeting and occasional 'best seller', which does create a common experience for a large sector of the public, it occurred to us that there exists in Israel a phenomenon which creates 'best sellers' of entire subjects, and thereby creates a literary experience common to the entire nation. Indeed, the findings of our study do show that books dealing with the Holocaust or the Six Day War were read by large parts of the population and, unlike books on most other subjects, are not limited to particular social groups. In other words, while the better educated are more likely to read serious books than the less well educated this difference is far less in evidence with respect to books about the Holocaust and the Six Day War. This finding was already anticipated where we noted the popularity of books on Israeli and Jewish subjects and where we noted the egalitarian distribution in the reading of reportage: reportage on Jewish and Israeli subjects refers, essentially, to the Holocaust and the War. Fully two-thirds of readers (about 50 per cent of the population) have read at least one book on the War and one book on the Holocaust.

Asked to specify the functions of reading about the Six Day War, most readers mention its role as a reinforcer of beliefs in the moral and physical superiority of the Israelis over their enemies. Others said it made the strategy of the War clear to them while still others said that it reminded them that the War's end was still a long way off. Minorities said that it reminded them of their personal experiences in the War (22 per cent) or that it strengthened their antipathy toward the Arabs (15 per cent).

Asked to specify the functions of reading about the Holocaust, 7 in 10 readers said that they read such books because 'we must not allow ourselves to forget what the Germans did'. Large groups of readers say that they read such books because they are still trying to understand how it happened, how human beings could have acted that way. A third of the readers say that these books give them the feeling that the danger of a holocaust is still current. The only important difference among the subgroups of readers relates to the obligation 'not to forget': more older people (8 in 10 of those over 50+) say this than younger people (6 in 10 of those under 29).

The collective function served by this literature is very evident. It serves as a basis of identification with the 'collective memory' of the people. It gives its readers a sense both of solidarity and security. It reinforces the need for continued alertness.

Another collective function served by book-reading is 'to strengthen ties with Jewish tradition'. Compared with the other media – television, radio, newspapers and cinema – the book is said to be the most important source for fulfilling this need.

However, while the book still retains some of its traditional functions as an instrument of national solidarity, analysis of the entire list of functions assigned to the book and to the other media confirms that, for most readers most of the time, the book is more closely associated with self than with collectivity.[24] For most of the population, the book fulfils personal cognitive needs. Thus, reading is associated with self-knowledge and self-realization, as well as with personal escapist needs; two-thirds of the reading public, for example, say that books help them overcome feelings of loneliness. For half of the reading public, the book supplies aesthetic pleasure, a concept which is certainly not in the traditional spirit. Books rank ahead of the other media as the medium which helps man most to 'know himself'.

The more detailed analysis in the following chapter will make clear that the primary functions attributed to the book have to do with self: self-improvement, self-knowledge, self-gratification. While some of this has an instrumental emphasis in the sense of preparing oneself to meet society, it is altogether different from the functions performed by television, radio and newspapers in *connecting* individuals to state and society.

9. *An Addendum on Adult Education*

As has been shown at several points, reading and study are closely connected in the minds of Israelis. It is a very far cry from the combination reading-knitting which appears in a recent marketing report by an English television research service.[25]

Nevertheless, like reading, study has also undergone a process of individualization and secularization. We have seen that about 30 per cent of Israelis are engaged in some form of adult education. But we must emphasize that this term includes courses in languages, in ceramics, and sewing – as well as more academic or traditional concerns. Those now studying consist of about 10 per cent of the least educated (0–4 years of schooling), about 15–20 per cent of the middle group (5–10 years) and about half of the best-educated group (11+). The latter is the only group that shows a decline with age – from 53 per cent at age 18–29 to 38 per cent in the over-50 group. This is because the group of young-and-well-educated includes those who are still students at institutions of higher learning.[26] But the interesting thing is that, overall, adult education does not decline with age, exactly as we saw in the case of reading. Nor is it associated with ethnic origin.

Altogether, about 40 per cent of those studying are doing so on their own. Eight per cent have a teacher; 3 per cent study by correspondence and 2 per cent with the help of radio or records. The other half of those studying do so within the framework of a formal institution. Most persons (70 per cent) who are actively studying do so several times per week.

Unlike the data on reading, however, the influence of religiosity is strongly evident in adult education. At each level of education, religious persons are more likely to be engaged in study than non-religious ones. At the lowest level of education, this difference is particularly marked. The rate of study among the low educated and observant is 3–4 times that of the non-observant of equal education.

If 'supply' were the determining factor, the cities would have the highest rate of participation in adult education: institutions, teachers, access are all presumably more characteristic of the densely populated large cities. On the whole, this is true. Studying is most frequent in the large cities where studying *privately* is least frequent. But the cities are surpassed by the kibbutzim where both the proportion engaged in some form of study and the proportion doing this themselves are high.

About half of those engaged in any form of adult education are studying something connected with their profession or occupation. The emphasis is on training and retraining for work. About one-fifth of those studying are learning languages. While this represents only 6 per cent (4 per cent if Hebrew is removed) of the total adult population, relatively it is a popular pursuit. Some of this has instrumental uses; some of it is for its 'own sake'. But it is a noteworthy phenomenon inasmuch as diversity of language skills, one of the great natural resources of the first generations in Israel, is rapidly disappearing from the second. We have seen already how overweaning is the success of the Hebrew language and here we see people making an effort to recapture something of their linguistic birthright.

About 15 per cent of those studying (4 per cent of the total population) are studying traditional subject matter, such as the Bible, the Mishna and the Talmud. It is in the older age group, especially those over 50, when instrumental pursuits lose ground and learning for pleasure and 'for its own sake' assumes greater importance. As one might expect, it is the traditional groups in the population which account for a large proportion of this particular form of spending leisure.

Yet, the commitment to study 'for its own sake' – the traditional preoccupation of the Jews – is still close to the surface. Inspired by the possibility of some sort of an Open University in Israel, we asked the following question: 'There is a proposal to broadcast studies of various kinds on television, providing that viewers are willing to prepare for these courses and to take examinations. Would you be interested in these studies? For what purpose?' The table (Table 12.5) shows that 51 per cent answered affirmatively. More important, perhaps, is that almost as many said they would be willing to go out of their homes if some nearby institution could offer them similar opportunity; indeed, it is the combination of broadcasting, correspondence and formal meetings which probably makes most sense in a small country like Israel. But even more important is that most people said that their chief interest in this kind of enterprise is not vocational and not for a degree but rather in study 'for its own sake'. There is good reason to believe, in fact, that adult education has a real chance in Israel. Inasmuch as it is a major link with the heart of Jewish tradition, albeit in secular form, and given the approaching five-day work week, the proposed expansion of community colleges and the proposed introduction of a second television channel, the time for planning in this field is surely now. But the planners would do well to note – both for the sake of the public and for the potential contribution to the continuity of the core of Jewish tradition – that the demand is *not* for vocational training. Nor, in our opinion, should study be as lonely a pursuit in Israel as the picture of an individual, his correspondence kit and his television set conjures up. Israel is too small, and too social, for that.[27]

10. *Summary*

This chapter has attempted to examine the place of the book in contemporary Israeli culture in the light of its central role in traditional Jewish culture. Certain clear-cut continuities are pointed out: proportionately more Israelis read at least one book more last year than did the people of Western European nations; the values of study and reading

TABLE 12.5 *Stated Purposes of Study via Broadcasting and Correspondence, by Age and Education**

Per cent

	Total (N=100%)	Training in trade	In-service training	Matriculation exams	B.A.	General studies (no exams)	Not interested	No opinion	
Age 18–29									
0–4 years education	(44)	15	–	–	–	25	55	5	100%
5–10 years education	(381)	25	5	4	1	29	30	6	100%
11+ years education	(552)	15	7	7	6	28	33	4	100%
Age 30–50									
0–4 years education	(268)	16	–	–	–	19	41	24	100%
5–10 years education	(683)	22	5	3	–	29	33	8	100%
11+ years education	(524)	15	6	3	5	34	33	4	100%
Age 50+									
0–4 years education	(204)	7	–	–	–	10	53	30	100%
5–10 years education	(524)	8	2	–	1	20	53	16	100%
11+ years education	(422)	14	1	1	3	28	47	6	100%
TOTAL POPULATION	(3602)	16	4	3	2	26	39	10	100%

* This was the question: 'There is a proposal to broadcast studies of various kinds on television providing that viewers are willing to prepare for these courses and to take examinations. Would you be interested in these studies? For what purpose?'

are highly regarded; the designation, 'People of the Book', is considered still applicable by large numbers of the population; the book is considered an important connection to Jewish tradition; the literature of the Holocaust and the Six Day War – two traumatic events in contemporary Jewish life – is very widely read and serves the purpose of fostering national solidarity and a feeling of collective identity and purpose, much as *the* Book used to do.

Many of these examples of continuity also show how the functions of the book and of study have undergone a process of secular transformation. The book is still important but some of its central functions have changed. Of these changes, the most significant, probably, is the fact that reading has become an individualizing rather than a collective experience, and the 'People of the Book' has become the people of books or the people of reading. The functions of the book as a source of supreme authority, as a giver of status and as a source of shared metaphors through which to understand the world have markedly declined. Paradoxical as it may sound, the simultaneous exposure of the entire population to a television programme may be more similar to the traditional function of the book as a source of integration and a provider of shared symbols than is the present-day reading of books by individuals, each sitting in his own corner.

Study has also become privatized, vocational and oriented to self-development whereas, in an earlier day, it was much more a group activity which ensured the continuity of a culture, a spiritual equivalent of patrolling the borders today.

Our findings suggest that it is highly unlikely that television will replace the book or pre-empt its social and psychological functions. As the level of education rises, in Israel and elsewhere, books will assume an increasingly important place in satisfying needs of self-realization.

Whether books and study will continue to symbolize something uniquely Jewish, and what share books and study will have in the shaping of the national character, still remains to be seen.

NOTES – CHAPTER TWELVE

1. By traditional Jewish society we refer here to that type of society which, according to Jacob Katz's definition, 'regards its existence as based upon a common body of knowledge and values handed down from the past'. From the historical point of view this is 'the whole of world Jewry, at least from the talmudic era (200 C.E.) up to the age of European Emancipation'. Despite the geographical dispersion of different parts of the

society, J. Katz emphasizes the social unity of the Jewish population based upon 'A common religion, nationhood and messianic hope'. In Jacob Katz, op. cit., pp. 3, 7.

2. Ibid., p. 162.
3. An analysis of the special characteristics of the Scholar of the Law is found in Ernst Simon's article 'Tomorrow's Jew in the Making, New Forces Reshape a Centuries Old Ideal', *Commentary*, Vol. 6, July 1948.
4. On the processes of spreading literacy see C. M. Cipolla, *Literacy and Development in the West*, Harmondsworth: Penguin, 1969.
5. Jacob Katz's analysis, on which these thoughts are based, refers to Max Weber's assertion that religious charisma and rationalism are the two crises that befall the institutions of traditional society. Hasidism was, in large measure, a populist reaction against the aristocracy of the learned; Haskalah was a reaction against the inhospitality of traditional Jewish society to secular culture.
6. S. N. Eisenstadt, *Israeli Society*, op. cit., pp. 368–71.
7. We intentionally preferred the more ambiguous 'people of Israel' (*am yisrael*) to the 'Jewish people'.
8. Based on replies to questions about primary and second activity. See Chapter Four for details.
9. See Robert Escarpit, *The Book Revolution*, Paris: UNESCO, 1966.
10. This operational definition of literacy makes no pretence at conceptual precision. It refers simply to persons who reported themselves as readers of at least one book per year.
11. We accepted the respondents' subjective definition of a book. Examination of the titles given us by respondents in answer to the question concerning the last book they read confirms that the subjective definition is not far different from the following accepted definition: 'A book is a non-periodical printed publication of at least 49 pages, exclusive of the cover pages', from *Recommendation Concerning the International Standardization of Statistics Relating to Book Production and Periodicals*, Paris: UNESCO, 1964.
12. Comparing our data with those from an NORC survey of number of books read per year by American readers yields the following table:

US (1962) Number of books	Per cent	Israel (1970) Number of books	Per cent
1–4	37	1–5	33
5–14	36	6–10	19
15–49	16	11–49	37
50+	11	50+	12
	100%		100%
	(N = 2845)		(N = 2782)

A cautious interpretation would be that the rate of reading, *among readers*, does not differ substantially between the two countries; if there is a difference, it somewhat favours Israel. For the American data, see Philip H. Ennis, *Adult Book Reading in the United States*, University of Chicago: National Opinion Research Centre, 1965.

13. See the comparative data in *Survey of Europe Today*, op. cit.
14. Joffre Dumazedier, op. cit. In Annecy, a town of 41,000, two-thirds of homes had books. The comparable figure in Israel is 95 per cent.
15. We surmise that in asserting that they owned a Talmud, many respondents might have had individual volumes of the Talmud in mind, rather than the complete set. Certain books of the Talmud are taught in the general schools, and textbook editions are purchased. Moreover, several large book campaigns, one of them sponsored by one of the evening newspapers, have made the entire set of the Talmud available in attractive and reasonably priced editions.
16. Ennis, op. cit., pp. 40–1.
17. Note here again that we are distinguishing between literacy – being able to read – and 'literacy' in the sense of actual reading. The question at hand is concerned with the habit of reading.
18. See Chapter Seven.
19. For the least educated group, where active readers are concentrated among young people (see Table 12.3), reading is also associated with youthful activity such as popular music. But the young-and-uneducated make up very few persons.
20. Some 1,100 of the 1,500 respondents volunteered information on the last book – the language, the author, the title, etc. The 600 identifiable titles were mentioned by some 900 respondents.
21. We know from another question in the study that 36 per cent of the population had read the book.
22. Robert Escarpit in the *Book Revolution*, op. cit., estimates from studies carried out in a number of countries that 3·5 is the average number of readers per copy for books.
23. In Israel, 55 per cent of those enrolled are regular borrowers, exchanging books at the rate of once a month or more.
24. The following chapter is a detailed discussion of the social and psychological functions of the different media.
25. As noted above. From ATV Networks Limited, *Midlands Activities Survey*, op. cit.
26. Twenty-seven per cent of the 18–29 age group are studying at such institutions. A fair proportion (16 per cent) are 'still' university students at age 30–50.
27. It is unfortunate that we did not think to explore the frequency, functions and attractiveness of group study. Thus, many of those who reported studying on their own – especially those engaged in religious study – may well be studying with groups of peers.

PART FIVE VALUES, CULTURE AND COMMUNICATION

CHAPTER THIRTEEN The Functions of the Mass Media: Connections to Self and Society

This chapter, continuing the last, sets out to do three things. First of all, it attempts to catalogue the needs or values which Israelis consider important. This list of needs is not meant to be representative either of all human needs or of all Israeli needs, but is biased, rather, in the direction of those needs which have been said to be served by the media of mass communications.

Having established which needs are deemed important, and by whom, we go on to assess the relative contribution of the several media to the satisfaction of each of these needs. We do this, admittedly, on the say-so of the respondents themselves, and thus are obviously going to have to mix respondents' images of the functions of the media together with reports of their actual use of them. The media in question are books, radio, television, newspapers and cinema.

Thirdly, and with respect to this same set of needs or values, we attempt to evaluate the importance of the gratifications obtained from the media with the gratifications obtainable elsewhere. In other words, we ask respondents to compare their uses of the media to other sources of need-gratification.

This method of approaching the media of mass communication is different from the conventional study of mass media 'effects'. Rather than ask: 'What do the media do to people?' this approach asks the question: 'What do people do with the media?' It is essentially a functional view.[1] It argues that people bend the media to their needs more readily than the media overpower them; that the media are at least as much agents of diversion and entertainment as agents of information and influence. It argues, moreover, that the selection of media and content, and the uses to which they are put, are considerably influenced by social role and psychological predisposition.

Viewing the media in this way permits one to ask not only how the media gratify and influence individuals but how and why they are differentially integrated into social institutions. Thus, if individuals select certain media, or certain types of content, in their roles as citizens, or consumers, or church members, insight is gained into the relationship between the attributes of the media (real or perceived) and the social and psychological functions which they serve. When Richard Crossman suggests, for example, that print is the medium most appropriate to democracy – referring to the preference of print for issues over personalities, and to the relative ease with which a reader can detach himself emotionally from what he is reading – he is suggesting a hypothesis concerning the compatibility between the attributes of a medium and the social institution of politics. The same thing holds true in the realm of the family when Donald Bogue suggests that print is the medium appropriate to the dissemination of family planning information – referring to the durability of print and the privacy in which it is consumed. Jean Cazeneuve suggests that the attributes of television provide modern man with the means to satisfy his primitive needs for taboo, magic and religion. These are hypotheses, of course, and do not mean, necessarily, that people act in these ways; they are questions for empirical research.[2]

Thus, we began by assembling as comprehensive a list as possible of social and psychological needs which have been said to be satisfied by exposure to the mass media. This list, taken from the literature, was supplemented by additional items, based on our own insights into the specific functions of the media in Israel. A variety of institutional areas – politics, family, religion and education – is represented as are the areas of self-identity, self-growth and self-gratification. The list was then pilot-tested and was subsequently reduced to thirty-five 'need statements' of the form: 'How important is it for you to spend time with your family?' or, 'How important is it for you to understand the true quality of our leaders?'

An example will make the procedure clear. We asked: 'How important is it for you to keep up with the way the Government performs its functions?' Respondents who answered that this need was 'very important' or 'somewhat important' for them, were asked: 'How much does listening to the radio help you to keep up with the way the Government performs its functions?' The same question was repeated five times – for radio-listening, television-viewing, newspaper-reading, book-reading and movie-going. (Only if a respondent had told us earlier in the interview that he is never exposed to a particular medium, he was not asked at all about the functions of that medium.) If the respondent's reply indicated that a given medium 'does not help', interviewers were instructed to probe in order to determine whether the medium simply does not help or whether it actually 'hinders' satisfaction of the particular need. In this way we attempted to take cognizance of the possible dysfunctions of each of the media as well. Finally, we asked: 'Is there something else besides these media which helps you to keep up with the way the Government performs its functions?' This last was an open-ended question.

In sum, our object was first to identify the felt needs of the population and of subgroups within the population. Then, for those respondents who answered that a given need was at least 'somewhat important', we sought to identify the extent to which each of the five media functions to fulfil these needs. Finally, we sought to compare the relative importance of the media with other means of fulfilling each need.

1. *The Relative Importance of the Various Needs*

Listing the needs in terms of their relative importance to respondents (Table 13.1) yields roughly three groups based on percentage cutting points. The list is headed by the need 'to feel pride that we have a State' (item 8), which was deemed 'very important' by 90 per cent of the sample. Indeed, the first group of eight items (items 8, 1, 14, 6, 35, 33, 26, 18) which were endorsed by 70 per cent or more of the respondents is dominated by what might be described as 'collectivity-oriented' needs, pertaining to integration in the nation and the family. Only two of the eight needs in this group – 'to raise my morale' and 'to feel that I am utilizing my time well' – can be described as 'personal needs'.

Lowest on the list is the need to 'escape everyday reality' (item 9), which was rated as 'very important' by only 16 per cent of the respondents. It is hardly a surprise that Israelis are high on national pride, familism and reality orientation, while the counterpart of these attitudes is a somewhat restrained – some would even say puritanical – attitude to self-indulgence. The goals which head the list seem to reflect a desire for assurance of belonging, and confidence that society and self are well thought of and running smoothly. More instrumental needs involving greater activity and participation, whether in the realm of self or society, are of lesser importance.

Background factors of various kinds are, of course, related to the differential importance attributed to various needs by different respondents. Thus, the higher the level of education, the larger the number of needs rated as 'very important'. Of the thirty-five items on the list, twenty-seven won higher endorsements from respondents of middle and high education as compared with the lesser educated. Only two needs were found to be negatively correlated with education, i.e. a higher percentage of the least educated than of the others considered them 'very important': these are the need to 'get closer to Jewish tradition' (item 21) and to 'strive for a higher standard of living' (item 32). Six other needs were related to level of education in a curvilinear way – respondents with medium (elementary) education rated them as 'very important' more frequently than either the lower or the higher educated.

There are similar connections with age. For example, the need 'to learn how to behave among others', or the need to 'get to know the true qualities of our leaders' are negatively related to age; that is to say, younger people attribute greater importance to these and other socializing needs than do older people. The same thing holds true for the group of needs associated with aesthetic and emotional experience.

TABLE 13.1 *List of Social and Psychological Needs*

Questionnaire item number		Per cent claiming need is very important
8.	To feel pride that we have a State	90
1.	To understand what goes on in Israel and in the world	87
14.	To spend time with the family	85
6.	To have confidence in our leaders	77
35.	To raise my morale	77
33.	To feel that I am utilizing my time well	72
26.	To know what the world thinks about us	70
18.	To be in a festive mood	70
34.	To know myself	66
13.	To experience beauty	64
19.	To order my day	63
24.	To participate in discussions with my friends	63
27.	To develop good taste	61
7.	To release tension	61
25.	To keep up with the way the Government performs its functions	60
12.	To feel satisfied with the way of life in Israel as compared with other countries	57
22.	To want to study or take courses	56
10.	To spend time with friends	55
32.	To strive for a higher standard of living	54
3.	To be entertained	54
23.	To learn how to behave among others	52
21.	To get closer to Jewish tradition	51
15.	To get to know the true qualities of our leaders	50
30.	To feel that I am influential	47
2.	To obtain useful information for daily life	47
17.	To feel that I am participating in current events	46
28.	To understand those who disagree with Government policy	41
29.	To feel that I am not always right	41
5.	To overcome loneliness when I am alone at home	37
11.	To feel that others think as I do	36
31.	To understand how the Arabs feel	33
16.	To re-experience events in which I was involved	32
20.	To participate in the experiences of other people	20
4.	To kill time	16
9.	To escape from the reality of everyday life	16

2. *Facets for the Classification of Needs*

As has already been noted, the list of needs came from the (largely speculative) literature on the social and psychological functions of the mass media. After compiling the list, we attempted to create a classificatory scheme which would encompass it. The scheme, consisting of three facets, is presented in Table 13.2.

TABLE 13.2 *Classification of Media-Related Needs*

A. Mode	B. Resource		C. Referent
1. To strengthen	1. Information, knowledge, understanding	*with respect to*	1. Self
2. To weaken	2. Gratification, emotional experience		2. Family
3. To acquire	3. Credibility, confidence, stability, status		3. Friends
	4. Contact		4. State, society
			5. Tradition, culture
			6. World
			7. Others, negative reference groups

Classifying the thirty-five needs on our list according to their resource and mode (Facets A and B), there emerge what seem to us five meaningful groupings:

1. Needs related to strengthening information, knowledge, and understanding – these can be called cognitive needs;
2. Needs related to strengthening aesthetic, pleasurable and emotional experience – or affective needs;
3. Needs related to strengthening credibility, confidence, stability, and status – these combine both cognitive and affective elements and can be labelled integrative needs;
4. Needs related to strengthening contact with family, friends, and the world – these can also be seen as integrative;
5. Needs related to escape or tension-release which we define in terms of the weakening of contacts with self and one's other social roles.

Adding the third facet, the referent (Facet C), finds the list heavily skewed toward two 'frames of reference' – the self and the socio-political collectivity.[3] This, however, may not be invalid, since most of the functions served by the media for the individual member of the audience are related either to the self or to his relations with his social environment and his society. Nonetheless it is unfortunate that the scheme was distilled only after the list was completed. Otherwise, we might have attempted to experiment with the missing elements.

TABLE 13.3 *Classification of Needs by the Three Facets*

	Self	Family	Friends	Society	Culture, tradition	World	Others	Total
1. Strengthen information, knowledge, understanding (cognitive)	3	–	2	5	–	1	2	13
2. Strengthen gratification, emotional experience (affective)	4	–	–	–	2	–	1	7
3. Strengthen sense of stability, confidence, status, etc. (integrative)	5	–	–	3	–	–	–	8
4. Strengthen contact	–	1	1	1	–	–	–	3
5. Weaken contact (escape)	4	–	–	–	–	–	–	4
TOTAL	16	1	3	9	2	1	3	35

3. *The Interrelationships among the Needs*

The next step beyond merely looking at the relative importance of the various items was to examine the interrelationship among them, as they emerge from the data. Specifically, we wanted to examine the extent to which items which had been coded *a priori* as similar actually cluster empirically. The coding is given in Table 13.4.

TABLE 13.4 *Coded List of Needs*

Questionnaire item number		Code*	Per cent claiming need very important
1.	To understand what goes on in Israel and in the world	A1, B1, C4	87
2.	To obtain useful information for daily life	A3, B1, C4	47
3.	To be entertained	A1, B2, C1	54
4.	To kill time	A2, B4, C1	16
5.	To overcome loneliness when I am alone at home	A2, B4, C1	37

6. To have confidence in our leaders	A1, B3, C4	77
7. To release tension	A2, B4, C1†	61
8. To feel pride that we have a State	A1, B3, C4	90
9. To escape from the reality of everyday life	A2, B4, C1	16
10. To spend time with friends	A1, B4, C3	55
11. To feel that others think as I do	A1, B3, C1	36
12. To feel satisfied with the way of life in Israel as compared with other countries	A1, B3, C4	57
13. To experience beauty	A1, B2, C1	64
14. To spend time with the family	A1, B4, C2	85
15. To get to know the true qualities of our leaders	A1, B1, C4	50
16. To re-experience events in which I was involved	A1, B2, C1	32
17. To feel that I am participating in current events	A1, B4, C4	46
18. To be in a festive mood	A1, B2, C5	70
19. To order my day	A1, B3, C1	63
20. To participate in the experiences of other people	A3, B2, C7	20
21. To get closer to Jewish tradition	A1, B4, C5	51
22. To want to study or take courses	A3, B1, C1	56
23. To learn how to behave among others	A3, B1, C3	52
24. To participate in discussions with my friends	A1, B4, C3†	63
25. To keep up with the way the Government performs its functions	A1, B1, C4	60
26. To know what the world thinks about us	A1, B1, C6	70
27. To develop good taste	A1, B1, C1	61
28. To understand those who disagree with Government policy	A1, B1, C7	41
29. To feel that I am not always right	A2, B3, C1†	41
30. To feel that I am influential	A1, B3, C1	47
31. To understand how the Arabs feel	A1, B1, C7	33
32. To strive for a higher standard of living	A3, B3, C1	54
33. To feel that I am utilizing my time well	A1, B3, C1	72
34. To know myself	A1, B1, C1	66
35. To raise my morale	A1, B2, C1	77

* For explanation of code, see text and Table 13.2, above. Note that in later stages of the analysis the category A3 (acquire) was combined with A2 (strengthen).

† Coded differently in later stages of the analysis. See footnote 7 below.

On the basis of the intercorrelations among all thirty-five items, we performed a factor analysis and also mapped the intercorrelations using Guttman's method for Smallest Space Analysis (SSA).[4] The results of the latter appear as Figure 13.1.

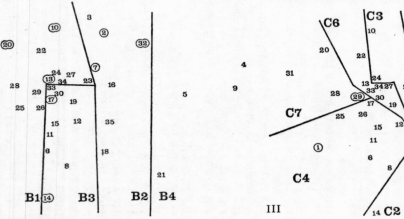

FIGURE 13.1 *SSA Map of Needs According to Facets**
(Two dimensions; coefficient of alienation 0.3)

I Division according to Facet A: A1 To strengthen; A2 To weaken.

II Division according to Facet B: B1 Information, knowledge, understanding; B2 Gratification, emotional experience; B3 Credibility, confidence, stability, status; B4 Contact.

III Division according to Facet C: C1 Self; C2 Friends; C3 Family; C4 State, society; C5 Tradition, culture; C6 World; C7 Others, negative reference groups.

* Circled numbers represent items which are 'out of place' from the point of view of the *a priori* classification.

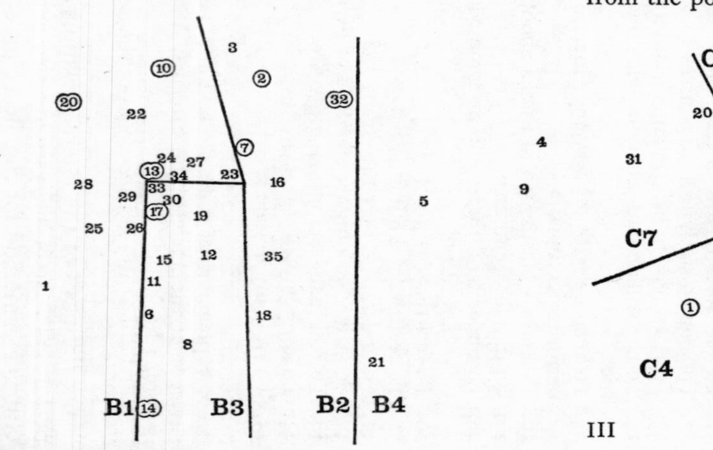

Close study of Figure 13.1 yields three observations:

1. Facet A, the 'mode', divides the map vertically in that category A2, which denotes the 'weakening' mode of media use and which includes items 4, 5, 7 and 9 (see Table 13.1), appears on the right-hand side. Of this group of 'escapist' items, only item 7 ('release tension'), is located at some distance, and appears to be different from the others.[5]
2. Facet B also divides the map in roughly vertical chunks in that the left-hand side of the map deals with cognitive matters (B1), proceeds via the integrative concerns of B3 (credibility, confidence, stability, status) to affectivity (B2) and contact (B4).
3. But probably the most important division of the map of intercorrelations is in terms of Facet C, the frame of reference. The spokes of a sort of wheel divide the clustered frames of reference. Two of the clusters refer to self (C1). Viewed in conjunction with the other facets, it appears that the right-hand cluster is a more affective self (B2, C1), and the left-hand cluster an integrative-cognitive one (B3–B1, C1). Going one step further, it is possible to think of the 'escapist' items (4, 5, 9) as representing the 'id'. In terms of the coding scheme, indeed, they might have been recorded as strengthening (A1), contact (B4) with one's *other* self rather than A2, B4, C1, and thus perhaps permitting us to abandon the notion of 'weakening' (and the first facet) altogether.

Another interesting aspect of this map is the suggestion that 'festivity' (item 18) and 'tradition' (item 21) are associated with 'family' (item 14).

Looking at the map as a whole, and considering that the items dealing with self (especially 'cognitive self') cluster near the centre, we attempt in Figure 13.2 (overleaf) an idealized representation of the overall structure of interrelations among the thirty-five items.

4. *The Functions of the Media*

Altogether, these representations of the empirical intercorrelations among the needs appear to give support to the *a priori* classification proposed in Tables 13.2 and 13.4. The next step, then, is to see whether the different clusters of needs are differently served by the several media. Ideally, in analyzing the functions of the media, one should separate the *attributes* of the media (e.g. print vs. picture) from their characteristic *contents* and from the typical *contexts* (e.g. public vs. private) in which they are consumed.[6] To some extent, we shall attempt to do this in what follows, but, obviously, this is not a question one can put to respondents: their rating of the helpfulness of the media with respect to each need is a composite of these elements. Table 13.5 shows how respondents ranked the media for each of the thirty-five needs, now divided into fourteen clusters.[7]

FIGURE 13.2 *Idealized Representation of Intercorrelations among Referents (Facet C)*

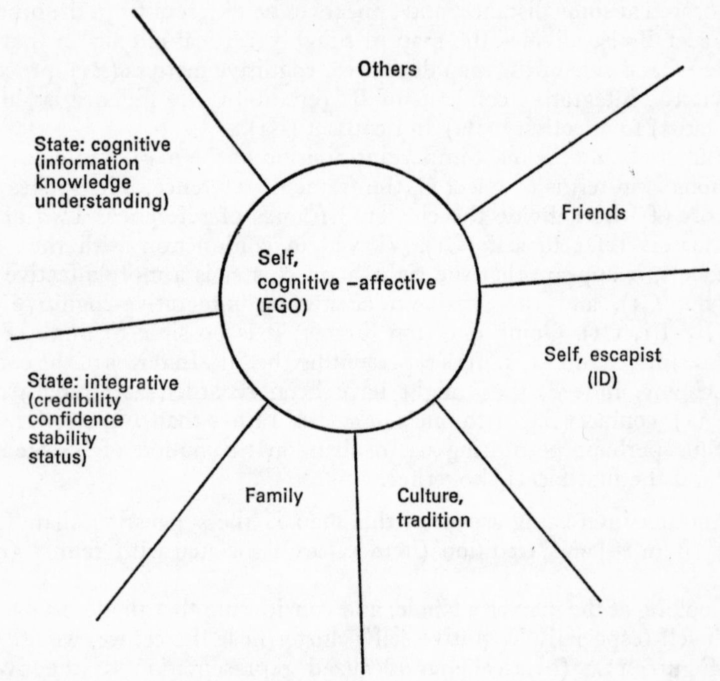

Consider first the items concerned with self (C1). Here the different media perform different functions depending on Facets A and B. Thus, when it comes to strengthening one's knowledge or understanding of self (A1, B1, C1) the key medium is the book, and the least important medium is the film. But the film is the key medium in enjoying oneself (A1, B2, C1) followed by television and the book; in this aspect, the newspaper functions least well as a perceived source of enjoyment. When it comes to the need for self-confidence, stability and self-esteem (A1, B3, C1), the newspaper is the most important medium followed by radio and television, books and films.[8]

The striking thing about these findings is how consistent they are. The theoretical groupings of needs yield almost perfect regularities in the rank order of the helpfulness of the media. Books cultivate the inner self; films and television give pleasure; and newspapers, more

TABLE 13.5 *The Helpfulness of the Media in Satisfying 'Important' Needs*

Code	Needs	Per cent claiming need is 'very important'	Ranking of media by per cent claiming medium is 'very helpful' for satisfying need*				
A1, B1, C1	*Strengthen knowledge, understanding with self*						
	(34) To know myself	66	B(31)	N(18)	R(15)	TV(14)	C(13)
	(27) To develop good taste	61	B(49)	TV(37)	R(35)	N(34)	C(33)
	(22) To want to study	56	B(63)	N(39)	R(28)	TV(27)	C(10)
A1, B2, C1	*Strengthen gratification, experience with self*						
	(35) To raise my morale	77	C(59)	TV(52)	B(49)	(R47)	N(34)
	(13) To experience beauty	64	C(55)	B(52)	TV(48)	R(30)	N(23)
	(7) To release tension	61	C(51)	B(47)	TV(43)	N(36)	R(35)
	(3) To be entertained	54	C(61)	TV(58)	R(48)	B(39)	N(32)
	(16) To re-experience events in which I was involved	32	B(36)	TV(29)	R(27)	C(26)	N(26)
A1, B3, C1	*Strengthen credibility, stability, status with self*						
	(33) To feel that I am utilizing my time well	72	N(47)	B(46)	TV(30)	R(30)	C(24)
	(19) To order my day	63	N(19)	R(17)	TV(13)	B(12)	C(7)
	(32) To strive for a higher standard of living	54	N(33)	TV(32)	C(27)	R(26)	B(26)
	(30) To feel that I am influential	47	N(20)	R(16)	TV(15)	B(15)	C(9)
	(11) To feel that others think as I do	36	N(44)	R(29)	TV(27)	(B24)	C(14)
A2, B4, C1	*Weaken contact with self*						
	(5) To overcome loneliness when I am alone at home	37	N(63)	B(62)	R(62)	TV(56)	C(29)
	(4) To kill time	16	TV(53)	N(52)	B(50)	C(47)	R(44)
	(9) To escape from the reality of everyday life	16	B(45)	C(44)	TV(31)	R(25)	N(25)
A1, B4, C2	*Strengthen contact with family*						
	(14) To spend time with the family	85	TV(36)	C(23)	R(17)	N(13)	B(8)
A1, B1, C3	*Strengthen knowledge, information with friends*						
	(24) To participate in discussions with my friends	63	N(56)	B(42)	TV(37)	R(37)	C(24)
	(23) To learn how to behave among others	52	B(40)	R(35)	N(30)	TV(29)	C(25)
A1, B4, C3	*Strengthen contact with friends*						
	(10) To spend time with friends	55	C(31)	TV(21)	N(13)	R(11)	B(8)
A1, B1, C4	*Strengthen knowledge, information, understanding with society, State, world*						
	(1) To understand what goes on in Israel and in the world	87	N(91)	R(77)	TV(59)	B(30)	C(11)

TABLE 13.5 *continued*

Code	Needs	Per cent claiming need is 'very important'	Ranking of media by per cent claiming medium is 'very helpful' for satisfying need*				
	(26) To know what the world thinks about us	70	N(85)	R(72)	TV(65)	B(28)	C(18)
	(25) To keep up with the way the Government performs its functions	60	N(84)	R(71)	TV(66)	B(21)	C(13)
	(15) To get to know the true qualities of our leaders	50	N(69)	TV(57)	R(53)	B(24)	C(12)
	(2) To obtain useful information for daily life	47	N(73)	R(57)	TV(35)	B(19)	C(8)
A1, B3, C4	*Strengthen credibility, stability, status with society, State*						
	(8) To feel pride that we have a State	90	N(68)	R(61)	TV(56)	B(37)	C(22)
	(6) To have confidence in our leaders	77	N(70)	R(58)	TV(53)	B(19)	C(10)
	(12) To feel satisfied with the way of life in Israel as compared with other countries	57	N(52)	R(40)	TV(40)	B(29)	C(28)
A1, B4, C4	*Strengthen contact with society, State*						
	(17) To feel that I am participating in current events	46	N(58)	TV(50)	R(49)	B(26)	C(17)
A1, B2, C5	*Strengthen experience with culture, tradition*						
	(18) To be in a festive mood	70	TV(41)	R(36)	N(28)	C(22)	B(19)
A1, B4, C5	*Strengthen contact with culture, tradition*						
	(21) To get closer to Jewish tradition	51	B(38)	TV(31)	R(30)	N(27)	C(9)
A1, B1, C7	*Strengthen knowledge, information, understanding of others*						
	(28) To understand those who disagree with Government policy	41	N(74)	R(55)	TV(50)	B(21)	C(11)
	(29) To feel that I am not always right	41	N(40)	R(28)	TV(25)	B(25)	C(11)
	(31) To understand how the Arabs feel	33	N(59)	TV(43)	R(42)	B(28)	C(13)
A1, B2, C7	*Strengthen gratification, experience with others*						
	(20) To participate in the experiences of other people	20	B(37)	TV(34)	N(33)	R(29)	C(28)

* B=book; TV=television: R=radio; N=newspaper; C=cinema.

than any other medium, give self-confidence and stability. The latter finding seems best interpreted in association with the idea of stability and reinforcement: it gives the day its framework (item 19); it tells me that others think as I do (item 11); it helps me feel influential (item 30); and so on.

This consistency in mass media use is not evident in the 'escapist' items (A2, B4, C1). Television is judged most helpful for killing time (item 4) followed very closely by newspapers and books; films and radio are considered somewhat less helpful for killing time, though on the whole the media seem to most almost equally useful for this purpose. The need 'to overcome loneliness when I am alone at home' (item 5) obviously puts film at a disadvantage and may do the same for television because broadcasting is limited only to a few hours in the evening when in most homes there is least loneliness. But these two items are less frankly escapist than the need to 'escape from reality' (item 9) which is best accomplished through books and films. Notice the similarity of this latter pattern to that of the media which help in the need 'to release tension' (item 7) which seemed, *a priori*, an 'escapist' item but which found its way, empirically, to the group of items whose subject is self-gratification (A1, B2, C1). The dimensions of the concept of 'escape' obviously require further clarification.[9] The management of 'time on my hands' is rather different from 'getting away from it all'.

The other regularity in these data is in the area of relationship with State and society. Regardless of whether the relationship is one of understanding or of pride, of confidence or connectedness, the rank-order of helpfulness of the media is completely uniform. Newspapers come first, followed by radio, then television. Books and film are far behind.

This pattern also holds for the understanding of others, perhaps particularly negative reference groups – Arabs, those who disagree with Government policy, and those who disagree with me (items 31, 28, 29, respectively). It will be recalled that strengthening one's own self-confidence and stability also fit this pattern in the sense that newspapers, radio and television came first. But note that in the case of self-confidence, books play a more important role than they do in the political arena.

Connections with the family (A1, B4, C2) are best fulfilled by television, as expected, just as connections with friends (A1, B4, C3) are best fulfilled by movies. Note that the need 'to participate in discussions with my friends' (item 24) is served, first of all, by newspapers and then by books, with television and radio in third place. Here is a difference between medium and message. It is the medium of film or television which contributes to friendship and familial solidarity, but the content of conversation is contributed by newspapers and books. It is more than a little surprising, one should add, to find that people do not give television as much credit as it intuitively seems to deserve as a topic of conversation.

5. *Division of Labour among the Media*

Summarizing briefly from the point of view of the media, we notice that the newspaper comes first, being the 'most helpful' medium in satisfying nineteen out of the thirty-five needs. It is the most helpful medium in fulfilling the needs to strengthen both information about and confidence in society. At the same time it satisfies some personal needs too, such as overcoming loneliness or strengthening stability and confidence in the State. It should be noted, however, that the primacy of the newspaper among all the media may be at least in part a function of the specific socio-political bias of the items on the list. On the other hand, as we have argued, perhaps this bias is indeed reflective of the range of functions which the newspapers perform especially in a country like Israel.[10]

The importance of the printed media for Israelis is demonstrated by the fact that the second medium, from the point of view of the number of different needs which it helps to satisfy, is the book. The main uses of the book are to satisfy personal needs of both cognitive and affective nature, such as to 'develop good taste', to 'know myself', to 'want to study', to 're-experience events in which I was involved'.[11] At the same time books were deemed helpful in escaping 'from the reality of every-day life' and in getting 'closer to Jewish tradition'.

In spite of its extreme popularity during the time of the study, television turned out to be 'most helpful' only with regard to three needs: 'to kill time', 'to spend time with the family' and 'to be in a festive mood' (which, as we have seen, has also been perceived as a family-oriented need). The discrepancy between the attention lavished on this medium and its rather limited 'uses' may again be the result of the specific structure of the list, or of the fact that exposure to television has not yet assumed a functional importance commensurate with its central position in the leisure time of the Israeli population.

A similar phenomenon pertains to radio. In spite of its total penetration there was not one single need on the list which was served best by radio. It came second in serving self-integrative needs, and cognitive and integrative needs related to State and society.

Finally, and not surprisingly, going to the movies was found to serve personal affective needs, such as 'to be entertained', 'to raise my morale' and 'to release tension', and social needs such as 'to spend time with friends'.

6. *The Effect of Education on Uses of the Media*

Since we know that the various needs are differentially important to persons of different levels of education, it is imperative to ask whether educational level is also associated with different patterns of media use. Thus, even though our analysis of media use relates, in each case, only to those persons for whom a given need is important, it may well be that persons of different levels of education rank the helpfulness of the media differently with respect to the same need.

Analysis of media preferences by educational level indicates that the printed media – the book and the newspaper – assume increased importance with increased education and the electronic media decline in importance. The reverse is true for the lesser educated, who find the electronic and visual media relatively more helpful for satisfying needs. Television, especially, appears to be very functional for persons of lower education, not only for satisfying personal-affective needs, as we have seen previously, but also for some of the cognitive needs, such as the need for information about society and the world, and reinforcing the wish to study.

More important for our purpose, however, is whether the ranking of the relative helpfulness of the media with respect to a given need varies by educational level. Here we find far less difference among the educational groups. In 6 of the 14 clusters of needs, virtually identical rankings were given by the three educational groups; for example, in needs having to do with understanding or feelings of confidence in matters of State, the ranking of the media for all groups was newspaper, radio, television, books and films. For 5 additional need clusters, the ranking of the media by the three educational groups was very similar. The major difference among groups in these latter clusters and in the 3 remaining ones on which there was a low level of concordance reflects the differential importance assigned to television and books, as has already been noted. Television is decreasingly helpful with increased education, while books are increasingly helpful. A clear example of this can be seen in the cluster of needs defined as to 'strengthen gratification, experience of self', as Table 13.6 reveals.

TABLE 13.6 *Ranking of the Helpfulness of the Media in 'Strengthening Gratification, Experience with Self' according to Education*

Low education	Television	Films	Radio	Newspaper	Book
Medium education	Films	Television	Book	Radio	Newspaper
High education	Book	Films	Television	Radio	Newspaper

The table shows clearly how television moves down and the book moves up the educational ladder. But while this represents an important trend, the rule, as we have noted, is for similarities of rankings to outnumber the differences. In other words, the individuals who indicate that a given need is important to them tend to evaluate the relative helpfulness of the several media in much the same way, regardless of their educational level.

7. *Overlapping Media; Overlapping Needs*

Having established which media are good for what purposes, we want to take one more look at an SSA mapping, this time to examine the extent to which persons who name a medium in response to a given need tend to name the same medium in response to another, or contrariwise, whether people tend to be so highly selective in associating media and needs that there are low intercorrelations among the usefulness of the same medium for different needs. Looking at the problem from the point of view of needs, we may find needs which are equally well served by different media and needs for which one medium but not another are deemed useful.

In order to answer these questions, we selected eight items from the list of needs – four each from the two polar extremes of the matrix of intercorrelations which formed the basis for Figure 13.1. Four of these items have to do with strengthening information and contact with State and society (items 1, 15, 25, 26: see Table 13.1), and four are needs relating to self-indulgence (items 3, 4, 5, 7). We intentionally chose these two groups since they are representative of the two major functions performed by the media – connection with society, and gratification of self – and because they give equal weight to the two sets of functions. Had we taken all thirty-five needs – which, as has been noted, gives greater weight to the socio-political area – the analysis we are about to undertake would have been biased by the roles ascribed to the media in the socio-political area.

Accordingly, we constructed a matrix of intercorrelations based on the evaluations of the usefulness of each of the five media for each of the eight items. Plotting these intercorrelations by means of the SSA technique (Figure 13.3) we can now turn to see how the map is organized. If media preferences predominate – that is, if a person who says books help him 'to get to know the true qualities of our leaders' also tends to say that books help him 'to escape from the reality of everyday life' – then we shall find clusters of correlations organized in terms of media. If, on the other hand, we find that a given need, when it is considered important, is served equally well by all media, we shall find needs at the centre of correlational clusters.

The map shows both patterns, although one is somewhat stronger than the other. The first pattern shows each medium with a distinct area of its own in which evaluations of the usefulness of that medium for all eight needs clearly cluster. Consider books, for example. Respondents who say that books are very helpful (or not very helpful) for killing time also say that books help (or don't help) in understanding leaders. Moreover, the correlations among the declared usefulness of

FIGURE 13.3 *SSA–1 Map of the Helpfulness of the Media for Satisfying Eight Needs*
(Two dimensions; coefficient of alienation 0·3)

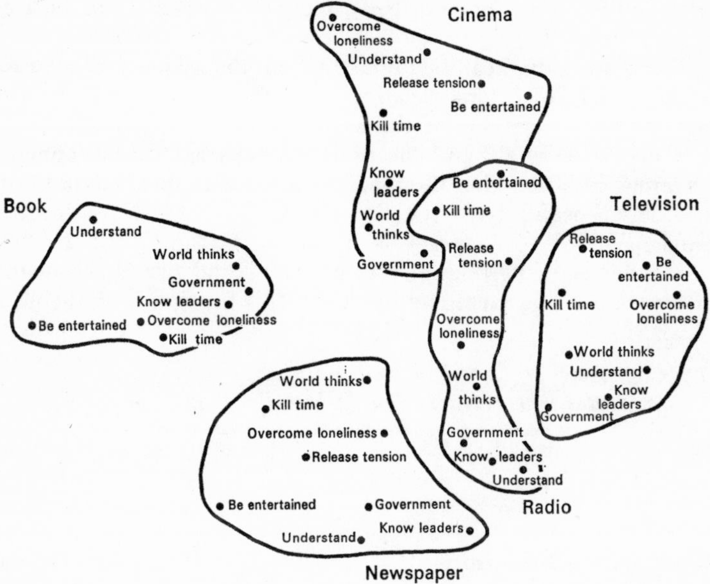

books over the eight different needs tend to be higher than the correlation among books and the other media in fulfilling the same need. This is what makes for the relative isolation of each medium from the others. Some are more isolated: books and television are the best examples; the others tend to spill over into each other rather more.

But there is a second pattern in this map, too, albeit a less visible one. Each of the spaces which enclose a medium can be subdivided into two. One half of the space, approximately, groups the political items; the other half groups the personal items. In other words, within each of the clusters which form about a given medium, the content areas form subclusters, showing that those who say that television is useful for getting to know one's leaders, for example, are more likely to say that it is also useful for understanding events at home and abroad than that it is useful, say, for reducing tension.

As soon as one notices this, another fact becomes apparent. The political uses of radio, television and newspapers are contiguous with each other, but not with those of film and books (which are also contiguous). The personal uses of radio and television are adjacent. These patterns suggest that (1) both political and personal uses of radio and television are closely allied; (2) the uses of newspapers for political needs are related to the political uses of radio and television, but the personal uses of the newspaper are rather different; (3) books and films are akin in their political uses (or non-uses), but are different from each other in their functions for the self.

Further information can be obtained from the map (or, more exactly, from the matrix of intercorrelations on which the map is based) by averaging the correlations of the helpfulness of each medium for all pairs of needs (28 in all) and comparing the average thus obtained.[12] A high average indicates that the medium is more diffuse – that is, that it is considered useful both for the satisfaction of socio-political and personal needs. A low average is indicative of the 'specificity' of the medium, that is, of its relevance to a limited and rather homogeneous set of functions. The averaging process yields the figures in Table 13.7.

TABLE 13.7 *Average Correlation of Helpfulness of each Medium for all Pairs of Eight Needs: How 'Specialized' are the Media?*

Television	0·66
Books	0·53
Radio	0·52
Cinema	0·43
Newspaper	0·42

From these data it appears that television is the most diffuse medium, that is, it is applied by its users to a wide range of functions, whereas movies and newspapers are the most 'specific' media. Books and radio are in-between. These findings seem to confirm also some aspects of the popular images about these media, such as the almost universal attractiveness of television for television fans, and the more specific informational function of the newspaper.

A similar analysis can be performed from the point of view of the functions. Instead of asking whether any given medium is specific or diffuse, one can examine the extent to which the nature of the function determines the selection of the medium which satisfies it. In other words, the question is whether functions of a given nature are associated with a specific medium, which, presumably, is perceived as more relevant, or more 'helpful' for satisfying this function. Again, we have computed the average of the correlations between the 'helpfulness' of each pair of media for every one of the needs selected for analysis. A high average signifies that all five media are 'helpful' for satisfying a given function. A low average means that the need is 'specific', in the sense that only one or two specific media satisfy it.

Following are the averages, in ascending order, of the correlations between the five media for each of the functions selected:

TABLE 13.8 *Average Correlation of Helpfulness of all Pairs of Media for each Function: How 'Specialized' are the Needs?*

To be entertained	0·31
To understand what is happening in Israel and in the world	0·39
To overcome loneliness when I am alone at home	0·43
To release tension	0·52
To kill time	0·53
To get to know the true qualities of our leaders	0·55
To keep up with the way the Government performs its functions	0·62
To know what the world thinks about us	0·63

It will be remembered that the eight functions on which this specific analysis is based were initially selected because of the polar distance between their cognitive-societal vs. affective-personal characteristics. The averaged correlations presented above indicate that, with one exception, listing the averages in ascending order conforms to the initial categorization of the functions. Thus, with the exception of 'to understand what goes on in Israel and in the world', the low-average functions belong in the affective-personal group, whereas the high-average functions are all of the cognitive-societal type. In other words, the affective-personal function appears to be more 'specific', in the sense that the media are more differentiated in satisfying them. Most specific seems to be the 'entertainment' function of the media, while the most 'general' functions, i.e. those functions served in a more undifferentiated way by all of the five media, are the straight informational functions. These findings seem surprising, since we usually tend to think of the entertainment function as one of the more universal functions of the media, that is, as a function which can be derived from exposure to any one of the media, while very few media, perhaps only the newspaper, are perceived as performing first and foremost an informational function. Yet, precisely the opposite appears to obtain: certain of the media are clearly differentiated from the others in their 'helpfulness' as agents of entertainment, while individuals who claim that one medium is helpful in providing them with socio-political information tend to say that the others are helpful too.

Finally, we looked at the interchangeability among the media. In other words, we examined the degree to which each pair of media performs similar functions, and therefore constitute functional alternatives for each other. This 'index of interchangeability' was computed by averaging the correlations which signify the extent to which each pair of media performs similarly with respect to all eight needs. The following table presents these averages in matrix form:

TABLE 13.9 *Matrix of Average Correlations of Helpfulness of each Pair of Media for all Eight Needs: Which Media are Interchangeable with which?*

	TV	Radio	Newspapers	Books	Cinema
TV	–	0·71	0·53	0·26	0·57
Radio		–	0·69	0·38	0·49
Newspapers			–	0·53	0·37
Books				–	0·51
Cinema					–

The data of Table 13.9 reveal that television and radio are highly interchangeable with each other while television and books are least so. In other words, people who say that television is helpful (or not) with respect to each of the needs, are very likely to say that radio is helpful (or not) with respect to the same needs. No such shadowing appears in the case of television and books.

Next to radio, the best substitute for television is the cinema (0·57). The visual entertainment function which both media serve apparently leads to this moderate degree of interchangeability. The documentary function of television also makes it somewhat interchangeable with newspapers.

This analysis of the interchangeability of television and the other four media provides a key to reading the matrix as a circumplex which shows each medium to be most interchangeable with its two closest neighbours.[13] Thus, radio's best substitutes are television, on the one hand, and newspapers on the other. The newspaper's best substitutes are radio and books. Books are most interchangeable with newspapers and cinema, while the best substitutes for cinema are books and television – although it should be noted that books and cinema are more insulated than the other three media.

These relationships among the media appear to reflect the complex ways in which the media overlap with each other. Thus, the media are classifiable first of all according to their mode of transmission – print vs. electronics. Secondly, they divide according to their mode of reception: television and cinema are received by watching and listening, radio by listening only, newspapers and books by reading. Thirdly, the media – as we have seen – differ in the range of their content (documentary, entertainment or both) and consequently in the needs that they serve. Thus, for example, books share the element of print with newspapers and the element of entertainment with the cinema. Radio shares both range of content and mode of transmission with television and the documentary coverage of the newspaper.

That television and newspapers are radio's best companions is of interest in the light of the findings reported in Table 13.6 where it was shown that people name television as helpful (or not) for a variety of needs but that their use of the newspaper is much more restricted. It is remarkable that radio is the best substitute for both the most specialized (television) and the least specialized (newspapers) media. Respondents apparently see in radio both a substitute for the versatility of television and, of all the media, the one that comes closest to fulfilling the documentary role of the newspaper.

8. *Satisfying Needs Elsewhere*

Although the needs with which we began were selected because of their presumed relationship to the mass media, it is still an empirical question whether these needs are also served by other means, and, indeed, whether the mass media or these other means are more helpful. In other words, even with regard to what we have described as media-related needs, functional alternatives to the media surely exist. In order to find out what these alternatives might be we asked, with respect to each need, what – if anything – the respondent found to be more helpful than the mass media for satisfying that need. This was presented as an open-ended question, and the list of 'functional alternatives' was compiled on the basis of the respondents' answers. It eventually included seventeen items, ranging from family and friends to sleep and drugs.

Table 13.10 presents the findings. Perhaps the first thing to notice is that even though the list includes only media-related needs, no single need was found to be served exclusively by the media. Indeed, the highest percentage of respondents claiming that 'nothing else besides the mass media' helps them to satisfy a particular need is 43 per cent. In other words, even in this case the other sources of gratification taken together equal the mass media in importance. Thus, even media-related needs must be looked at in the perspective of the larger context of human

TABLE 13.10 *Primary Sources of Need Satisfaction*

Code	Needs	Is there anything that helps more than the mass media? (open-ended question) No, per cent saying nothing helps more than media	Yes, per cent saying something helps more (most frequent mentions)*		Yes, per cent saying something helps more (other mentions)†	Per cent don't know or 'nothing helps'
A1, B1, C1	*Strengthen knowledge, understanding with self*					
	(34) To know myself	18	Friends Family	26 15	20	21
	(27) To develop good taste	26	Activities Friends	20 12	22	20
	(22) To want to study	23	Lectures Work	31 8	19	19
A1, B2, C1	*Strengthen gratification, experience with self*					
	(35) To raise my morale	15	Friends Family	23 18	34	8
	(13) To experience beauty	20	Activities Hobbies	26 9	30	15
	(7) To release tension	15	Friends Sport	18 11	39	10
	(3) To be entertained	16	Friends Activities	27 17	33	7
	(16) To re-experience events in which I was involved	21	Friends Family	36 11	14	18
A1, B3, C1	*Strengthen credibility, stability, status with self*					
	(33) To feel that I am utilizing my time well	23	Work Family	15 10	34	18
	(19) To order my day	24	Work	20	26	30
	(32) To strive for a higher standard of living	25	Work Friends	15 15	19	26
	(30) To feel that I am influential	15	Friends Family	32 18	17	18
	(11) To feel that others think as I do	23	Friends Family	44 8	8	17
A2, B4, C1	*Weaken contact with self*					
	(5) To overcome loneliness when I am alone at home	25	Hobbies Friends	15 12	39	16
	(4) To kill time	17	Friends Hobbies	16 10	33	16
	(9) To escape from the reality of everyday life	25	Friends Sport	15 7	28	18
A1, B4, C2	*Strengthen contact with family*					
	(14) To spend time with the family	16	Family Holidays	42 11	17	14
A1, B1, C3	*Strengthen knowledge, information with friends*					
	(24) To participate in discussions with my friends	29	Friends Activities	27 6	17	21
	(23) To learn how to behave among others	25	Friends Family	34 5	16	20

A1, B4, C3 *Strengthen contact with friends*					
(10) To spend time with friends	15	Friends Activities	46 7	18	14
A1, B1, C4 *Strengthen knowledge, information, understanding with society, State, world*					
(1) To understand what goes on in Israel and in the world	36	Friends Lectures	27 11	12	14
(26) To know what the world thinks about us	43	Friends Lectures	18 15	6	18
(25) To keep up with the way the Government performs its functions	41	Lectures Friends	20 18	7	14
(15) To get to know the true qualities of our leaders	35	Lectures Friends	26 14	7	18
(2) To obtain useful information for daily life	33	Friends Family	31 7	10	19
A1, B3, C4 *Strengthen credibility, stability, status with society, State*					
(8) To feel pride that we have a State	25	Holidays Friends	33 7	19	16
(6) To have confidence in our leaders	36	Lectures Friends	20 16	11	17
(12) To feel satisfied with the way of life in Israel as compared with other countries	30	Friends Lectures	16 6	22	26
A1, B4, C4 *Strengthen contact with society, State*					
(17) To feel that I am participating in current events	35	Friends Holidays	19 7	19	20
A1, B2, C5 *Strengthen experience with culture, tradition*					
(18) To be in a festive mood	12	Holidays	46	31	11
A1, B4, C5 *Strengthen contact with culture, tradition*					
(21) To get closer to Jewish tradition	15	Holidays Prayer	49 11	12	13
A1, B1, C7 *Strengthen knowledge, information, understanding of others*					
(28) To understand those who disagree with Government policy	35	Friends Lectures	27 18	4	16
(29) To feel that I am not always right	19	Friends Family	42 13	10	16
(31) To understand how the Arabs feel	33	Lectures Friends	23 17	9	18
A1, B2, C7 *Strengthen gratification, experience with others*					
(20) To participate in the experiences of other people	22	Friends Family	43 10	11	14

* 'Activities' refers to cultural activities of all kinds (theatre, cinema, etc.); 'holidays' includes religious and/or national holidays. Item 18 (A1, B4, C5), 'to be in a festive mood', is served equally by religious holidays (24 per cent) and national holidays (22 per cent). Religious holidays exclusively are named for item 21 (A1, B4, C5), 'to get closer to Jewish tradition'.

† Detailed percentages are given for the two most predominant 'functional alternatives'. The rest, with lower per cent, have been lumped together as 'other'.

needs of which these form but a small segment, as well as in terms of the variety of means by which these needs can be, and actually are, satisfied.

Looking at the table again we notice that, relatively speaking, the highest percentage of endorsements for the mass media as the 'most helpful' means for satisfying a need is won by the group of socio-politically-related needs, both on the cognitive level (strengthening knowledge, information, understanding) and on the integrative level (strengthening confidence and stability). Thus, for example, of those who described as important the need to 'know what the world thinks about us', 43 per cent claimed that nothing else besides the media helps in satisfying that need. A slightly lower, though still quite high, vote for the media was given with respect to such socio-political needs as 'have confidence in our leaders', 'feel satisfied with the way of life in Israel as compared with other countries', 'feel that I am participating in current events' and 'get to know the true qualities of our leaders'. The role of the media in overcoming distance is obvious too, in the dominant role played by the media in helping to understand opposition groups ('understand how the Arabs feel' and 'understand those who disagree with Government policy'). What is surprising, perhaps, is how frequently interpersonal communication (friends and lectures) competes with the mass media even here.

In the realm of personal needs the role of the media declines, and face-to-face contacts, primarily with friends, become more salient. This is especially true with regard to such needs as 'to know myself', 'to be entertained', 'to raise my morale', 'to feel that others think as I do' and 'to feel that I am influential'. Friends are thus the main source of support for strengthening personal confidence and security, while they are also the best framework within which tension can be released and where one can 'learn how to behave among others'. It is interesting to note that with respect to most of these needs the family, though still mentioned quite frequently, lags far behind reference to 'friends'.

Of considerable importance in satisfying socio-political needs are also public lectures of various kinds. This seems to be a fairly popular substitute for some of the functions which are commonly attributed to the mass media. Likewise, integrative functions such as the need 'to feel pride that we have a State', 'to be in a festive mood' or 'to get closer to Jewish tradition' are provided for primarily by national and religious holidays.

9. *Summary*

The media of mass communication are thought to satisfy a variety of needs arising from social roles and psychological dispositions. These needs, typically, take the form of (1) strengthening or weakening (2) a connection – cognitive, affective, integrative (3) with some referent – self, friends, family and tradition, social and political institutions, others. A group of needs selected for study was found to cluster empirically in these terms.

The object of this chapter was to identify the 'uses' made of the media in the gratification of these social and psychological needs, or, in other words, in the achievement of personal and social goals. Methodologically, it rests on the assumption that people are aware of their needs and are able to identify the sources of their satisfaction.

Israelis rank identification with State and family as matters of the highest importance. They want to know that society and self are worthy. Active participation in civic affairs and self-fulfilment seem somewhat less important. 'Escapist' needs are rated very low in importance.

Respondents were asked to indicate the extent to which each of five media contributes to the gratification of the needs in question, and to assess the relative helpfulness of the media compared with other sources of need-satisfaction. The principal findings were these:

1. For all needs examined, the non-media sources (combined) were deemed more gratifying than the mass media. Friends, holidays, lectures and work were often said to be more important sources of gratification than the media.

2. The greater the 'distance' from a referent – social, physical or psychological – the more important the role of the media. Yet, interpersonal communication – formal and informal – competed even in such areas as connection to political leadership and negative reference groups.

3. Certain comparative processes – such as striving for a higher standard of living, or satisfying oneself that one's time is well spent or that one's country is a good place in which to live – appear to be well served by the media. So are 'escapist' needs. On the whole, however, friends are more important than the mass media in needs having to do with self-gratification, even 'to be entertained'!

4. For individuals who say that matters of State and society are important to them, the rank-order of the usefulness of the media in serving these needs is entirely consistent regardless of the educational level of the respondent. Newspapers are the most important medium, followed by radio, then television. Books and films are far behind. Altogether, the centrality of the newspaper for knowledge and integration in the socio-political arena cannot be overstated.

5. Needs having to do with self invoke different kinds of media, depending on the specific functions involved. Knowing oneself – the cognitive needs associated with self – is best served by books; enjoying oneself is associated with films, television and books; while the newspaper contributes to self-regulation and self-confidence. The individuated character of book-reading, the social character of film- and

television-viewing, and the simultaneity of exposure to the newspaper apparently link attributes of these media with the needs they serve best.

6. In satisfying needs associated with self, books are more helpful for the better educated, while television is more helpful for the lesser educated. Particularly in the area of self-gratification, books and television exchange places as educational level increases.

7. Television is useful for killing time, but not as a medium of 'escape'. The presence of television at the hearth apparently makes it unsuccessful as an agent of insulation from the demands of ego and of others.

8. Film and television, respectively, contribute to the maintenance of friendship and familial solidarity. However, the topics of conversation which these relationships engender are provided by newspapers and books.

9. Television is the least specialized of the media: persons who say that television is helpful for one set of needs tend to say that it is helpful for the other. The cinema and newspaper are most specialized in this sense: the one serves self-gratification and sociability, the other, participation in the socio-political order.

10. Needs in the social and political sphere are served by more media than are needs in the sphere of self-gratification. The use of newspapers, radio and television for political functions are highly correlated while the two electronic media cater to the self-serving functions in similar ways.

11. Examining the media in terms of their 'interchangeability' – that is, in terms of the extent to which they serve similar functions – reveals a circular relationship whereby each medium (as a point on the circle) is most similar to its two nearest neighbours. The circular order consists of television, radio, newspapers, books, cinema and back to television. These adjacent functions may be explained in terms of shared technical attributes, overlapping content, and the social contexts in which the media are consumed.

Finally, it should be noted that media-related needs are not necessarily needs generated by the media. Most of them predate the emergence of the media and, properly, ought to be viewed within the wider range of human needs. As such, they always have been, and still are, satisfied in a variety of ways, most of them quite unrelated to the mass media. The surprising thing, perhaps, is to realize the extent and the range of the media's encroachment on the 'older' ways in which social and psychological needs are satisfied. We do not believe that Israeli society is very different in this respect from other developed societies.

NOTES – CHAPTER THIRTEEN

1. See Charles Wright, *Mass Communication: A Sociological Perspective*, New York: Random House, 1959. For a recent example of research in this tradition, see Denis McQuail, Jay G. Blumler and J. R. Brown, 'The Television Audience: A Revised Perspective', in McQuail, ed., *Sociology of Mass Communications*, Harmondsworth: Penguin, 1972 and *Studies in Broadcasting*, Vol. 9, Tokyo: NHK, 1973.
2. See Richard Crossman, 'The Politics of Viewing', *New Statesman*, 76, 1968, pp. 525–30; Jean Cazeneuve, *La société de l'ubiquité*, Paris: Denoel, 1972; and Donald Bogue, 'Recommendations for a Sociologically Correct Program of Family Planning in India', in Kiser, ed., *Research in Family Planning*, Princeton: Princeton University Press, 1962.
3. The three facets taken together yield 84 possible combinations. The coding of the 35 needs in terms of these three facets filled 19 of the 84 three-dimensional boxes, with 8 of the boxes containing two or more items. Thus, for example, the need 'to understand what is going on in Israel and in the world' (item 1) is coded A1, B1, C4; the need to 'learn how to behave among others' (item 23) is coded A3, B1, C3; the need to 'escape from the reality of everyday life' (item 9) is coded A2, B4, C1. This *a priori* coding of all items is reported with minor amendments in Table 13.4.
4. As already explained (Chapter Eleven) this method graphs the distance between all items in the matrix of intercorrelations as an inverse function of the size of the correlations; the higher the correlation between any two items, the smaller the distance between them in the map. A number of sources of distortion are possible, e.g. two items may fall close to one another, though they are not highly correlated, owing to the similarity of their relationships with all other items. More basic is the problem of whether the matrix of correlation is well described in a two- (or three-) dimensional space. For details see Louis Guttman, 'A General Nonmetric Technique . . .', op. cit. The factor analysis – the starting point for which is the same matrix of intercorrelations employed in the Smallest Space Analysis (SSA) – is not presented here. The results obtained correspond rather closely.
5. It has therefore been reclassified for subsequent analysis; see footnote 4 for details. This, taken together with the findings concerning the different media which serve these 'escapist' needs (see Table 13.5 and discussion in text), raise further questions concerning the dimensionality of the concept of escape. Note, too, the large proportion of the population which affirms tension release as an important need, compared with the minorities agreeing to the other 'escapist' needs (items 4, 5, 9).
6. For example, Berelson's reference to the newspaper as a 'tool for daily living' is a content function, while the 'ritualistic and near-compulsive character' of newspaper-reading appears to be an attribute function. Similarly, for Mendelsohn's discussion of the provision by radio of 'vicarious and identificatory participation in newsworthy happenings' on the one hand, and 'companionship' on the other. While these functions

are analytically distinguishable, it is not clear to what extent members of the audience conceive of the media separately from their characteristic content. One wonders whether different content would affect popular images of television as 'escapist', newspapers as 'informative' and books as providers of 'culture' – functions which will be discussed below. We do not claim to have succeeded in separating these different functions of the media in the questions which were addressed to respondents. The analysis, at a number of points, attempts to sort out the three types of functions, however. See Bernard Berelson, 'What Missing the Newspaper Means', in Lazarsfeld and Stanton, eds., *Communication Research 1948–49*, New York: Harper, 1950, and Harold Mendelsohn, 'Listening to Radio', in Dexter and White, eds., *People, Society and Mass Communication*, New York: Free Press, 1964.

7. Some minor revisions of typology are introduced here. First, we group category A3 ('to acquire') with category A1 ('to strengthen'), in order to reduce the total number of different groupings. Secondly, we have introduced 'correlations' in our coding of 3 items, based on the findings of the SSA and factor analyses. The first of these corrections is in item 7, 'to release tension'. Originally coded as an 'escapist' item (together with items 4, 5, 9) the empirical analysis (see below) places it as A1, B2, C1 (strengthen gratification of self). Item 29, 'to feel that I am not always right', has been displaced from A2, B3, C1 (weaken stability of self) to the present A1, B1, C7 (strengthen understanding of others). Similarly, item 24, 'to participate in discussions with friends', was formerly A1, B4, C3 (strengthen contact with friends) and is now A1, B1, C3 (strengthen knowledge of friends).
8. It will be recalled that questions about the media were put only to those who said that a given need was at least 'somewhat important' to them, and that questions about each of the media were put only to persons who had minimal accessibility to the medium in question. Thus, persons who did not view television (about 60 per cent of the population owned sets at the time of the study; another 25 per cent had regular access) were not asked to rate television's helpfulness in achieving any of the needs, just as questions about the helpfulness of books were put only to book readers (22 per cent reported that they do not read books at all). In other words, the percentages in Table 13.5 are based on the total number exposed to each medium, and the base varies, therefore, from medium to medium. The media are then ranked in terms of the percentage which considered each medium 'very helpful' in achieving the need in question.
9. See Elihu Katz and David Foulkes, 'On the Use of Mass Media as Escape: Clarification of a Concept', *Public Opinion Quarterly*, 26, 1962, pp. 377–88.
10. Compare Alex Edelstein's rather similar findings for Yugoslavia and the United States. See 'An Alternative Approach to the Study of Source Effects as Mass Communication', *Studies of Broadcasting*, 9, 1973.
11. This function was probably reinforced by the fact that during the period in which the fieldwork was carried out the Israeli book market was flooded with books of reportage on the Six Day War.

12. In this and the next table, means were preferred to other measures of central tendency precisely because they permit extreme cases to exert disproportionate influence.
13. The circumplex is also discernible in Figure 13.3 where the five media fall into the same circular order.

CHAPTER FOURTEEN Cultural Integration: Zionists, Israelis and Jews

In the previous chapter, we saw the primacy of concern with the State, not only as a political entity but also, and perhaps primarily, as the supreme collective symbol. The 'need' to 'feel pride that we have a State' was considered 'very important to me' by most people. Similarly, in an earlier chapter, we found that Independence Day, Yom Haatzmaut, was the holiday that had 'meaning' for more people than any other.

The State is a new-old idea in Judaism. It is the return to the homeland – albeit not a modern Western state – to which Jewish prayers have been addressed for millennia. Given the generations of prayer, suffering and struggle, it should come as no surprise that the State is not simply a legal and institutional framework. Indeed, in the spirit of our argument throughout this volume, the State is another example of secular transformation, one which gives new expression to the collective identity and interdependence of the Jews.

Some writers see this transformation as short-lived. Indeed, they see the emergence of the State as the beginning of 'the end of the Jewish people'.[1] Out of the collective yearning and striving of the Jews, they say, there will emerge a new people, the Israelis, who will rapidly lose their connections with Jews and Judaism. The cosmopolitanism of the people without a land will lead to the provincialism of a people with a land. The creativity that went with sophisticated marginality will give way to more local concerns. The game of State will supersede the universal and transcendental. The substitution of nationhood for ethnicity and religion will weaken ties to the Jews abroad who will, increasingly, assimilate, while within Israel Jews will simply become Israelis. Gloomier prophets think worse than that: they argue that when peace comes, the seeming solidarity of the Israelis will reveal a patchwork of ethnic, religious and ideological differences which will be difficult to hold together. Their concern is not with the quality and content of Jewish nationhood but with its viability. They are unsure of its cultural integrity.

The opposing argument sees the State as of the essence of Jewish continuity. Israel is the Jewish dream come true. It is the drama of reassembling people who have tenaciously maintained a common identity, a language, a literature, a culture. Far from abandoning its ties with Jews abroad, it will serve Jews everywhere as a centre of cultural and religious authority and creativity. And the relationship will be mutual: the Jews abroad will rally, in their own ways, in support and response. Within Israel, moreover, there will emerge a cohesive society and culture based on the old and the new.

What does the future hold? Which of these theses is the more likely? We cannot look very far into the future, of course, but some of the data collected in this study have bearing. Viewing culture in the broadest sense, we can hardly overlook these questions. The elements of identity, continuity and change are the *content* of leisure and communication. The policy-maker concerned with the quality of Sabbath and holidays, the book, the electronic media, the arts – in short, with the uses of leisure – must consider these questions, for some of the essence of the Jewish future is implicit in the ways they are answered. The holidays, the media, the arts have the function of 'agenda setting' for societies; they influence what people talk and think about. Their effect is to focus attention on issues and values.

Ideally, we should have liked to be able to point explicitly to connections between patterns of values and patterns of leisure activity; but as we shall see, these are not easily discerned. In other words, we tried, but unsuccessfully, to relate participation in various types of leisure activity to the holding of distinctive opinions and attitudes about Judaism and Zionism and to value orientations more generally. But we found very few such relationships. Perhaps the relationships between values and cultural consumption *are* very weak, as Steiner and others have suggested.[2] Perhaps it is because we had to limit our analysis to patterns of *exposure* and *use* of the various leisure activities without being able to explore variations in exposure to different types of *content*. Indeed, common sense would maintain that it is content rather than frequency of exposure that is related to values. We doubt it; but are unable to exclude the possibility that this may be so.[3] The interaction of patterns of culture (in the sense of values) and patterns of Culture (in the sense of art) is more subtle than that. Celebrating a particular holiday probably has no direct, measurable effect on opinions and attitudes; why expect more from a television programme?

We believe, rather, that in *the long run* there is a process of mutual reinforcement between culture and Culture.[4] To this point, we have speculated on the implications of various types of leisure attitudes and behaviour for Jewish continuity and change, and for the integration of Israeli society. Here, we want to examine these questions head-on. We will ask to what extent central values are shared by Israelis of different generations, different levels of education, different commitments to religion, and so on. We want to see how, and how well, Israeli society is holding together, and to what extent there is a basis for the emergence of a common culture and Culture.[5]

1. *How Salient is Jewishness in the National Identity of Israelis?*

We ask, first of all, how salient to Jewish Israelis is the fact of their being Jewish? Thus, we know from the previous chapter how central is their concern with, and pride in, the State. We saw that half of the respondents said it was 'important' for them to feel an attachment to tradition, although this need was not among the highest on the list of 'important things'. Here we are attempting to determine how much Israelis are concerned with their Jewishness, how much thought they give to it, whether it plays a part in their ideas about nationhood.

One index of the extent of concern with Jewish identity and continuity is the salience of concern with the destruction of the Jews of Europe in the Nazi era. This is a subject which receives widespread and continuous attention in the schools, in the media, on the holidays, in the synagogues. It is a subject which a large share of Israelis know first-hand from having lived in Europe during this period. The young and immigrants from Eastern countries can only have learned about it from others. It is referred to as 'the Holocaust'.

We asked: 'Does the matter of the Holocaust which befell the Jews of Europe – the fact that six million Jews were destroyed by the Nazis – preoccupy you?' Four per cent said it did not; 1 per cent said they did not know what it was. Virtually everybody said yes. We then asked: 'How often do you think about it?' Twenty-seven per cent said 'very often'; one-third said 'often'; another third said rarely or very rarely. Table 14.1 gives the replies by education, ethnicity and generation.

Countries of origin are, of course, the key to reading the table. Among those born abroad, the Europeans are haunted by the Holocaust: most of them think about it frequently. Yet, half of those born in Asia or Africa are preoccupied as frequently. The difference between the two groups is very large, relatively speaking, but one cannot overlook the substantial proportions of non-Europeans who dwell on the tragedy.

In the Israel-born generation, it is the children of the Europeans who change. Only half are as occupied with the problems as their parents. Moreover, the difference between the ethnic groups has disappeared: the frequency among children of Eastern immigrants who say they 'often' think about the Holocaust, is equal to that among children of immigrants from the West or the children of parents who themselves were born in Israel.

Level of education makes no difference – either in the first or the second generation. The only possible exception is to be found among the first generation of immigrants from the East, whose better-educated members give thought to the Holocaust somewhat more often.

We asked further whether the threat of another holocaust exists in our generation, in the sense of a physical danger to any section of the

	Total (N=100%)	Per cent preoccupied with Holocaust: Very frequently	Frequently	Occasionally	Rarely	Never	Has not heard of Holocaust	No opinion	
0–4 years education									
Born in Asia–Africa	(185)	12	31	23	11	8	6	9	100%
Born in Europe–America	(42)	48	42	10	–	–	–	–	100%
Israel-born; father born in Asia–Africa	(14)	(29)	(36)	(29)	(7)	–	–	–	100%
Israel-born; father born in Europe–America	(3)	–	–	–	–	–	–	–	–
Israel-born; father born in Israel	(5)	–	–	–	–	–	–	–	–
5–10 years education									
Born in Asia–Africa	(334)	15	32	32	12	5	1	3	100%
Born in Europe–America	(387)	52	27	15	4	1	–	1	100%
Israel-born; father born in Asia–Africa	(68)	16	28	37	9	4	1	4	100%
Israel-born; father born in Europe–America	(39)	26	36	26	10	2	–	–	100%
Israel-born; father born in Israel	(29)	14	45	28	3	10	–	–	100%
11+ years education									
Born in Asia–Africa	(177)	14	41	33	8	3	1	–	100%
Born in Europe–America	(513)	34	38	21	5	2	–	–	100%
Israel-born; father born in Asia–Africa	(33)	12	39	40	6	3	–	–	100%
Israel-born; father born in Europe–America	(141)	9	42	36	9	4	–	–	100%
Israel-born; father born in Israel	(28)	21	25	50	4	–	–	–	100%
TOTAL POPULATION	(1998)	27	34	26	7	3	1	2	100%

Jewish people. Fully 70 per cent of Israeli Jews say that such a danger exists! Most of these think it may happen abroad; almost half think it might also be possible within Israel. Neither age, education nor country of origin makes much difference in these feelings. If Israelis seem cocky sometimes, there is a deep-seated apprehension underneath. At least this was so in 1970, during the tense days of the war of attrition over the Suez Canal; but it probably holds just as true today.

In this most elemental sense, at least, it is evident that the physical existence of the Jewish people is a matter of concern to Israelis. Moreover, it is a matter of shared concern. In the second generation, neither ethnic origin nor education affects this 'memory' of the events of thirty years ago. A sense of anxiety continues to exist about the present physical security of the Jews.

It follows that Israelis might be expected to feel strong ties of kinship with their fellow Jews abroad. This is confirmed in our data. Seventy-five per cent agree that 'the Jewish people cannot continue to exist without the existence of the State of Israel', and an even larger proportion says that they themselves 'feel hurt' when they hear that Jews abroad have been hurt. Slightly smaller proportions – but very large majorities – agree that the existence of the State is dependent, reciprocally, on 'strong spiritual connections with the Jews abroad'. They endorse, for example, a statement saying that they feel as if they are being praised when they hear that Jews abroad have been praised.

These feelings of interdependence are somewhat affected by age, education and religiosity in the sense that the young, the better educated and the irreligious are slightly more detached. The most important of these differences, perhaps, is in the feeling of younger people that Israel is less dependent on the support of the Jews outside than vice versa; Table 14.2 shows this difference. But while this is a trend that wants watching, the overall affirmation of interdependence is evidenced by a strong majority of all sectors of the population.

From the concern over the physical and spiritual survival of the Jews, it seems a natural conclusion that 'the defence and refuge which the State of Israel gives to every Jew' is seen as the primary justification for the Jewish right to its land. We asked: 'What is the basis of our right to live in the land of Israel [*eretz yisrael*]? How important is each of the following reasons?' From Table 14.3 which gives the distribution of replies it is evident that while a majority considered each of the reasons 'important' or 'very important', the right to a place of refuge and defence is foremost.

The next four reasons are given almost equal weight. Leading somewhat in importance is the fact of Zionist settlement on the land; that is to say, the fact that Jewish settlers took the initiative in coming and doing. This was the revolution of the labour movement in Zionism

TABLE 14.2 *Strength of Connection Between Jews in Israel and Outside*

	Per cent affirming that:			
Age	Israel is spiritually dependent on Jews abroad	The Jewish people cannot continue without existence of Israel	Feel proud when Jews abroad are praised	Feel hurt when Jews abroad are insulted
18–24	53	74	77	79
25–29	61	73	68	75
30–34	64	81	73	78
35–39	61	76	73	78
40–44	72	75	81	75
45–49	76	78	79	84
50–54	78	85	77	89
55–64	80	81	86	91
65+	74	78	86	87

against those who thought that the legal and political arrangements all ought to be made in advance. It represents an image of the peaceful conquest of land – either as if the Arabs did not exist, or hoping that this will be a venture from which both Jews and Arabs will benefit together. It contrasts, obviously, with rights based on military struggle to which a slightly smaller number subscribe.

These three are the existential bases of Israel's right, although the right to refuge has deep echoes in the Jewish past. The third and fourth

TABLE 14.3 *Legitimacy of Jewish Rights in the Land*

	Per cent who say reason is				
	Very important	Important	Not important	No opinion	
Refuge and defence provided by Israel for all Jews	78	14	3	5	100%
Zionist settlement in the land	63	26	5	6	100%
Yearning through the generations to return to homeland	59	27	7	7	100%
Birthright, dating to biblical times	57	25	12	6	100%
Military conquests beginning with War of Independence	53	25	16	6	100%
Decision of United Nations (to partition Palestine)	38	24	31	7	100%

TABLE 14.4 *Legitimacy of Jewish Rights in the Land*

		Per cent who say 'very important'					
	Total (N=100%)	Refuge and defence for all Jews	Zionist settlement	Longing for return	Birthright from Bible	Military conquests	U.N. decision
Age 18–29							
0–4 years education	(28)	(65)	(46)	(56)	(67)	(70)	(46)
5–10 years education	(209)	78	58	56	54	56	34
11+ years education	(393)	79	60	43	45	50	35
Age 30–50							
0–4 years education	(124)	74	52	71	80	61	38
5–10 years education	(406)	82	68	64	60	58	43
11+ years education	(326)	82	67	58	49	50	38
Age 50+							
0–4 years education	(110)	81	66	72	73	64	44
5–10 years education	(288)	81	71	76	73	60	45
11+ years education	(265)	85	75	66	59	52	45
TOTAL POPULATION	(2095)	78	63	59	57	53	38

reasons on the list, however, are genuinely traditional: the longing to return to Zion throughout the generations, and the birthright promised to our forefathers in biblical times. These – together with the first – are the 'Jewish' bases of Israeli rights.

The most important thing about the figures in Table 14.4 is their essential similarity. The most marked differences among the groups in the table – though even these are not large – are to be seen in the replies to the two 'traditional' reasons: the longing for Zion and the biblical birthright. The young and better educated are more reserved about these historical and traditional claims. But the homogeneity of the table is its most important message.

The 'traditional' reasons have considerably greater importance in the eyes of religious persons, as might be expected. Indeed, the rights to the heritage of the biblical forefathers is ranked foremost in importance by the religiously observant. And the traditional longing for Zion is as important as the fact that Israel affords refuge and defence to all Jews today. These differences between the religious and secular segments of the population, however, do not lead to a depreciation of any of the other reasons. While the rank order of the importance of the reasons is somewhat different, all six reasons are as strongly, or more strongly, endorsed by the religious groups as by the secular ones. Religion strengthens Zionism.

In the judgement of all, then, the State rests on both existential and Jewish rights. International law, at least as expressed in the U.N. decision of 1948, is considered less important by far.

On the whole, then, a concern with Jews as a people preoccupies Israelis, and Jewishness is surely an important part of their own identities. While we have had only limited opportunity to examine the meaning of these attachments, it does seem fairly evident that the manifest attachment is an ethnic one; to the Jewish people, rather more than to its religious traditions and ideas.

2. *The Role of Israel in Jewish Identity*

A specific question about the components of Jewish identity permits further examination of this impression. We asked: 'How much do the following influence the feeling that you are a part of the Jewish people and want to be a part of the Jewish people?'[6] Seven items were listed as reported in Table 14.5.

Four of every five Israelis affirm the *existential* reason. The very fact that I am here in the homeland, they say, makes me feel part of the Jewish people. Two-thirds associate their feelings of Jewish identity with the will for Jewish *continuity*: an awareness of the age-old struggle to stay alive as it was transmitted from generation to generation right down to the home in which they were raised. Smaller proportions – but still clear majorities – cite the history of Zionist settlement and the whole of Jewish history, as well as the ethics and religion of the Jewish people. Thus, contemporary peoplehood – building on the tenacious will to live – appears to be the basis of Jewish identity. The sense of having 'returned' seems to be at the root of it, and it is this basis in Jewish peoplehood, in turn, which connects the identity of those who have already come with the haven which they offer as a

TABLE 14.5 *Bases of Jewish Identity*

	Per cent who say reason is				
	Very influential	Influential	Not influential	No opinion	
Fact that I live in the homeland	80	12	3	5	100%
Jewish people's will to live	68	22	5	5	100%
Upbringing in my parents' home	64	23	9	4	100%
History of recent settlement in the land	51	34	10	5	100%
Ethics of the Jewish people	49	30	15	6	100%
Jewish religion	48	25	23	4	100%
Jewish history of 3,000 years	46	28	23	3	100%

right to those who are yet to come. 'I am Jewish because I am here', goes the answer to the question of Jewish identity. 'And the legitimacy of my being here is explained by those who have yet to come and by the efforts of those who came before me.' That is the answer to the previous question, of the Israeli right to the land. Note that the emphasis is 'I am Jewish because I am in Israel' rather more than 'I am in Israel because I am Jewish.'

Religious and secular Israelis differ, as shown in Table 14.6. Once again, we find the order of priorities conceived differently by the two groups. Just as in the discussion of the legitimacy of Jewish settlement in Israel, we see here that the religiously observant give first place to religion: 'Being religious makes me feel Jewish.' Much higher proportions of the observant assign influentiality to Jewish ethics and to Jewish history, without lowering the extent of their support for any of the other principles of Jewish identity. Thus, even the recent history of Zionist settlement – which ranks last among the observant – is affirmed as frequently by religious Israelis as by secular ones. Once again, then, we find the religious placing religion ahead of Zionism, while their commitment to Zionism remains as fervent as the others. Indeed, their Zionism is grounded in faith. And faith adds a fervour to the existential needs of the present and the sense of continuity with the past.

TABLE 14.6 *Bases of Jewish Identity, by Education and Religiosity*

	Total (N=100%)	Per cent who say reason is 'very influential'						
		Fact of my being here in homeland	Jewish will to live	Home education	History of Zionist settlement	Ethics of Jews	Jewish religion	3,000-year Jewish history
Attends synagogue every Sabbath and holiday								
0–4 years education	(90)	73	64	69	55	70	81	70
5–10 years education	(180)	80	70	76	53	62	77	56
11+ years education	(124)	86	87	90	58	80	89	74
Attends synagogue on occasional Sabbaths and holidays								
0–4 years education	(52)	84	76	76	54	67	76	46
5–10 years education	(177)	81	69	71	54	56	63	52
11+ years education	(168)	86	77	69	51	60	56	50
Attends synagogue on high holidays only								
0–4 years education	(75)	78	69	69	42	61	62	50
5–10 years education	(347)	81	62	64	51	45	45	40
11+ years education	(291)	85	73	66	58	40	33	38
Never attends synagogue								
0–4 years education	(42)	77	67	64	38	56	59	49
5–10 years education	(188)	81	62	53	53	37	29	39
11+ years education	(334)	82	67	51	50	37	21	34
TOTAL POPULATION	(2068)	80	68	64	51	49	48	46

That the religious group place religion ahead of Zionist history as a basis of Jewish identity is not so surprising. That the young do the same is a matter of considerable interest. Table 14.7 reveals that the 18–29 age groups downgrade the past. Relative to their elders, they find morality and history – personal, Zionist and Jewish – less relevant to their Jewish identity. Religion, however, is as important to the young as to the old, and relatively, therefore, religion moves up to fourth place in the rank-ordering of the young.

It would certainly be mistaken to conclude, on the basis of these findings, that the young are more religious than their elders. They are not; although they are not much less religious either. It may be correct to conclude that young people are sceptical of the high-sounding principles and abstract slogans on which the return to Zion and the renaissance of Jewish mission were predicated, and as a result, they do not so readily dismiss State and synagogue as 'tangible' anchors of identity. The lesser importance for younger people of historical and ethical rhetoric makes religion more salient, almost by default. Young people will have more trouble than their elders in grappling with the secular transformation of Jewishness if the alternatives of history and ethics are not so readily accessible to them.[7]

The only certain interpretation of Table 14.7 is that young people find the existential reasons – the fact of being here in the homeland, the fact of being alive and wanting to remain alive, and the fact of their attachment to home – the more compelling explanations of their feelings of Jewish belongingness. They are not more religious than their elders; rather, they are more reserved than their elders about history and ethics, less so than about religion.

3. *The Attributes of the Jewish People*

Still another way of looking at this same set of problems is implicit in the set of questions we asked about the characteristics that best define the Jewish people today. We chose a list of stereotypes which have been used – at various times – to characterize the Jewish people, and asked respondents how characteristic they thought they were of the people of Israel today. Here the importance of the ethnic attributes far exceeds that of the religious attributes. What's more, the young people are as likely as their elders to emphasize the importance of the ethical and the ethnic, and are *less* likely than their elders to agree that religious beliefs and practices are characteristic. Of course, it must be borne in mind that this series of questions asked respondents to act as *observers* of their society rather than to report their own inner beliefs.

Table 14.8 reports the percentage of the population who indicated that a given attribute was 'very characteristic' of the Jewish people

TABLE 14.7 *Bases of Jewish Identity, by Age and Education*

	Total (N=100%)	Per cent who say reason is 'very influential' Fact of my being here in homeland	Jewish will to live	Home education	History of Zionist settlement	Ethics of Jews	Jewish religion	3,000-year Jewish history
Age 18–29								
0–4 years education	(28)	(58)	(54)	(77)	(31)	(50)	(58)	(46)
5–10 years education	(209)	73	61	60	41	41	49	38
11+ years education	(339)	83	72	58	40	40	42	33
Age 30–50								
0–4 years education	(124)	78	71	69	53	66	71	55
5–10 years education	(406)	83	65	65	52	49	50	42
11+ years education	(326)	85	71	65	57	47	38	46
Age 50 +								
0–4 years education	(110)	82	68	63	45	67	75	60
5–10 years education	(288)	85	69	70	61	55	58	57
11+ years education	(265)	87	78	74	68	61	41	57
TOTAL POPULATION	(2095)	80	68	64	51	49	48	46

today, thus giving that attribute the highest rating possible on a four-point scale.[8]

TABLE 14.8 *Endorsements of Different Characteristics of the Jewish (Israeli) People Today**

	Per cent who say 'very characteristic'
1. Concern over peace among the nations	62
2. Self-sacrifice for the ideals of the people (*kiddush hashem*)	61
3. Attitude of sanctity toward human life	58
4. A nation that does not rely on others	58
5. Emphasis on the importance of family life	56
6. Diligent and ambitious	52
7. Progressive social thought	50
8. Stubbornness – 'a stiff-necked people'	49
9. A well-developed sense of justice	47
10. Mutual responsibility among all sectors of the people: 'All Israel is responsible one for the other'	46
11. The feeling that we as a people must set an example for other nations	45
12. The feeling of superiority in talent (intellect) over other nations	41
13. A special attitude to books ('People of the Book')	38
14. Keeping tradition	38
15. The feeling of moral superiority over other peoples	34
16. A belief in a God who watches over us	32
17. Love of learning (*torah*) for the sake of learning	28
18. Greed (money, profits)	26
19. Modest way of life and satisfaction with little	19
20. Clannishness (shutting oneself off from outsiders)	18
21. Anticipation of the Messianic era	17
22. Ability to laugh at ourselves	16

* One attribute has been dropped from this list and the discussion in the text: 'Lack of a sense of beauty'. Because of its formulation in the negative, where all other traits were positively formulated, it appears to have confused many respondents.

A quick glance through the table is enough to discern how positively and self-confidently Israelis view themselves.[9] Their self-image is made of altruism (items 1, 2) and reliability (6); mutual dependence (2, 5, 7, 10) but stubborn independence of others outside (4, 8). It is infused with a sense of commitment to social justice and progressive social thought (3, 7, 9). A majority of Israelis find these terms 'very characteristic'.

Strong minorities have a sense that there is a Jewish mission in the world (11, 12, 15), and that traditional values are still alive (13, 14, 15, 16, 17). But it is also clear that some of the latter are on the wane (19, 21).

Taking only those values that were judged to be positive[10] it is possible to verify this intuitive 'factor analysis' of what seems to be the manifest content of the items in the table. Using the SSA technique to map the interrelations among these items we find them distributed with respect to each other in the manner portrayed in Figure 14.1. The map suggests a spoke-like arrangement of the items with the value of family (5) at its hub; in other words, a view of the nation as family-oriented is central to the perceived characteristics of the people.

FIGURE 14.1 *SSA–1 Map of Characteristics of Jewish (Israeli) People* (Two dimensions; coefficient of alienation 0·2)

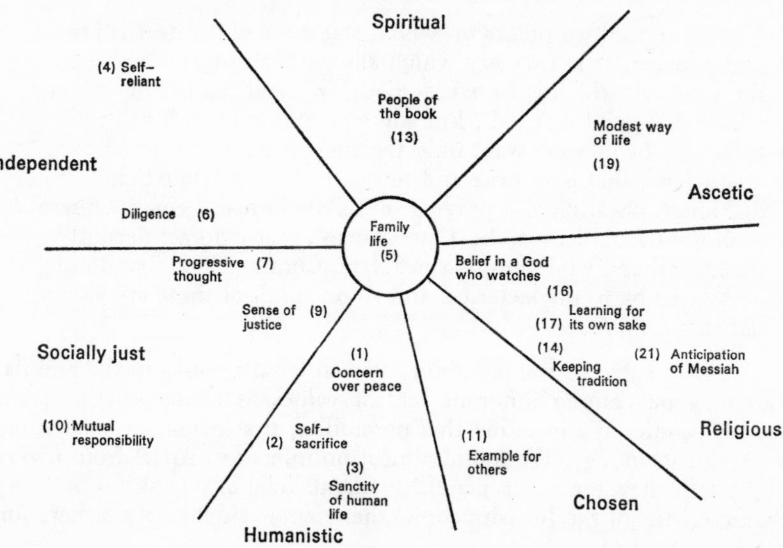

It will be seen that the right-hand side of the map includes most of the traditional religious values: religious beliefs and practices, asceticism and the idea of mission. The left-hand side consists of more secular values, although most of these also have an ethical quality, such as the values of social justice and of mutual responsibility. The values of peace, of life, of self-sacrifice – what we have labelled humanity – constitute a bridge between the more religious and the more secular sides of the map. So does the concept of the Book which lies as close to the secular-humanistic values as to the religious ones.

The clustering of traditional religious beliefs and practices on the one side of the graph, and the values of social justice on the other is an interesting mirror of the schism which entered Judaism at the time of the Enlightenment: the ethical and the 'religious' (in belief and ritual practice) became disconnected. The map reflects this. The two sets of values, in other words, are not correlated. They may inhere in some of the same persons; or they may not.

An equally graphic description of this problem is cited by Professor Dov Sdan in his discussion of the distinction that was drawn, in the Haskalah period, between the concepts of 'Jew' and 'man'.[11] An essay by Ben-Zion Alfas, notes Sdan, elaborates on the observation that one side of the Tablets of the Law (Commandments 1–5) deals with the relationship between man and his Maker, while the other side (Commandments 6–10) concerns ethical relations among persons. Figure 14.1 presents almost the very same picture.

> These are the two pillars on which stand the old concern 'Jew and Judaism', the two legs which allow a man to walk upright: the right leg which is called 'a good Jew', and the left leg which is called 'a good man' . . . But some people want to break the tablets in two. Some want only the right-hand side – to be a 'good Jew', that is to pray and to recite Psalms, while being dishonest, cheating and preying on fellow human beings. Others grab the left tablet – to be a 'good man', that is to act decently toward others, while limping in relationship to God, abandoning belief, Sabbath, phylacteries, and so on. Both of these are clowns, dancing on one leg.

The map suggests the possibility that different groups in the population may be naming different sets of values as characteristic of the Jewish people. We examine this possibility, first of all, by examining the influence of age. We found almost no influence. Apart from a very slight tendency for older people to name religious qualities as 'very characteristic' of the Jewish people, there is no evidence of a generation gap in these data.

Nor is education a strongly differentiating factor. Only religiosity genuinely discriminates among these characteristics. At each educational level, the more observant persons are more likely to assert that traditional religious attributes – of belief, study, ascetic living and mission – characterize the Jewish people today. The sense of mission – that the feeling that 'we as a people should set an example to others' – is still very strong even among the least religious.[12]

This same pattern – where the well educated and the more secular are more reserved about the idea that the Jews have any special ethical mission – is also evident in another set of questions. We asked: 'Is it desirable, in your opinion, that social relations in the State of Israel should be more moral than those in other countries or should they be the same as in other countries?' Two-thirds of the population said that Israel should be 'more just'. A like proportion said Israel should be more active than other nations in the fields of culture and learning. Just about half said that Israel ought to be 'more just' than other nations with respect to social legislation (56 per cent) and international relations (48 per cent). Forty-two per cent said that 'Israel should treat its hostages from Arab countries better than they treat those of our people who fall into their hands.'

Examining these data by religiosity – while holding constant age and education – reveals again that religion, but not age or education, influences replies. Religious people assert that Israel should be more moral than other nations. Only with respect to attitudes toward Arab prisoners is there no difference by degree of religiosity. There is some indication of a reversal on this question: the secular well-educated respondents are most insistent (63 per cent) on this question of treatment of Arab prisoners; with respect to all the other issues, however, this group are least likely to assert that Israel ought to be different from other nations. But, on the whole, neither education nor age is a determining factor.

We must reiterate, again and again, that these are self-images. The Israelis think well of themselves; and they expect a lot of themselves. One question which, unfortunately, has not been asked is whether they think their behaviour lives up to these expectations.

One sobering thought does arise from the data, however. We have seen the high regard in which Israelis hold human life and humanistic relationships. We asked respondents whether they thought that war, and the constant tension, affects these values. 'Is the assumption correct', we asked, 'that the prolonged war makes people insensitive so that they lose respect for their own lives and the lives of others?' Half the population agrees with this statement, thus tempering some of the lofty ideals with some stark reality. The distribution of replies, moreover, is unaffected by sex, education, ethnicity or religiosity. Curiously, it is not affected by age either, although one might have good reason to expect a different set of reactions from young people who are closer to the front than from their elders: the society as a whole is well experienced in such matters it seems, and again, young and old seem quite alike.

4. *Tentative Summary*

It is more than patriotism which holds the people together. It is a clear

TABLE 14.9 *Feeling of Chosenness and Sense of Mission, by Education and Religiosity*

	Total (N=100%)	Per cent who say: Be more moral in international relations	Be more moral in interpersonal relations	Have more just social legislation	Be more active in cultural-educational affairs	Treat its prisoners of war better than others
Attends synagogue every Sabbath and holiday						
0–4 years education	(90)	76	80	72	80	27
5–10 years education	(180)	72	82	76	80	33
11+ years education	(124)	68	80	71	85	44
Attends synagogue on occasional Sabbaths and holidays						
0–4 years education	(52)	72	78	74	82	42
5–10 years education	(177)	51	73	60	69	38
11+ years education	(168)	52	77	60	76	44
Attends synagogue on high holidays only						
0–4 years education	(75)	57	72	61	67	46
5–10 years education	(347)	50	69	55	68	33
11+ years education	(291)	30	57	39	64	49
Never attends synagogue						
0–4 years education	(42)	57	73	66	69	28
5–10 years education	(188)	44	60	50	60	44
11+ years education	(334)	33	60	53	64	63
TOTAL POPULATION	(2068)	48	68	56	68	42

sense of peoplehood which extends beyond the boundaries of the State. But its emphasis is on living people: those who came and reclaimed the land, those who are yet to come and those who are here. The sense of danger still looms large, and the feeling of being home permeates not only Israeli identity but Jewish identity as well. It also gives a sense of efficacy: being here we can do something for the others.

There is a very high regard for the traditions of Judaism and a feeling that the Jews are, and have to strive to be, ethically superior. Yet, this affirmation of the sense of mission is not directly reflected in the personal sense of Jewish identity which is much more closely tied to existential realities. And despite an awareness of the past and a glorification of tradition, the salience of the present is far greater. The past – biblical history, the diaspora, even recent Zionist history – is more salient to older persons than it is to the younger. It is most salient of all among the religious groups.

The downgrading of the historical and ethical among the young gives a more prominent place to religion, by default. This does not mean, as we have seen, that young people are unaware of the ethical imperatives of the Jewish people. No less than their elders, they say that the values of altruism and social justice characterize (and ought to characterize) the Jewish people today, but they do not feel that these attributes bear on their own identities just as they do not invoke tradition or history to justify either their own identities or their rights in the land.

The picture is not a simple one, and we must reiterate that our data are inadequate to the subtle and difficult set of problems to which this chapter presumes to address itself. Nevertheless, it seems altogether clear that Jewish and Israeli identities are thoroughly interwoven. 'I am Jewish because I am in Israel' and 'Israel exists for the Jews who have come and who may yet come' are the predominant themes. The sense of tradition, of history, of ethical attributes are all alive – but it is the sense of present peoplehood which is most salient. Inferring the future from the attitudes of youth, we may say that there is an even greater emphasis on present than on past, and a tendency to see the interdependence of Israel and the Jews outside as growing more one-sided.[13]

5. *Social and Normative Integration*

The differences between young and old are *not* large, however, and there is only little evidence of a generation gap. On most things, young people are like their elders. They are somewhat less observant: 20 per cent of the younger men go to the synagogue every Sabbath and holiday as against 35 per cent of those over 50. But, of course, this may change as the young grow older. The young are somewhat more present-oriented and existential as we have seen. They are more reserved about the relevance for their own identities of high-minded ideals and historical continuity, but they are aware of these and affirm both their applicability to the Jewish people and the desirability of their perpetuation.

When young people and their elders were asked explicitly which of the characteristics of the Jewish people are more typical of youth and which are more typical of older people, most were said to characterize both groups equally. There were some differences: the older generation was seen as more religious, more family-oriented and more ascetic, while younger people were judged more pleasure-oriented, more present-oriented and more rebellious (even though history might well find the parental generation objectively more rebellious). But even when differences between the generations are perceived, there is almost complete agreement in perceptions: younger and older people share the same judgements about the differences that exist, where they do.

Our conclusion, then, is that the generation gap is small. The data do not support those who feel that the young have lost faith in their elders, that they are less confident about the legitimacy of the Zionist enterprise.

But what of the other possible cleavages in Israel society? What can we conclude concerning the gaps between ethnic groups, or about differentials in education and income?

Differences between educational groups in matters discussed in this chapter are smaller than the differences among the age groups. Apart from the very strong correlation between educational level and religiosity – and the implications of religiosity for Jewish and Israeli identity – the extent of normative integration in the society, over these matters, is very striking. On other matters, related to class and ethnicity, there are more serious differences. Thus, the higher the education, the greater the demand for large income differentials between different sectors of the working population. Education, of course, is directly related to income.[14]

Education is also directly related to ethnicity. As we have seen, education levels most ethnic differences, meaning that Jews of different ethnic origin act and think remarkably alike provided they have the same number of years of schooling. But very few do: few Western immigrants or their children have only an elementary-school education, and few Eastern immigrants or their children reach the university.

But in matters of culture and ideology, certain ethnic differences persist even after education is held constant. We saw certain examples in the chapter on 'going out'. Differences in theatre-going, for example, continue to characterize the second generation, even when educational level is held constant.

Actually, there is quite a lot of optimism about the future of ethnic relations. We asked our respondents for their opinions about the relationship among the ethnic groups 'today' and 'four years ago, about a year before the Six Day War'. On a nine-point scale (where 9 is the top), the score for the population as a whole is 6·2. This represents an improvement as compared with the earlier period about which we asked.[15] In the first generation – for both time periods – it is the

TABLE 14.10 *Estimated Goodness of Ethnic Relations among Jews in Israel*

(Average score on a nine-point scale:
1 = poor relations, 9 = excellent relations)

Country of origin and generation	Appraisal of Relations today (1970)	four years earlier
Born in Asia–Africa	5·7	5·3
Born in Europe–America	6·8	5·7
Israel-born; father born in Asia–Africa	6·3	5·4
Israel-born; father born in Europe–America	6·0	5·2
Israel-born; father born in Israel	6·1	5·1

Westerners who are more sanguine about the situation. In the second generation, this difference between the estimates of the two groups disappears; if anything, the Easterners are more optimistic.

As for the desire for organization along ethnic lines – political, economic and cultural – several important observations can be made. All groups, regardless of ethnicity, generation or education, favour the continuity of ethnic pluralism in culture, that is, in things having to do with customs, holidays, music and the like. Over half want to maintain ethnic ties for this purpose. Sixty per cent of the population affirm the desirability of ethnic organization for the purpose of mutual economic aid with support somewhat more concentrated among the elementary-educated groups. One-third of the population wants ethnic organization to take a political form. This opinion is slightly more characteristic of Eastern than Western groups, of older than younger, and of lower educated rather than better educated. A potential for the politicization of ethnicity may be lurking here.

In a series of questions about relations with Arabs, the influence of education and ethnicity are both apparent: the better educated are more favourable to Arab rights, more willing to make friends with Arabs and the like. Jews of Western origin are more favourable than those Jews who come from the Moslem countries. About one-third of the population

TABLE 14.11 *Willingness for Personal Friendship with an Arab, by Education and Ethnicity*

	Total (N=100%)	Per cent who say: Certainly willing	Depends on circumstances	Unwilling	Certainly unwilling	No opinion	
0–4 years education							
Born in Asia–Africa	(183)	9	13	27	48	3	100%
Born in Europe–America	(42)	10	29	35	26	–	100%
Israel-born; father born in Asia–Africa	(14)	14	7	50	29	–	100%
Israel-born; father born in Europe–America	(4)	*	*	*	*	*	100%
Israel-born; father born in Israel	(5)	*	*	*	*	*	100%
5–10 years education							
Born in Asia–Africa	(329)	21	24	25	28	2	100%
Born in Europe–America	(384)	30	29	23	15	2	100%
Israel-born; father born in Asia–Africa	(68)	25	21	34	21	–	100%
Israel-born; father born in Europe–America	(39)	28	41	5	23	3	100%
Israel-born; father born in Israel	(27)	37	15	30	15	4	100%
11+ years education							
Born in Asia–Africa	(177)	28	29	17	24	1	100%
Born in Europe–America	(509)	38	36	15	10	1	100%
Israel-born; father born in Asia–Africa	(32)	25	41	19	16	–	100%
Israel-born; father born in Europe–America	(141)	40	41	9	10	–	100%
Israel-born; father born in Israel	(27)	37	48	7	7	–	100%
TOTAL POPULATION	(1981)	29	29	20	20	2	100%

is 'certainly' prepared to befriend an Arab and an additional third would do so under certain conditions. About 40 per cent would not. The better educated (11 years of schooling or more) are four times more likely to answer in the affirmative. Age makes no difference whatever; education is the predominant influence.

On the whole, it is our opinion that age, education and ethnicity do not loom large as barriers to normative and social integration of the Jewish community of Israel. Others may think otherwise. We know there have been recent ethnic tensions. We know that the correlation between ethnicity on the one hand, and education-income on the other, is explosive. We know that there is talk of a generation gap, and even of a moral 'crisis' which allegedly is taking the form of unethical practices in business and bureaucracy. There is an alleged rise in hedonism and individualism. Our data lend little support to these gloomy perceptions.

Even the most divisive factor that we have been able to identify – religion – is not as divisive as it seems. It is true that religion, more than any other factor, is associated with the widest range of difference in the consumption of culture, in identity, in the perception of national characteristics and the like. But in the area of moral integration at least, the religious community is no less Zionist and no less ethnic or existential than their secular fellow citizens. They are simply more religious, and put religion ahead of the other bases of identity, national legitimacy and national character. Yet, the potential for conflict is more apparent here than anywhere else, as far as our data are concerned.

6. *Values and the Consumption of Culture*

In the previous chapter, we saw some relationship between patterns of media use and patterns of values: certain media are more closely associated with certain kinds of needs.

As far as the values discussed in the present chapter are concerned, there is essentially no association with different patterns of the consumption of culture. We had hoped to find such differences, of course, but they are not apparent, with the single exception of religion. Religious observance is negatively associated with almost all aspects of the consumption of culture. It is particularly visible in the case of participation in out-of-home activities, but also apparent in the lower consumption of leisure activities inside the home. Attendance at lectures and participation in study are, however, positively associated with religiosity.

But is this a question of values or way of life? The Jewish religion, of course, is both. It is highly prescriptive of the daily round of activities. In the latter sense, it may be that religious people are simply less 'free' – they have less discretionary leisure – to participate. It may also be true that the content of some popular culture is offensive to religious people.

As far as other values are concerned, it is very difficult to find associations between them and patterns of the consumption of culture that are not better explained by their joint association with education and age. However, it may be worth noting that one set of activities appears to be associated with the value of 'experiencing beauty' and another set with the importance of 'being entertained' or 'releasing tension'. Correlates of the orientation to beauty are concerts and museums, while correlates of the orientation to entertainment are night clubs, popular music and television-viewing. Activities such as cinema and theatre are related to both types of orientation.

On the whole, however, we are forced to the conclusion that values and leisure patterns are not highly related. Following George Steiner, we might suggest that one reason is that modern society has disconnected values from art and culture.[16] No relationship exists, says Steiner, between the consumption of high culture and moral beliefs and behaviour. It is a myth, he argues, to believe in the greater ethical influence of classical music or serious art.

But we cannot really answer this question in the present study, for two reasons. First of all, it is difficult to answer because of the relationship between value patterns and demographic variables such as religion or education which 'explain' differences in the consumption of culture better than do values. Secondly, and more seriously, we cannot go deeply into this problem because our study did not focus primarily on the *content* of culture. It will take another study, of a somewhat different kind, to explore this question further.

NOTES – CHAPTER FOURTEEN

1. See Georges Friedmann, *The End of the Jewish People?*, New York: Doubleday & Co., 1967. In a remarkable essay entitled, 'On the Intellectual Preeminence of the Jews in Western Europe', Thorstein Veblen anticipated this problem many years ago. See M. Lerner (ed.), *The Portable Veblen*, New York: Viking Press, 1950.
2. George Steiner, *In Bluebeard's Castle*, London: Faber, 1972. Steiner argues the absence of contemporary relationship between ethical behaviour and the partaking in 'high' culture or 'fine' arts.
3. While certain areas of content – of books, television, films, holidays, etc. – have been explored in this study and reported in the preceding chapters, it is technically impossible to cross-tabulate these with value patterns because, as will be recalled, not all questions were asked of all respondents.

The value questions and the media-content questions were not on the same questionnaire.

4. Unfortunately, such long-run relationships are not easily accessible to observation by empirically minded social scientists.
5. Before beginning to tread this difficult ground, however, it would be well to emphasize that our study was not designed to answer questions put in quite this form: that is to say, we had not formulated our original intentions in quite this way, and therefore the data presented here have had to be adapted to the purpose at hand rather than adduced ready-made.
6. A careful discussion of this problem may be found in Simon Herman, *Israelis and Jews*, op. cit.
7. It suggests that the Ministry of Education may be succeeding where it thought it was failing, and failing where it thought it was succeeding. In the much discussed Programme for Jewish Consciousness, the Ministry has been attempting to make Jewish customs and beliefs more familiar to children in the secular schools. The assumption underlying this programme is that ignorance of the tradition is increasing, that younger Israelis find themselves uncomfortable in ceremonial roles, etc. While this may be true, it is ironic that some of the more secular bases of Jewish identity are giving the young at least as much trouble.
8. The question refers to the 'people of Israel' (*am yisrael*) which is here rendered (correctly) as the Jewish people. The connotation is to Jews everywhere, not just in Israel, but it is inescapable that some respondents would perhaps have thought it referred to the Jews in Israel.
9. Since the items were formulated positively, and there were more desirable than undesirable traits, there is a basis for the methodological objection that respondents were being invited to express positive attitudes. Perhaps so. But a comparative study of self-images of Jewish, Arab and German students using a different technique, supports our conclusion that the Israeli self-image is highly positive. See Kalman Binyamini, 'On the Images of Israelis, Americans, Germans and Arabs in the Eyes of Israeli Youth', *Megamot* (Hebrew), 16, 1969, pp. 364–75.
10. An analysis of the intercorrelations among these items, using the SSA technique, groups a set of 'negative' attributes and a large cluster of 'positive' ones. It is clear from this analysis that 'satisfaction with a modest way of life' is considered positive and traditional, whereas 'greed' (18) is negative. Other non-positive values are 'stubbornness' (8), 'clannishness' (20) and surprisingly, the ability to laugh at oneself (22).
11. In Dov Sdan, *Betzetcha Uveoholecha*, Tel Aviv: Massada, 1966, p. 46 (Hebrew).
12. The least educated (0–4 years) are omitted from the table. At each level of religiosity, they behave as do the religious and uneducated.
13. We do not know, of course, whether young people will retain their attitudes as they grow up, or become as past-oriented as their elders.
14. 'What income differentials ought there to be – or oughtn't there to be differentials at all – between people working in different occupations or in different jobs?'

Monthly income (IL)	Per cent replying 'large' or 'very large' differentials (on six-point scale)
0– 399	26
400– 599	30
600– 799	28
800– 999	35
1000–1249	39
1250–1499	46
1500–1949	47
1750+	51
TOTAL	34

15. Since our study was completed, there was an outbreak of inter-ethnic tension, mostly having to do with economic problems, and symbolized by the emergence of the so-called Black Panthers. Whether this changed anything fundamental is doubtful, though it certainly made the educational-economic differentials between the ethnic groups more salient.
16. See Steiner, op. cit.

CHAPTER FIFTEEN Cultural Policy in a Small Nation: An Agenda for a Meeting with Policy-Makers

There is no easy relationship between research and policy. Researchers who conclude their studies with 'policy recommendations' and blithely assume that their will will be done are simply deluding themselves. Researchers who *really* are interested in policy know that the road from library or laboratory to government is a difficult one – whatever route one takes. Some researchers preach revolution to implement their findings: Marx is the obvious example. Others, noting the need for change, expend great energy in frontal attack on establishments and in the demand for reform: Ralph Nader's research-based campaigns in the United States are an example. But effective reforms are also achieved more quietly, by researchers who are willing to consider policy-making also from the policy-makers' point of view.

It is easy to caricature the policy-maker as a bureaucrat who fears nothing so much as change. Some are. Others are quite receptive to ideas for change, yet they find (sometimes to their relief) that the requisite political, organizational or material resources are not available to them. The researcher with experience in applying social research knows that he must also understand the context in which policy is made before he can hope for the implementation of his findings.

All of this presumes, however, that the researcher is clear about how his findings *ought* to be implemented. This is only rarely the case. Much more frequent is the situation where the researcher has no clear idea of the alternative ways in which his findings may be implemented, and needs the policy-maker to help in their translation. Nor should one underestimate the policy-maker's potential assistance to the researcher in the interpretation of his findings. Often, at some point where the results of research are unclear to the researcher, the response of the policy-maker may be illuminating.

However one looks at the relationship between policy-making and applied research, then, the beginning of wisdom is for policy-maker and researcher to talk together. Short of revolution or campaigns for radical reform, the process of interpreting findings and translating them into actionable terms can only begin where researcher and policy-maker make the concerted effort of understanding each other. Otherwise, the policy-maker will dismiss the research as unrealistic and the researcher will dismiss the policy-maker as politician or bureaucrat – and nothing will happen.

The present study had a good start in this respect: indeed its original impetus, as has been noted, came from the Minister of Education himself. But no Minister can get very far without the support and interest of his permanent staff: in the present instance, some of the senior staff showed interest, others did not. During the fieldwork and the analysis of findings, however, the rate of interaction between policy-makers and researchers fell off; this was surely the fault of the researchers, who, caught up in the introverted world of coders, computers, collegial teamwork and limited budgets, are pleased to be left alone to get on with it. And the truth is that one can go on and on – probing ever more deeply – into the never-ending puzzles and riddles of data analysis.

As the analysis drew to a close, the dialogue between researchers and policy-makers showed signs of renewal. Two committees of the Knesset – the Labour Committee and the Education Committee – each devoted several sessions to close inspection of the results. The Labour Committee considered the implications for proposed legislation to increase the number of non-working days, ultimately leading to the institution of a five-day working week. The Education Committee considered the overall implications of the study for the formulation of policy in the field of culture and the arts.

In addition to the Knesset committees, the results were examined by the National Council on Culture and the Arts; by the Association for Adult Education; by the subcommittee of the Council for Higher Education (the Lifson Committee) charged with formulating policy for post-secondary education; by the Librarians' Association; sports groups and others. And the press gave the report considerable coverage.

But all this is only a beginning. In this concluding chapter, then, we can do no more than propose an agenda for the discussion of implications. Note again that we are not pointing to clear-cut implications, but, rather, to issues which need airing. These might serve as a basis for the dialogue out of which policy might emerge.

1. The first and most fundamental issue, perhaps, is the question of whether there is room or need for an explicit cultural policy in a democratic society. Aren't *laissez-faire* and the guarantee of maximum freedom for expression the best cultural policy both for producers of cultural materials and for their consumers?

Even those who wish the answer were yes must be aware that that is not now the case and probably never will be the case. Although no cultural policy has been formally pronounced in Israel (and in most other countries), the everyday acts of the legislative and executive branches of government have clear-cut consequences for culture and the arts. The Ministry subsidizes theatre and does not subsidize popular music; the Ministry subsidizes some theatre groups and not others;

some Israeli-made films are granted a rebate of taxes and some are not; the making of a 'serious' Israeli film is an almost impossible financial risk; the playing of the music of Wagner and Richard Strauss is still largely taboo; broadcasting, by and large, *avoids* religious subjects on the Sabbath; most cultural establishments are closed on the Sabbath; the number of working hours is prescribed; the municipality builds football fields in most neighbourhoods, not golf courses; there is a very stiff tax on travel abroad; Western classical music, attended by some 15 per cent of the population, is very heavily subsidized; bread is subsidized, but not books; very large quantities of public funds and energy go into the planning of the Independence Day Celebrations; there is a revival of interest in the teaching of Arabic, and even Yiddish – after years when these languages were not much encouraged. This is not quite the cultural dictatorship of an authoritarian regime whose elite is fully prepared to dictate the rules for both artists and audiences; it is, rather, a mix of freedom and paternalism, centralism and individual initiative, tradition and modernization. But the situation is not so different in most democratic states.[1]

What is the cultural policy underlying all of this? Is there one? Ought it to be made explicit and thus subject to public debate? Different people will give different answers to these questions, but it is difficult even to hope – if such is one's hope – that the foreseeable future will see a decline in the Government's share in *de facto* policy-making in the field of culture. Why not then make those policies explicit? Zionism had a more or less explicit cultural policy for the revival of the basic culture. Is that still alive? Has it succeeded? What of the obvious orientation toward European culture and the basic disinterest in Oriental culture? Shouldn't that be discussed?

For the fact is that culture is political. It affects votes, it affects the national consensus, it affects tourism, it affects international relations, it affects the national image abroad. In the case of Israel, it affects the Jews of the whole world – and perhaps Christians and Moslems too. Governments placate ethnic and regional groups by giving them support for their local cultures; governments put the image of their nation forward through cultural manifestations; governments show recognition for each other through the exchange of culture and communication.

The problems of new and small nations in this respect are all the greater. Many of them – like the African nations – must mould a national identity out of tribal and regional particularisms; and they must find means of unifying their culture for the purpose of trans-national communion. By contrast, many of the Asian nations, those with ancient national cultures, have the problem of coping with modernization: What are the ways of blending old and new? Can modern mass media help, or do they only hinder? How can they avoid being overwhelmed, culturally speaking, by the international tidal wave of 'the free flow of information' which inevitably gives an advantage to the politically and culturally strong nations? Israel has both sorts of problems. It is trying to blend disparate streams of ethnic culture into a national culture, and it wants that culture to be a synthesis, of some sort, between the traditional and the modern. It has, after all, a commitment to Jewish continuity.

But how Jewish should Israel be? Does Jewish mean religious? How much encouragement should be given to the continuity of ethnic cultures? What if somebody were to come right out and proclaim that Israel wants to be a European culture – with European values and European arts?

These are subjects for debate, and some of the data of the present study speak to them.

2. There is the problem of increased leisure. The population is in favour of reducing the work week; so, it appears, are many of the leadership. Only the consciousness of the national security and the fear of further inflation appear to be holding back the appropriate legislation.

But what will be done with the additional time? The religious groups hope that the secular activities now pursued on the Sabbath will be transferred to another day. Most people, religious and irreligious alike, will simply do more of what they now do on non-work days.

Surely those charged with cultural policy cannot simply ignore this prospect. First of all, there is the question of which day – Friday, Sunday, or a day in the middle of the week? Will activity cease altogether on the new day off – or might it be useful to allow people to do their shopping and their business with government on this day? The choice which will eventually be made will have clear implications also for the character of the Sabbath.

And what new cultural opportunities will be offered with the five-day week? Surely, this is one of the great historic opportunities for renascent Israeli culture. How could one wish for more – if one is concerned with cultural policy – than to plan for the culture of another, unspoken-for Day of Leisure? And yet, to the best of our knowledge, nobody is giving this problem any thought whatever!

3. Indeed, what of Jewish continuity? How will Israel give expression to its heritage? Study and reading, the two traditional means of 'life-long education' in Judaism, are now individualized and secularized. Study is career-oriented, and reading is for self-gratification.

Our research gives support to those who contend that there is an active desire for *adult education* in Israeli society. Moreover, the demand is for education for-its-own-sake rather than career-oriented education. Indeed, this kind of organized or spontaneous study has always existed in Israel, and may be gaining momentum.

It can be argued that adult education is the modern-day equivalent of the lifelong education provided for in traditional Judaism. What better way to plan for the new day of leisure than by infusing it with Jewish continuity? What better way to infuse Jewish continuity than by associating the added day with an attractive programme of adult education?

4. Or, perhaps the Sabbath should be the day. With added leisure, the question of the character of the Sabbath will loom even larger. Today, it is the only day off; tomorrow, it will be one of two days. It can either lose its character altogether and melt into an amorphous weekend, or reassert itself as the Sabbath.

Cultural policy-makers are giving little thought to the Sabbath. That, at least, is the impression given by the policy-makers' silence on the subject. Of course, cultural policy-making is not usually defined in this way, so perhaps there is little reason for surprise. The debates and the policy-making process concentrate on such things as subsidizing the arts or how to sensitize people to aesthetic values – worthy causes in themselves – but, surely, the character of the Jewish Sabbath is no less important a problem for the Council on Culture and the Arts.

In the early days of the *yishuv*, the 'traditionals' – that is, the not-necessarily-religious people who cared for the continuity of Jewish culture – instituted the *oneg shabbat*, a community event on Friday night or Saturday morning. This is an example of the kind of innovation which might be the subject of policy-making whether inside or outside of Government: how to make the Sabbath meaningful for the 75 per cent of the population which is not orthodox?

Should the restrictions now in force – those which close most places of culture on the Sabbath – be lifted? Sizeable proportions of the population think so; equally sizeable proportions think not.

Should greater investment be made for the fast-growing activity of Sabbath outings in the family automobile? Summer Saturdays will see increasing traffic jams as the mobile population increases.

Or should other provision be made? Should the Sabbath, perhaps, be the day for Adult Education? How can broadcasting and the other arts contribute, if at all? Has the synagogue anything to offer to the less-than-orthodox?

Is anybody willing to debate these things?

5. From the Sabbath to the holidays. We have shown that the holidays are undergoing transformation in their meaning. We have shown how

the holidays that lend themselves to nationalistic and familistic transformations appear to be holding their own, while the most spiritual of holidays, Yom Kippur, puzzles a sizeable minority.

The entire question of the content of holidays deserves serious thought – not necessarily in Government. Yom Haatzmaut (Independence Day) is still struggling for definition, and considerable thought and effort have gone into the day. The religious community is somewhat divided over its religious status, though it seems likely that it will be absorbed into the religious calendar. But, once again, the problem is that of the non-orthodox. Military parades, it is agreed, are not enough – perhaps not even desirable. Street celebrations are desirable, but how to give them the spontaneity they once had?

The institutionalization of memories is one of the marks of Jewish holidays, and one wonders whether the Holocaust has found its proper setting. We found that the memory is salient, but we do not know how it will continue through the generations. Unfortunately, we did not study the extent to which the Day of the Holocaust has meaningfully incorporated these memories. Jewish holidays have always absorbed added meaning: perhaps Tisha B'av or another of the holidays of tragedy should encompass the memory of the Holocaust and perhaps Passover should encompass the new Independence?

Altogether, the subject of holidays as custodians of memories and as ceremonial reaffirmation of communal values urgently needs to be studied and planned for.

6. The dangers of nationalism are evident throughout the study. The supreme pride in the State, the dazzling self-image of the people together with the perpetual security threat, point to a lurking chauvinism, which some would claim is quite widespread. For the non-religious, Jewish identity and Israeli identity are almost indistinguishable.

The Jewish antidotes to chauvinism are several: the sense of mission is one of these, if the ideal of social justice underlies it. The sense of the spirituality of the individual (as in a holiday like Yom Kippur) is another. The salience of the connection to Jews outside of Israel is a third.

Indeed, the consciousness of Jewish identity that connects Jews everywhere is still very strong in Israel, though there is a decline in this sense of interdependence in the second generation. The second generation is also less keenly concerned with the past, ancient or recent: altogether it is more present-oriented. This, too, is a legitimate concern of the makers of cultural policy: it is the connection between Jews of Israel and the Jews outside, and between the Jews of today and the Jews of yesterday, that will keep Israel from being just another new nation, and even worse, a self-satisfied one.

7. There is a race, as we have seen, between ethnicity and education. Ethnic differences are large in many cultural pursuits. Some of these are differences in tradition or style, and there is a desire for differentiation to continue, as in religious practices or the arts. Is anybody paying attention to this?

Other differences between the ethnic groups are more divisive, and undesired (at least by most people). The data of this study, and others, show that education can overcome these differences. That means that if one compared the university-educated son of an immigrant from Yemen with an equally educated son of a Czech immigrant, there would be little to distinguish them in occupational attainments, cultural pursuits and values. The same would hold true if one compared elementary-school-educated sons of the two groups. The trouble is that there are extremely few Yemenites who make it to the university and very few Czechoslovakians who don't. This makes a problem for social research: but we can take it. The problem is more difficult for cultural policy. And the problem is well known.

Less well known is that a similar problem connects age and education. Increased age leads to increased withdrawal from out-of-home cultural activities of every kind – whether film, theatre, concerts, lectures, or just visiting – except when higher education intervenes. If an individual has had the benefit of a secondary-school education, or even better, a university education, the dulling and isolating effects of age can be overcome. Dozens of statistical tables in this study bear that out.

The problem of the cultural policy-maker is to help the less well educated of the present generation overcome the constraints of age. The least well educated are also the most minimal consumers of the media, and least in contact with other people – even family – which makes their isolation more acute.

8. The new cities represent a similar kind of problem. Compared with the old-established settlements of like size, the new towns need help. Their inhabitants complain that there are not enough opportunities for spending leisure appropriately, and that there is a lack of companionship. This experience that one's neighbours are more 'remote' has been noted in new towns and housing settlements in other societies as well. One study found, for example, that there were thought to be fewer baby-sitters in a new housing estate as compared with an established neighbourhood.

We have shown that persons of equal education have rather equal access to the supply of culture regardless of where they live. But, again, 'equal education' in the new towns and many small places is equally low, and therefore, the perception that they do not have 'enough' facilities for spending leisure, is not a false perception: lower-educated people at least see the institutions of culture in the large cities and old towns, even if they don't use them very often.

9. This, in turn, raises the more conventional question of the democratization of the arts, and the democratization of access. Is it fair for the society to subsidize symphony orchestras when so few people attend concerts, and when those who do can afford to pay? Is it fair that no comparable popular art is subsidized in this way, except perhaps for the local film industry which receives a few million Israeli pounds per year via tax exemption?

Which are the popular arts that deserve to be subsidized? The Report of the Arts Council in Great Britain recently sparked a similar debate. How about television? Perhaps the society should invest much larger sums in this medium, considering the proportion of people's free time which it commands.

The theatre seems to be a viable popular art, engaging sizeable proportions of the less well educated as well. The Ministry of Education has mounted an elaborate programme of bringing theatre to new towns and smaller places. Some effort has been made to effect movement in the reverse direction as well; that is, to bring audiences to the big cities. This two-way flow highlights one of the central aspects of the issue of the democratization of the arts: that of the relationship between the cultural centre and the periphery. While the outflow of culture from the centre to the provinces is highly institutionalized (a centralized mass media system does precisely that), the need to encourage cultural production in the provinces and to bring the best of it to the attention of the centre is one of the tasks of cultural policy-makers which needs to be more widely recognized.

10. There is an obvious connection between these concerns and the stimulation of indigenous creativity. It is perhaps ironic, though understandable and probably inevitable, that much of the culture consumed by the Israelis, who belong to a highly creative people, is imported from the outside, and that even some of its indigenously created culture reflects imitative influences of imported materials. Ninety per cent of the films shown, 50 per cent of the television programmes and a large share of stage plays and of books purchased and read come from abroad. Some of it is translated (as in the theatre and books) and some of it is subtitled (as in television and the cinema).

One might debate and try to evaluate the pros and cons of this phenomenon. Surely no small nation can be culturally self-sufficient. Some would argue that the very notion of self-sufficiency in the field of culture is essentially parochial. But the issue is not either/or. Rather, it is the protection and encouragement provided for indigenous creativity while at the same time avoiding cultural parochialism and insularity.

There is some evidence that the film industry in Israel may finally be at a take-off point. The number of home-made films has increased, but that in itself is a very questionable blessing if it were not for the fact that there are signs of a concomitant growth in more serious efforts. The Ministries of Education and of Commerce and Industry have given thought to supporting these efforts, and are now offering, in addition to the tax rebate, the opportunity of positive reward for those who are prepared to risk making a try at a 'good' Israeli film.

Recognition and encouragement for play-writing have also been institutionalized in recent years, though one may ask whether any of this is enough to attract and support promising young people in the theatre.

These are the areas to which policy-makers have given thought, and often with success. Attention also needs to be given to the more modern arts of broadcasting, popular music, design and so on.

11. The investment in culture, however, cannot succeed ultimately without giving careful attention to the education of the consumer of culture. Knowing how to view a film or a television programme is as important, these days, as knowing how to read a book or a newspaper – not that many people approach these arts as critically as they might.

The education of the consumer of culture and mass communication begins at home and school, of course, but like all of education it is a lifelong task. It thus properly belongs in the realms of the cultural policy-maker and the adult educator.

12. Finally, we would like to recommend for this agenda the continuation of empirical research on the subjects discussed in this volume. As time goes by, and, particularly, as policy is made and implemented, it is useful and interesting to measure the changes that take place in the opinions, attitudes, practices and leisure patterns of the population. An effort should also be made to collect comparable data from other societies, which would make systematic comparative analysis possible. These efforts should be carried out periodically, perhaps every five or ten years. For only through such continuing studies of 'social and cultural indicators' do societies learn to observe and evaluate themselves.

NOTE – CHAPTER FIFTEEN

1. For a discussion of cultural policy in societies, see Raymond Williams, *Communications*, London: Chatto & Windus, 1966 (revised ed.); also for

the discussion of the Annual Report of the Arts Council of Great Britain, see Paul Harrison, 'Beauty and the Beast', *New Society*, Vol. 22, No. 530, 30 November 1972, p. 512; and Karen King and Mark Blaug, 'Does the Arts Council Know What It is Doing?', *Encounter*, Vol. XLI, No. 3, September 1973, pp. 6–16. For a discussion of cultural policy in Israel, see S. N. Eisenstadt, *Israeli Society*, op. cit., Chapter 10, and the recent *Cultural Policy in Israel* by Y. Melkman, in the UNESCO series, Paris: 1973.

APPENDIX On Sampling

During the course of the fieldwork, interviews were conducted with 3,697 people, living in fifty-six different communities, and representing the entire Jewish population of Israel over eighteen years of age.

The sample was drawn from the electoral register for 1969, which includes the names of all citizens over eighteen. Since the fieldwork was carried out in mid-1970, the minimum age of the respondents was at that time nineteen years. Because of past experience in surveys of this sort, which had indicated that use of the electoral register for sampling purposes leads to a fairly high drop-out rate, an initial sample of 8,000 names was drawn. Thus, the rate of completed interviews is slightly less than 50 per cent of the initial total sample. The main causes of sample drop-outs were as follows: address unidentifiable – 28 per cent; refusals – 15 per cent; language difficulties (interviewers were instructed to conduct the interview only in Hebrew and under no circumstances to attempt their own translations of questions) – 9 per cent; unknown at the address specified – 8 per cent; moved – 8 per cent; respondent not found at home in three visits – 7 per cent; respondent sick, hospitalized or deceased – 5 per cent; Army service – 3 per cent; other causes – 17 per cent.

The distribution of the sample among the different types of communities was determined so as to represent the distribution of the total Jewish population among three categories of communities differentiated by size:

1. Urban communities with a population of 20,000 and over;
2. Urban communities of a population between 2,000 and 20,000;
3. Rural communities with a population under 2,000.

The selection of the fifty-six communities sampled, out of the total of 779 Jewish communities, was carried out in consultation with the Division on Statistical Methods of the Central Bureau of Statistics of the Government of Israel. Their assistance is hereby gratefully acknowledged.

The three categories of settlements mentioned above were also used for selecting the number of settlements from each category. In the first category all twenty-five cities and towns with a population of over 20,000 were included in the sample. The second category of settlements, with a population of 2,000 to 20,000, includes forty-eight settlements of which ten, randomly selected by size, area, and age of the settlement, were included. The third category includes 706 rural settlements of which twenty-one were selected to represent all types of settlements (non-collective villages as well as semi-collective moshavim and collective kibbutzim) by size and age of settlement. Thus the distribution of settlements included in the sample according to their size is as follows: 45 per cent (twenty-five) large urban settlements; 18 per cent (ten) small urban settlements; and 38 per cent (twenty-one) rural settlements. The population of the sample, however, is distributed somewhat differently: about 70 per cent in large urban settlements, 20 per cent in small urban settlements; and about 10 per cent in rural settlements. This distribution is based on actual distribution of the population by size of place of residence.

The settlements in the sample are distributed almost evenly between old settlements and new settlements. (The distinction between old and new settlements is based on the definition of the Central Bureau of Statistics: old settlements are defined as those which had been settled before the establishment of the State of Israel in 1948; new settlements include those which were initially established after 1948 or those in which the majority of the population settled after that time.)

In order that the sample adequately represent total Jewish population, a basic ratio of 1 : 609 was decided upon. According to this ratio, a total of 4,000 interviews should include 2,848 from large urban settlements, 696 from small urban settlements, and 456 from rural settlements. The following table presents these data in summary form:

Sample Design by Type of Settlement and Sampling Ratio

Type of settlement	No. of settlements in sample	Registered voters in sample settlements	Sampling ratio	No. in sample
Large urban	25	1,209,050	1 : 424	2,848
Small urban	10	61,509	1 : 88	696
Rural	21	6,343	1 : 14	456
TOTAL	56	1,276,902		4,000

INDEX